W9-BNB-253

Cervantes.

863.

CERVANTES

Modern Critical Views

Henry Adams
Edward Albee
A. R. Ammons
Matthew Arnold
John Ashbery
W. H. Auden
Jane Austen
James Baldwin
Charles Baudelaire
Samuel Beckett
Saul Bellow
The Bible
Elizabeth Bishop
William Blake
Jorge Luis Borges
Elizabeth Bowen
Bertolt Brecht
The Brontës
Robert Browning
Anthony Burgess
George Gordon, Lord
  Byron
Thomas Carlyle
Lewis Carroll
Willa Cather
Cervantes
Geoffrey Chaucer
Kate Chopin
Samuel Taylor Coleridge
Joseph Conrad
Contemporary Poets
Hart Crane
Stephen Crane
Dante
Charles Dickens
Emily Dickinson
John Donne & the Seven-
  teenth-Century Meta-
  physical Poets
Elizabethan Dramatists
Theodore Dreiser
John Dryden
George Eliot
T. S. Eliot
Ralph Ellison
Ralph Waldo Emerson
William Faulkner
Henry Fielding
F. Scott Fitzgerald
Gustave Flaubert
E. M. Forster
Sigmund Freud
Robert Frost

Robert Graves
Graham Greene
Thomas Hardy
Nathaniel Hawthorne
William Hazlitt
Seamus Heaney
Ernest Hemingway
Geoffrey Hill
Friedrich Hölderlin
Homer
Gerard Manley Hopkins
William Dean Howells
Zora Neale Hurston
Henry James
Samuel Johnson and
  James Boswell
Ben Jonson
James Joyce
Franz Kafka
John Keats
Rudyard Kipling
D. H. Lawrence
John Le Carré
Ursula K. Le Guin
Doris Lessing
Sinclair Lewis
Robert Lowell
Norman Mailer
Bernard Malamud
Thomas Mann
Christopher Marlowe
Carson McCullers
Herman Melville
James Merrill
Arthur Miller
John Milton
Eugenio Montale
Marianne Moore
Iris Murdoch
Vladimir Nabokov
Joyce Carol Oates
Sean O'Casey
Flannery O'Connor
Eugene O'Neill
George Orwell
Cynthia Ozick
Walter Pater
Walker Percy
Harold Pinter
Plato
Edgar Allan Poe
Poets of Sensibility & the
  Sublime

Alexander Pope
Katherine Ann Porter
Ezra Pound
Pre-Raphaelite Poets
Marcel Proust
Thomas Pynchon
Arthur Rimbaud
Theodore Roethke
Philip Roth
John Ruskin
J. D. Salinger
Gershom Scholem
William Shakespeare
  (3 vols.)
  Histories & Poems
  Comedies
  Tragedies
George Bernard Shaw
Mary Wollstonecraft
  Shelley
Percy Bysshe Shelley
Edmund Spenser
Gertrude Stein
John Steinbeck
Laurence Sterne
Wallace Stevens
Tom Stoppard
Jonathan Swift
Alfred, Lord Tennyson
William Makepeace
  Thackeray
Henry David Thoreau
Leo Tolstoi
Anthony Trollope
Mark Twain
John Updike
Gore Vidal
Virgil
Robert Penn Warren
Evelyn Waugh
Eudora Welty
Nathanael West
Edith Wharton
Walt Whitman
Oscar Wilde
Tennessee Williams
William Carlos Williams
Thomas Wolfe
Virginia Woolf
William Wordsworth
Richard Wright
William Butler Yeats

These and other titles in preparation

Modern Critical Views

CERVANTES

Edited and with an introduction by
Harold Bloom
Sterling Professor of the Humanities
Yale University

CHELSEA HOUSE PUBLISHERS
New York ◊ Philadelphia

Library of Congress Cataloging-in-Publication Data
Cervantes.
    (Modern critical views)
    Bibliography: p.
    Includes index.
Summary: A collection of critical essays on Cervantes
and his works. Also includes a chronology of events in
the author's life.
    1. Cervantes Saavedra, Miguel de, 1547–1616—
Criticism and interpretation. [1. Cervantes Saavedra,
Miguel de, 1547–1616—Criticism and interpretation.
2. Spanish literature—History and criticism] I. Bloom,
Harold. II. Series.
PQ6351.C47 1986   863'.3   86–17114
ISBN 0–87754–722–X (alk. paper)

Contents

Editor's Note

This book brings together what I judge to be the best critical essays and commentaries available in English on the works of Cervantes, arranged here in the chronological order of their original publication. I am grateful to Eden Quainton for his erudition and judgment in helping to edit this volume and to Sandra Ferdman for supplying translations where necessary.

My introduction considers *Don Quixote* under the categories applied to the order of play in the *Homo Ludens* of J. Huizinga, and compares the Don and Sancho to Shakespeare's Falstaff. Two of our century's major scholarly critics begin the chronological sequence. Leo Spitzer analyzes what he calls "linguistic perspectivism" in *Don Quixote*, perhaps finding in Cervantes a precursor of Nietzschean perspectivism, with its interpretive interplay. In an excerpt from his famous study, *Mimesis*, Erich Auerbach acclaims Cervantes as the largest single instance of a continuous gaiety in the representation of ordinary reality in Western literature. Auerbach, like Spitzer, views the perspectivism of Cervantes as a humane avoidance of traditional moral judgments.

Ortega y Gasset, a man-of-letters in the tradition of Cervantes, gives us a very brief but pungent allegorization of the Don's exuberant reaction to Master Pedro's puppet show, a reaction that is analogous to the reader's hallucinatory yielding to the enchantment of fable. Even more in the spirit of Cervantes is the magnificent, early piece, "Pierre Menard, Author of *Don Quixote*," by the contemporary Argentine master Jorge Luis Borges, whose hilarious irony takes us back to the art "of deliberate anachronism and erroneous attributions" in Cervantes himself.

The late Michel Foucault, who substituted his own archaeological Structuralism for more traditional history-of-ideas, reads the Don partly as an allegory of writing, and partly as a true knight-errant who is questing for similitudes. Foucault can be said to conclude the first movement in this book, since our remaining essays are stricter instances of current modes of scholarly literary criticism.

In *Persiles and Sigismunda,* Cervantes's evening-song, Manuel Durán gives an incisive account of the author's favorite among his own works, with particular emphasis upon its famous "Prologue," in which Cervantes deliberately takes a valedictory stance toward his readers. The picaresque, Cervantes's truest mode, is brilliantly analyzed by Roberto González-Echevarría, who deconstructs the mode as a series of turning points that "allude to the origin and organization of writing through a metaphoric field of allusion drawn from sexuality."

Mary Gaylord Randel, ruminating upon *La Galatea,* reads the work as an allegorical or ironic defense of poetry, a defense that acknowledges the limits of language while finding in poetry the language of limits. In a cognate account of the *Exemplary Novels,* Cervantes's short stories, Juan Bautista Avalle-Arce discovers how varied are the transformations that Cervantes, in his quest for reality, brought about in the traditions of the picaresque.

The theme of the trickster, sly hermeticist and anarchist of the spirit, is tracked throughout Cervantes by Ruth El Saffar, who judges Cervantes to have appropriated for reality much of the dream world, by his manipulations of the trickster image. In a final essay, Alban Forcione reads the hallucinatory intensity of the witch Cañizares in "Colloquy of the Dogs" as what can be termed the apocalypse of Cervantes, a vision of the last things as a fearsome descent into the grave.

Introduction

"The text of Cervantes and that of Menard are verbally identical, but the second is almost infinitely richer." That superb irony is the culmination of "Pierre Menard, Author of *Don Quixote*," one of the earliest of the fictions of Jorge Luis Borges. Hidden in it is a deeper irony; Cervantes is one of those few Western writers who cannot be surpassed: the Yahwist (primary author of Genesis, Exodus, Numbers), Homer, Dante, Chaucer, Montaigne, Shakespeare, Milton, Tolstoy, Proust. These are the masters of representation who have fashioned a reality that contains us. In contrast to these, even writers as strong as Virgil, Spenser, Goethe, Blake, Wordsworth, Dickens, Whitman, Flaubert, Joyce, Kafka, Freud, seem partial. The Virgilian and Freudian reality principle is ultimately a taking into account of all the conditions imposed upon us by nature, yet Virgil and Freud do not compel us to see aspects of nature or the given that otherwise we might not come to see. Cervantes and Shakespeare so represent reality as to cause otherwise hidden aspects of reality to appear.

Carlos Fuentes tells us that *Don Quixote* "illustrates the rupture of a world based on analogy and thrust into differentiation," the world of Cervantes and of Shakespeare. If that is correct, then it pertains also to Homer and Dante, Tolstoy and Proust, which is to say that Fuentes has expressed not a temporal truth but an insight into the highest order of literary representation. Something vital in the individual rhetoric of the strongest masters of representation destroys traditional analogies and creates fresh differences. We can name that vitality in Cervantes by Hazlitt's critical term *gusto*. Don Quixote and Sancho Panza both incarnate a primal exuberance—at once ethos or character, logos or cognition, pathos or personality—that is utterly memorable through its gusto.

Nietzsche taught us that the memorable always is partly reliant upon pain. We forget easier pleasures, but not those so difficult that they also comprehended severe pain. This Nietzschean, pragmatic test for the Sublime is akin to Wittgenstein's test for love, probably because both Nietzsche and Wittgenstein were the sons of Schopenhauer. "Love is not a feeling," Wittgenstein wrote, because: "Love, unlike pain, is put to the test. We do not say: that was not a true pain, because it passed away so quickly."

We remember the Don and Sancho, always, because they give us a difficult pleasure, in which much pain is mixed, and we love them, always, because Cervantes puts our love for them to the test. Their greatness is dialectical in regard to one another; they educate one another in reality, and in all the orders of reality. One of those orders is play, as beautifully outlined in the *Homo Ludens* of J. Huizinga. Like their great contemporary, the Falstaff of Shakespeare's *Henry IV, Part 1*, the Don and Sancho achieve their essential being in the world of play, or freedom. If everything is a metaphor, except when we play, then Falstaff, the Don, and Sancho achieve a reality beyond the metaphoric. And the Don and Sancho are more fortunate than Falstaff, because they have one another, whereas poor Falstaff learns, in *Henry IV, Part 2*, that he has no one.

Play, being disinterested and secluded (of ideal time and place), creates or is a kind of order, an idea of order that is temporary and limited, but with its own perfection or beauty. Huizinga reminds us also that play has its tensions, lest we suddenly find we have "come off" its rules, and he relates these tensions to the secrecy that play affords its adepts, who are different from us because they are secluded away from us in the sphere of rules of a game that we do not know, or can come to know only by observing and by listening.

II

The play of the world, as Don Quixote conceives it, is a sublimely purified vision of chivalry, a game of knights-errant, damozels beautiful and virtuous, enchanters both wicked and potent, ogres, giants, and island kingdoms where the shrewd Sancho might exercise his pragmatic wisdom. Falstaff, surveying the corpse of the chivalric Sir Walter Blunt, splendidly declares: "I like not such grinning honor as Sir Walter hath. Give me life, which if I can save, so; if not, honor comes unlook'd for, and there's an end." Don Quixote, though committed to precisely the opposite stance, nevertheless shares with Falstaff the kingdom of play, and we do not sense that there would be any spiritual conflicts between these superb figures if they met in that kingdom. We hear the Don in Falstaff, and a reduction of the grand Sancho in the hypocritical Prince Hal, when they prepare to play the scene in which King Henry IV will denounce his heir:

> FALSTAFF. Well, thou wilt be horribly chid tomorrow when thou comest to thy father. If thou love me, practice an answer.
> PRINCE. Do thou stand for my father and examine me upon the particulars of my life.
> FALSTAFF. Shall I? Content. This chair shall be my state, this dagger my sceptre, and this cushion my crown.
> PRINCE. Thy state is taken for a join'd-stool, thy golden sceptre for a leaden dagger, and thy precious rich crown for a pitiful bald crown!
> FALSTAFF. Well, and the fire of grace be not quite out of you, now shalt thou be mov'd . . .

The fire of play is almost quite out in the Prince, and he is not much moved, but we are. As in Falstaff (until Hal destroys him by renouncing him), the fire of play cannot abandon Don Quixote. Cervantes, more even than Rabelais, more even than the Shakespeare of the great clowns and of Falstaff, represents reality with a continuous gusto and buoyancy. What counts most about the Don is neither his obsession nor his courage. It is the greatness or sublimity of his unflagging playfulness, as when his neighbor protests to him that "your Grace is neither Baldwin nor Abindarráez but a respectable gentleman by the name of Señor Quijana," and the Don replies:

> I know who I am, and who I may be, if I choose: not only those I have mentioned but all the Twelve Peers of France and the Nine Worthies as well; for the exploits of all of them together, or separately, cannot compare with mine.

"I know who I am, and who I may be, if I choose," is the Don's credo, even as Falstaff's is: "No, that's certain, I am not a double man; but if I be not Jack Falstaff, then am I a Jack." As for the difference between these grand representatives of *homo ludens,* we may start with Don Quixote confronting the possibility of battling lions and saying, with a slight smile: "Lion whelps against me?," and then rejecting, with contempt, the lionkeeper's insistence that his lions have no thought of attacking the knight:

> My dear sir, you had best go mind your tame partridge and that bold ferret of yours and let each one attend to his own business. This is my affair, and I know whether these gentlemen, the lions, have come to attack me or not.

This is only the apparent antithesis to Sir John Falstaff declining to have been slaughtered by Douglas, "that hot termagant Scot":

> Counterfeit? I lie, I am no counterfeit. To die is to be a counter-
> feit, for he is but the counterfeit of a man who hath not the life
> of a man; but to counterfeit dying, when a man thereby liveth, is
> to be no counterfeit, but the true and perfect image of life indeed.
> The better part of valor is discretion, in the which better part I
> have sav'd my life.

There is only a touch of discretion in the Don's valor, but there is a plethora in Sancho's, yet like Falstaff, Sancho pragmatically is as playfully valorous as the Knight of the Mournful Countenance. Don Quixote's dole-fulness and Falstaff's wit, the Don's mad courage and Falstaff's vital dis-cretion, are the same qualities turned inside out. An essential gaiety informs the sense of freedom in Cervantes and Shakespeare alike, a freedom that incarnates the will to play. The world awaits the writer who could bring the Don and Falstaff onto one stage simultaneously, or into the pages of one book, to hold converse together. For the Don is no more insane than the superb Falstaff is. They are the two authentic literary representations that Nietzsche longed for: true overmen, figures without a superego, humans beyond the necessity of turning aggression against the self, or most simply, defiers and deniers of the death drive.

III

Had Cervantes given us only Don Quixote, it would have been more than enough. The astonishment of his masterwork is that its title is inade-quate, since the book is not only *The Adventures of Don Quixote de la Mancha,* but just as much the adventures of Sancho Panza. "The Truth about Sancho Panza" is the title of perhaps the finest of Kafka's parables, a parable that is certainly the most illuminating criticism of Cervantes yet written:

> Without making any boast of it Sancho Panza succeeded in the
> course of years, by devouring a great number of romances of
> chivalry and adventure in the evening and night hours, in so
> diverting from him his demon, whom he later called Don Qui-
> xote, that his demon thereupon set out in perfect freedom on the
> maddest exploits, which, however, for the lack of a preordained
> object, which should have been Sancho Panza himself, harmed
> nobody. A free man, Sancho Panza philosophically followed Don

Quixote on his crusades, perhaps out of a sense of responsibility, and had of them a great and edifying entertainment to the end of his days.

What is strongest in Kafka's insight is the primacy given to Sancho Panza, whose corporeal understanding or bodily ego provides the ground from which imagination or the Don rises up. Don Quixote cannot harm the world or disturb the flow of the mundane, because there is no object for his exploits except Sancho, and Sancho has diverted the demonic drive out into the "perfect freedom" of the beyond, as here in the magnificent chapter 28 of part 2, where the two inseparables quarrel, the occasion being a rare Falstaffian moment on the Don's part:

> When a brave man flies, he must have discovered some odds or foul play; and it is the business of prudent captains, to reserve themselves for better occasions. This maxim was verified in Don Quixote, who, by giving way to popular fury, and the evil intention of that incensed squadron, took to his heels, and, without paying the least regard to Sancho, or the danger in which he left him, moved off to such a distance as he judged sufficient for his own security. He was followed by Sancho lying across the ass, as we have already observed, who, by that time he was brought up to his master, had just recovered the use of his senses, and fell from Dapple at the feet of Rozinante, all battered and bruised, and in an agony of pain.
>
> The knight dismounting to search his wounds, no sooner perceived he was sound from head to foot, than he thus accosted him in angry tone: "In evil hour, you must understand braying, sirrah! Where did you learn it was convenient to talk of halters in the house of a man that was hanged? To the tenor of braying, what bass could you expect but the basting of a cudgel? You have reason to thank God that, instead of receiving a benediction with a pole, you have not been crossed with a scymitar." "I am at present in no condition to answer," said Sancho; "for, methinks I talk through my shoulders; let us mount and depart from this place, and I shall make an end of my braying; though I shall never be weary of telling as how knights-errant run away, and leave their honest squires beaten to chaff and pounded to cinders, in the power of their enemies." "There is a wide difference between flying and retreating," answered Don Quixote; "for you must know, Sancho, that valour which is not founded on the base of

discretion, is termed temerity or rashness; and the achievements of a rash person ought to be ascribed rather to good fortune than courage. I own, therefore, I have retreated, but not fled, and in so doing have imitated a great number of valiant chiefs, who reserved themselves for more dignified occasions: and of these instances histories are full, but I omit rehearsing them at present, because the recital would be of no advantage to thee, or entertainment to myself."

By this time Sancho, being set upon his ass again by Don Quixote, who likewise mounted Rozinante, they jogged along softly, in order to shelter themselves in a grove that appeared at the distance of a quarter of a league; and the squire every now and then heaving up a most profound ah! accompanied with piteous groans, his master desired to know the cause of such bitter ejaculations. To which question the squire replied, that from the extremity of his rump to the top of his head, he felt such intolerable pain as was like to deprive him of his senses. "The cause of that pain," said Don Quixote, "must doubtless be this; as the pole or staff by which you have suffered was long and large, it extended over thy whole back, comprehending all those parts that now give you pain; and if it had reached still farther, the pain would have been more extensive." "'Fore God," cried Sancho, "your worship has taken me out of a huge uncertainty, and resolved the doubt in delicate terms. Body o'me! was the cause of my pain so mysterious, that there was a necessity for telling me, I feel pain in those parts that were cudgelled? Had my shins ached, there might have been some reason for guessing at the cause of their aching; but, surely there is no great witchcraft required to tell me that my back aches, because it was crossed with a quarter-staff. In good faith! sir master of mine, our neighbour's care hangs by a hair. Every day I see more and more how the land lies, and how little I have to expect from keeping your worship's company; for, if you left me to be cudgelled at this time, we shall, upon a hundred different occasions, return to our late blankettings and other such toys; and though this misfortune has fallen upon my shoulders, the next may light upon my eyes. Abundantly better should I have done, but, I am such a barbarian, that in all the days of my life, I never did well; I say again, abundantly better should I have done, had I returned to my house, my wife, and my children, and maintained and brought them up with what Providence should please to bestow; rather than lag after your worship in this manner, through roadless roads and pathless paths, drinking bad liquor and eating worse food; then when I come to sleep, 'Brother squire, measure out seven feet of ground; and if you choose to be more at your ease, take as much more, for the saddle is in your own hand, and lay yourself out to your heart's desire.' Would to God I could see the first man who meddled with knight-errantry burnt to a cinder; at least the first booby who chose to be squire to such wiseacres as all former knights-errant must have been. Of the present, I say nothing; as your worship is one of the number, I hold them in respect, because I am sensible, that in speeching and understanding, you know a point more than the devil himself."

"I would venture to lay a good wager, Sancho," said Don Quixote, "that now while you are permitted to speak without the least hindrance, you feel no pain in any part of your body. Proceed, child, and out with every thing that comes into your head, or tarries at your tongue's end; for, provided you are free from pain, I shall convert into pleasure that disgust which proceeds from your folly and impertinence; and if you are so much bent upon returning to your house, your wife and your family, God will not suffer me to oppose your resolution. You have some of my money in your hands; recollect how long it is since we set out on this my third sally; then reckon what you might and should have earned monthly, and be your own paymaster." "When I worked for Thomas Carrasco, father of Bachelor Sampson, who is your worship's acquaintance," answered Sancho, "I earned two ducats a month, besides my victuals: with your worship I know not what I can earn, though well I know that the squire of a knight-errant has a much more troublesome office than that of a farmer's servant; for, in fact, we who serve husbandmen, let us work never so hard through the day, and happen what will, have a hot supper out of the pot at night, and lie in a good bed, which I have never enjoyed since I have been in your worship's service, except for that short space of time that we stayed in the house of Don Diego de Miranda; and bating the good chear I found among the scum of Camacho's kettle, and my eating, drinking and sleeping at the habitation of Basilius, all the rest of the time I have slept on the hard ground, under the cope of heaven, exposed to what you call the inclemencies of the weather, living upon cheese-

parings and crusts of bread, and drinking cold water, sometimes
from the brooks and sometimes from the springs we met with in
the by-places through which we travelled."

We are never more moved by and with Sancho than when he cries out:
"'Fore God, your worship has taken me out of a huge uncertainty, and
resolved the doubt in delicate terms. Body o'me! was the cause of my pain
so mysterious, that there was a necessity for telling me, I feel pain in those
parts that were cudgelled?" Sancho, I think, might have desired to dispute
Erich Auerbach's contention that Cervantes does not take his work's play
very seriously: "He looks at it; he shapes it; he finds it diverting; it is also
intended to afford the reader refined intellectual diversion." That makes Cervantes rather too much like Walt Whitman's "real me" or "me myself," who
is both in the game and out of it, and watching and wondering at it. Cervantes is both Sancho and the Don, and all three of them take the game very
seriously indeed, but taking play seriously is a mode very much its own, the
mode we call freedom.

As a fierce lover of Falstaff, I find that all his moments are my favorite
moments, but the best of all comes in the midst of battle, when Prince Hal
requests the knight's sword, and is offered the great wit's pistol instead:

> PRINCE. Give it me. What? is it in the case?
> FALSTAFF. Ay, Hal, 'tis hot, 'tis hot. There's that will sack a city.
> *The Prince draws it out, and finds it to be a bottle of*
> *sack.*
> PRINCE. What, is it a time to jest and dally now?
> *He throws the bottle at him. Exit.*

Falstaff, like Cervantes, has both the Don and Sancho in him. It is indeed
always the time to play, to jest and dally, even in the very midst of battle.
The order of play is the only idea of order that Falstaff acknowledges. The
Don and Sancho, in their very different ways, are shadowed by darker in-
tensities than Falstaff is, though his prophetic fear of being rejected by the
Prince is dark and intense enough. Don Quixote plays until reality intrudes
and destroys the game, and then he dies. Sancho survives, even though he
has learned to play as well as his teacher, though in an earthier mode. Perhaps
the Don was the writer in Cervantes, and Sancho the reader in Cervantes;
perhaps they are the writer and the reader in each of us.

LEO SPITZER

Linguistic Perspectivism
in the Don Quijote

Much, though not too much, has been written about Cervantes's master novel. Yet, we are still far from understanding it in its general plan and in its details as well as we do, for instance, Dante's *Commedia* or Goethe's *Faust*—and we are relatively further from an understanding of the whole than of the details. The main critical works of recent years, which represent gigantic strides forward toward the understanding of the whole, are, in my opinion, Américo Castro's *El pensamiento de Cervantes* [*Cervantes's Thought*], in which the themes of Cervantes's poetry of ideas are stated, and Joaquín Casalduero's article "La composición de 'El Ingenioso Hidalgo Don Quijote de la Mancha,' [The Composition of *Don Quixote*]," in which the artistic architecture of the novel, as based on the themes recognized by Castro, is pointed out. As for the style of the novel, Helmut Hatzfeld, in his book *Don Quijote als Wortkunstwerk,* has attempted to distinguish different "styles" determined by previous literary traditions (the pastoral or chivalric styles, the style of Boccaccio, etc.)—without, however, achieving what I should call an integration of the historical styles into one Cervantine style in which the personality of the writer would manifest itself. Perhaps it is better not to break up the unity of a work of art into historical units which, in any case, are extraneous to Cervantes and, instead, to proceed according to a method by which one would seek to move from the periphery toward the center of the artistic globe—thus remaining within the work of art. Any one outward feature, when sufficiently followed up to the center, must yield us

From *Linguistics and Literary History: Essays in Stylistics.* © 1948, © 1976 renewed by Princeton University Press.

insight into the artistic whole, whose unity will thus have been respected. The choice of the particular phenomenon, then, would appear to be of secondary importance: any single one must, according to my ideology, give final results.

Accordingly, I shall choose certain linguistic phenomena (of, at first glance, slight importance for Cervantes's artistic cosmos) which I shall attempt to reduce to a common denominator, later to bring this into relationship with the "pensamiento," the *Weltanschauung* of Cervantes.

Any reader of the *Quijote* is struck by the instability of the names of the main characters of the novel: in the first chapter we are told by Cervantes that the protagonist has been called, by the sources of "this truthful story," alternatively Quixada, Quesada, or Quixana (this last, according to Cervantes, being the best "conjecture"); from this assortment the "ingenioso hidalgo [ingenious gentleman]" chose, before starting his knightly career, the name that he was to bear in the whole book: Quijote. When, at the end, he is cured of the fever of quixotism and repudiates *Amadis de Gaula* and the rest of the novels of chivalry, he recovers his unpretentious prosaic original name (part 2, chap. 74): "ya no soy don Quixote de la Mancha, sino Alonso Quixano a quien mis buenas costumbres me dieron renombre de Bueno [I am no longer Don Quixote de la Mancha, but Alonso Quixano whose good habits gave him the name of Good]"; and the final scene of his Christian death and regeneration seems rounded out by a kind of rebaptism, as this "loco [crazy man]" becomes a "cuerdo [sane one]" (the change of name is thrice mentioned in this final chapter, as if the author wanted to din it into our heads that the old Adam is dead); in his will, "Quixano" calls his niece Antonia by the name Quixana, as if to emphasize that he is now a "bourgeois rangé" to the extent of having a family bearing his own (everyday) name. The first-mentioned name Quixada is also used in recognition of the reasonable side of the protagonist's nature: earlier (1.5) he was referred to, by an acquaintance who knew him in the days before his madness, as "Señor Quixada." Again, just as Quesada, Quixada, or Quixana became a Quijote when he fancied himself a knight, so, when his chivalric dreams seemed about to give way to those of pastoral life, he imagines himself to be called "el pastor Quijotiz [the shepherd Quijotiz]" (and his companion, Sancho Panza, "el pastor Pancino [the shepherd Pancino]"). In another episode, Dorotea, who plays the role of Princess Micomicona (1.30), feigns that her presumptive rescuer is called "(si mal no me acuerdo,) don Azoto o don Jigote [if I do not remember wrongly, don Azote or don Jigote]." And the Countess Trifaldi jocundly endows him with the superlative for which she seems to have a predilection: "Quijotísimo." As for his epithet "de la Mancha [of La Mancha]," this is coined (1.1) after Amadis de Gaula. Later, he will be called by the name, first given him by Sancho, "el caballero de la Triste Figura [the Knight of the Mournful Countenance]," still later by "el caballero de los Leones [the Knight of the Lions]" (in 2.27–29, this change is strongly emphasized, and a certain character is rebuked by Sancho for having disregarded the distinction).

It is obviously required by chivalric decorum that whoever enters the sphere of the knight Don Quijote must also change his or her name: Aldonza Lorenza > Dulcinea ("nombre a su parecer músico y peregrino y significativo [a name which seems musical, wandering, and meaningful]"), Tolosa > doña Tolosa, la Molinera > doña Molinera (1.3), and the anonymous nag receives the name of Rocinante ("nombre a su parecer alto, sonoro y significativo [a name which seems lofty, melodious, and meaningful]": note the parallel wording appearing in the justifications for the names given to Dulcinea and to the nag); incidentally, the ass from which Sancho is inseparable is not deemed worthy of a change of name that would be indicative of a change of rank. Although Sancho Panza, the peasant squire, undergoes no change of name similar to that of his master, and is resolved always to remain (governor or no governor) plain Sancho without the addition of "don" (2.4), there is some uncertainty in regard to his name, too, since, in the text of Cide Hamete Benengali, the Arabian chronicler whose manuscript Cervantes purports to have found at the moment when other sources gave out (1.5), there is a picture of thick-set Sancho with "la barriga grande, el tallo corto, y las zancas largas [a big belly, of short body and long legs]," bearing the inscription: "Sancho Zancas."

It is, however, in regard to the name of Sancho's wife, that the greatest confusion obtains: Sancho calls her first "Juana Gutiérrez mi oislo [Juana Gutiérrez, my old lady]" (1.7); a few lines later, he ponders whether a crown would fit "la cabeza de Mari Gutiérrez [upon the head of Mari Gutiérrez]"— which change the more intelligent commentators, seeking to avoid bringing the charge of inconsistency against Cervantes, rightly explain by the fact that *Mari* had come to represent simply a generic and interchangeable name for women. But in part 2, chapter 5, Sancho's wife calls herself Teresa Cascajo; from then on she is either Teresa Panza or Teresa Sancho, "mujer de Sancho Panza [wife of Sancho Panza]"; of the name Teresa itself she says (2.5): "Teresa me pusieron en el bautismo, nombre mondo y escueto.... [they named me Teresa at my baptism, a pure and simple name]." Evidently we have to do with a woman named Juana Teresa Gutiérrez, who becomes a Juana Panza or Teresa Panza when called after her husband, or ... Cascajo when called after her father. Occasionally, however, according to the mood of the situation, she may be called "Teresaina" (2.73) or "Teresona" (2.67: because of her "gordura [fatness]").

There are other cases, slightly different from those enumerated so far, in which the ignorance and weak memory of Sancho seem to create a "polyonomasia": here we can hardly think in terms of different traditions offered by chroniclers (as in the case of the names of Quijote), or of popular variation (as in that of the names of Sancho's wife): Sancho must multiply names simply because all the forms of names that he retains are only approximations to the real ones; they are variable because he cannot take a firm hold on them; he indulges in what linguists call "popular etymologies," i.e. he alters names according to the associations most convenient to his intellectual horizon. Sometimes he offers several variations, but even when only one alteration is involved, the effect of polyonomasia still remains because of the fact that the real name is also present in the reader's mind. Mambrino (1.19–21), of whose helmet he speaks, becomes "Malandrino" (a "moro"), "Malino [= the Evil One]," or "Martino" (a common first name); Fortinbras > feo Blas (1.15), Cide Hamete Benengeli > ". . . Berengena" (2.2; this Sancho justifies with the remark: ". . . los moros son amigos de berenjenas [Moors are great friends of eggplant]"), Señora Rodriguez de Grijalva > Señora González (2.31), Magalona > "la señora Magellanes o Magalona" (2.41). A similar alteration of names is practiced by the *ama* who (1.7) contends that the books which we know to have fallen prey to the *auto-da-fé* (1.6) had been ravished by the sorcerer Muñaton: Don Quijote corrects this to "Frestón." "Never mind Frestón or Tritón," answers the ama, "provided it is a name ending in *-ton*": word forms that are unalterable for the learned Don Quijote are quite exchangeable in the mind of the uncultured ama.

The names of the Countess Trifaldi are in a class by themselves since, in addition to the instability of names conditioned by a masquerade, there are involved the alterations to which Sancho is prone: here there coexist polyonomasias of the first and second degrees. The Countess is first (2.36) introduced to us (by her messenger Trifaldi de la Barba) as "la condesa Trifaldi, por otro nombre llamada la Dueña Dolorida [the countess Trifaldi, otherwise called the Distressed Duenna]"; one of the two names is her authentic one, the other her "name within the world of romance" (just as Don Quijote is also the "Caballero de la Triste Figura"). When she appears in the pageant (2.38) of the *carro triunfal* her name "Trifaldi" is given the following explanation: "la cola, o falda, o como llamarla quisieren, era de tres colas [the tail or skirt, or whatever you want to call it, had three flounces]"; the "mathematical" (geometrical) figure of her skirt with three flounces (or trains?) is so striking that every spectator must interpret her

name as "la Condesa de las Tres Faldas [the Countess of the Three-Skirts]."
But the scrupulous chronicler Benengeli who, like Cervantes, seems to care
about even the minor details of the fiction-within-the-fiction, is said by Cervantes to have stated that the character was really called "la Condesa *Lobuna*"—allegedly because of the presence of wolves in her domain (he adds
that, according to onomastic traditions in princely houses she would have
been called "la Condesa Zorruna" if foxes had been prevalent in her domain)—but that she had dropped this name in favor of the more novel one
derived from the form of her skirt. Now, this etymology of the name "Trifaldi," as stated by the chronicler (and as made evident to the eye of the
spectators who see the masquerade skirt), had been somewhat anticipated
by Sancho's popular etymology in part 2, chapter 37: "esta condesa Tres
Faldas o Tres Colas (que en mi tierra faldas y colas, colas y faldas todo es
uno) [this Countess Three-Skirts or Three-Tails (where I'm from, skirts or
tails, tails or skirts, it comes to the same thing)]." Ultimately we are presented
with an array of (possible) names for the same character: la Condesa Trifaldi,
de Tres Faldas, de Tres Colas (the latter name would be due to what the
modern linguist in his jargon calls "synonymic derivation"), Lobuna ("Zorruna" again being a "synonymic derivative"), Dueña Dolorida—a list as
impressive as that of the names of Don Quijote.

Now those commentators who, in general, take the line of emphasizing
the satiric intent of Cervantes, will point out that the variety of names attributed to the protagonist by Cervantes is simply an imitation of the pseudo-
historical tendencies of the authors of chivalric novels who, in order to show
their accurateness as historians, pretend to have resorted to different sources.
In the case of the names of Sancho's wife, some commentators point out, as
we have seen, that the polyonomasia is due to the onomastic habits of the
period; in the alterations of the name "Mambrino" they usually see a satire
on Sancho's ignorance; in the case of the Condesa Trifaldi I have seen no
explanation (Rodríguez Marín's edition points out possible "historical"
sources for the costume itself of "tres colas o faldas"). But, evidently, there
must be a common pattern of thought behind all these cases, which would
explain (1) the importance given to a name or change of name, (2) the etymological concern with names, (3) the polyonomasia in itself.

Now it happens that just these three features are well known to the
medievalist (less, perhaps, to students of Renaissance literature): they ultimately derive from Biblical studies and from ancient philology: one need
only think of Saint Jerome's explanation of Hebrew names or of Isidore's
"Etymologies"—and of the etymologizing habits of all great medieval poets.
The names in the Bible were treated with seriousness; in the Old Testament

the name, or rather the names of God were all-important (Exod. 6:2–3: "I am *Iahve,* and I have appeared to Abraham, Isaak and Jacob as *El Schaddai,* under the name of Jahve I was not known to them," cf. Exod. 3:14); the many *nomina sacra* revealed the many aspects through which the divine might make itself felt. Nor does the importance of the name decrease with the New Testamentary divinity (Christ is Immanuel). And, in the New Testament, a tendency appears which will have great influence on medieval chivalry: the change of name subsequent to baptism will be imitated by the change of name undergone by the newly dubbed knight. In all these sacred (or sacramental) names or changes of names, etymology plays a large part, because the true meaning (the etymon) may reveal eternal verities latent in the words—indeed, it was possible for many etymologies to be proposed for the same word, since God may have deposited different meanings in a single term: polyonomasia and polyetymology. Both these techniques are generally applied to a greater degree to proper names than to common nouns—because the former, "untranslatable" as they are by their nature, participate more in the mysterious aspect of human language: they are less motivated. In proper names the medieval mind could see reflected more of the multivalence of the world full of arcana. The Middle Ages were characterized by an admiration as well for the correspondence between word and thing as for the mystery which makes this correspondence unstable.

By all this I do not mean to deny that Cervantes followed the models pointed out to us by the commentators: what I do say is that, in doing so, he was also following certain accepted medieval patterns (which, however, he submitted to a new interpretation: that of his critical intelligence). It is possible, for example, in the case of the name "Trifaldi," to see on the surface a medieval imagination at work: the name is given an interpretation (*Trifaldi = tres faldas*) which, from our modern linguistic or historical point of view, is evidently wrong but which would have delighted a medieval mind, ever ready to accept any interpretation offering a clarification of the mystery of words. The ancient and medieval etymologies are indeed rarely those a modern linguist would offer, trained as he is to respect the formational procedures current in human language; the aim of those etymologies was to establish the connection between a given word and other existing words as an homage to God whose wisdom may have ordained these very relationships. The etymological connections that the medieval etymologist sees are direct relationships established between words vaguely associated because of their homonymic ring—not the relationships established by "historical grammar" or those obtained by decomposition of the word into its morphological elements. In other words, we are offered edifying ideal possibilities, not deterministic historical realities; Isidore will connect *sol* and *solus* because of the ideological beauty of this relationship, not sol and ἥλιος as the comparative grammarian of today must do.

But, if the equation Trifaldi = tres faldas represents a "medieval" etymology, Cervantes himself did not take too seriously his own etymologizing: he must have been perfectly well aware of the historically real explanation— that which prompted him to coin the word. Trifaldi is evidently a regressive form from *Trifaldín,* which name, in turn, is the farcical Italian *Truffaldino* "nome di personaggio ridicolo e basso di commedia" (Tomm.-Bellini); the reference to *truffare* "to cheat" is apposite, in our story, given the farcical episode intended to delude Don Quijote and Sancho. Thus the name of the messenger Trifaldín is (historically) not a diminutive of Trifaldi, as it might seem but, on the contrary, was preexistent, in Cervantes's mind, to the name of the mistress. The etymology of "tres faldas" is, historically speaking, entirely out of place. We have to face here the same para-etymological vein in which Rabelais (facetiously imitating medieval practice, while exemplifying the joyous freedom with which the Renaissance writer could play with words) explained the name *Gargantua* by *que grand tu as* [sc. *le gosier*]! and *Beauce* by [*je trouve*] *beau ce* [sc. *pays*]. In this story, the para-etymological play with names serves to underline the deceitfulness of outward evidence; what for Quijote and Sancho are wondrous events are, in reality, only *burlas* [jests] in a baroque world of histrionics and disingenuity.

The disingenuous procedure of offering such "medieval" etymologies as would occur to his characters (for the simpleton Sancho as well as the learned Arab Benengeli are medieval primitives) is also exemplified in the case of the nag Rocinante, whose name is interpreted by Don Quijote in the style of Isidore: the horse was a "rocín antes"—which may mean either "a nag before" ("previously a nag," "an erstwhile nag") or "a nag before all others": "antes de todos los rocines del mundo." Two explanations are given of one word, as was the general medieval practice—not the *one* historically true significance according to which the name was actually coined: viz. *rocín* + the noble and "literary" participial ending *-ante*. Cervantes was perfectly aware of the correct etymology but he allowed his medieval Don Quijote to offer a more "significant" one. He knew also the explanation of the name Quijote (= *quij*- "jaw" + the comic suffix *-ote,* derived from *jigote* etc.), while his protagonist, who adopted this name, thought of it as patterned on *Lanzarote.*

Thus we may conclude that, while, for the medieval world, the procedures of polyonomasia and polyetymologia amounted to a recognition of the working of the divine in the world, Cervantes used the same devices in order to reveal the multivalence which words possess for different human minds: he who has coined the names put into them other meanings than those conceived of by the characters themselves: a Trifaldín who is for Cervantes a *truffatore,* a cheater or practical joker, is understood by Don Quijote and Sancho to be the servant of a Countess Trifaldi who wears a three-flounce skirt.

Perhaps this procedure is symptomatic of something basic to the texture of our novel; perhaps a linguistic analysis of the names can carry us further toward the center, allowing us to catch a glimpse of the general attitude of the creator of the novel toward his characters. This creator must see that the world, as it is offered to man, is susceptible of many explanations, just as names are susceptible of many etymologies; individuals may be deluded by the perspectives according to which they see the world as well as by the etymological connections which they establish. Consequently, we may assume that the linguistic perspectivism of Cervantes is reflected in his invention of plot and characters; and, just as, by means of polyonomasia and polyetymologia, Cervantes makes the world of words appear different to his different characters, while he himself may have his own, the coiner's, view of these names, similarly he watches the story he narrates from his own private vantage point: the way in which the characters conceive of the situations in which they are involved may be not at all the way in which Cervantes sees them—though this latter way is not always made clear to the reader. In other words, Cervantes's perspectivism, linguistic and otherwise, would allow him qua artist to stand above, and sometimes aloof from, the misconceptions of his characters. Later we will have more to say about what lies behind this attitude of Cervantes; suffice it for us here, where we are given the first opportunity to look into the working of the (linguistic) imagination of the novelist, to have summarily indicated the relationship between his linguistic ambivalences and his general perspectivism.

If, now, we turn back for a moment to Sancho's mispronunciations of names—which, as we have seen, was one of the contributing factors to the polyonomasia of the novel—we will recognize a particular application of Cervantes's linguistic perspectivism at work: to Sancho's uncultured mind, "Mambrino" must appear now as "Malino," now as "Martino," etc. In this, there is no suggestion of smugness on the part of Cervantes, as there might be with modern intellectual writers who would mock the linguistic "abuses" of ignorant characters; Cervantes presents "Malino," "Martino," etc., simply as the "linguistic appearances" of what, for Don Quijote, for example, can evidently be only Mambrino. This lack of auctorial criticism in the face of so much linguistic relativity tends to shake the reader's confidence in estab-

lished word usage. Of course, we are apt to rely on the correctness of Don
Quijote's use of words and names; but who knows whether the knight, who
is so often mistaken in his attempts to define reality (as he is precisely in his
identification of the helmet of Mambrino), has hit this time upon the right
name, whether this name is not as much of a dream as are the fantastic
adventures he envisions (we are reminded of the baroque theme *par excellence* ". . . que los sueños sueños son [even dreams are dreams]")? Why
should, then, "Mambrino" and not "Malino" or "Martino" be the name
representing *reality*? The same insistence on "correctness" of word-usage,
as applied to the nonexistent, occurs in the scene where Quijote listens to
the ama's cock-and-bull story of the theft of the books by "the sorcerer
Muñaton," and finds nothing to correct therein but the name: not "Muñaton" but "Freston": Freston and Mambrino are names correct in irreality
(in books), representing naught in reality. Evidently we are offered in Don
Quijote a caricature of the humanist who is versed in books and bookish
names, but is unconcerned as to their valid relationship to reality (he has a
pendant in the *licenciado,* to whom Don Quijote tells the fantastic story of
his descent to the "cueva de Montesinos [Cave of Montesinos]," and who is
outspokenly qualified by Cervantes as a "humanista").

In these two incidents we have a suggestion of a theme which informs
our whole novel: the problem of the reality of literature. I belong with those
critics who take seriously Cervantes's statement of purpose: "derribar la
máquina mal fundada de los libros de caballería [to topple the ill-founded
machinery of chivalric romances]"; this statement, which indicts a particular
literary genre, is, in fact, a recognition of the potential danger of "the book."
And, in its larger sense, the *Quijote* is an indictment of the bookish side of
Humanism, a creed in which, seventy years earlier, Rabelais had so firmly
believed, and an indictment of the "word-world" in which the Renaissance
had delighted without qualms. Whereas the writers of the Renaissance were
able to build up their word-worlds out of sheer exuberance, free to "play"
linguistically because of their basic confidence in life—with the baroque artist
Desengaño, disillusionment is allowed to color all things of the world, including books and their words, which possess only the reality of a *sueño.*
Words are no longer, as they had been in the Middle Ages, depositories of
truths nor, as they had been in the Renaissance, an expansion of life: they
are, like the books in which they are contained, sources of hesitation, error,
deception—"dreams."

The same linguistic perspectivism is present in Cervantes's treatment of
common nouns. For the most part we have to do with the confusion, or the
criticism, engendered by the clash of two linguistic standards determined

mainly by social status. Here, too, in this continuous give-and-take between cultured and uncultured speakers, there is given a suggestion of linguistic relativism that is willed by Cervantes. The opposition between two different ways of speech takes different forms: it may be Sancho who is interrupted and corrected by Don Quijote: in 1.32 [*hereje o*] *flemático* is corrected to *cismático*; in 2.7 *relucido > reducido*; 2.8 *sorbiese> asolviese*; 2.9 *cananeas > hacaneas*; 2.187 *friscal > fiscal*. Particularly interesting are the cases in which the term used by Sancho and the correction offered by Quijote are in the relationship of etymological doublets (popular and learned developments of the same root): (1.12): *cris - eclipse, estil - estéril* (how admirably has Cervantes anticipated the discoveries of nineteenth-century linguistics!). Again, it may be a question of Sancho's reaction to the language of the knight which the squire either misunderstands (in 1.8 Quijote's *homicidios* "murders" is transposed by Sancho into the more familiar, semipopular doublet *omecillos* "feuds") or fails to understand (in 2.29 Quijote must explain the meaning of *longincuos* [longuinquous] ("*por longincuos caminos* [by longuinquous paths]"), which he "translates" by *apartados* [remote]). In general, Don Quijote shows more tolerance for linguistic ignorance (in regard to the longincuos just mentioned, he excuses Sancho with the words: "*y no es maravilla que no lo entiendes, que no estás to obligado a saber latín* [and it is no wonder you do not understand, as you are not obligated to know Latin]") than his uncultured associates (who seem more concerned with things than with words) do for linguistic pedantry: they often blame the knight for his *jerigonza* [gibberish] (1.11), for his *griego* [Greek] (1.16). And, when Don Quijote reproves Sancho for his use of *abernuncio* instead of *abrenuncio* [By no means], the squire retorts: "*Déjeme vuestra grandeza, que no estoy agora para mirar en sotilezas ni en letras mas o menos* [Leave me alone your worship, as I am not interested in subtleties nor in letters, more or less]" (similarly, in 2.3, when the *bachiller* Sansón Carrasco corrects *presonajes* to *personajes* [personages], Sancho remarks: "*Otro reprochador de voquibles tenemos! Pues andense a eso y no acabaremos en toda la vida* [So we have another word-corrector here! Let's go on or, at this rate, we shall not be finished in a lifetime]"). Sancho adopts the attitude of a Mathurin Régnier, opposing the "éplucheurs de mots"! It may happen that the same Sancho, the advocate of naturalness in language, turns purist for the moment for the edification of his wife, and corrects her *revuelto* [revolved] to *resuelto* [resolved] (3.5); but then he must hear from her lips—oh, relativity of human things!—the same reproach he was wont to administer to his master: "*No os pongáis a disputar, marido, conmigo. Yo hablo como Dios es servido, y no me meto en más dibujos!* [Don't start a quarrel with me, husband. I talk as God pleases, and I don't worry about using fancy words]" (Here, she is referring to the language of God, Who, as Sancho himself had already claimed, is the great "Entendedor [Understander]" of all kinds of speech). Another example of the linguistic intolerance of the common people is the retort of the shepherd who has been corrected for having said *mas años que sarna* [older than Sarna] instead of . . . *que Sarra* [than Sarra]: "Harto vive la sarna [Sarna lives long enough]," he answers, "y si es, señor, que me habéis de andar zaheriendo [= 'éplucher'] a cada paso los vocablos no acabaremos en un año [and if, sir, you are going to reproach me repeatedly for my words, we shall not finish in a lifetime]." In this case Don Quijote apologizes, and admits that there is as much sense to the one as to the other expression (in other words, he is brought to recognize the wisdom of "popular etymology"). Indeed, Don Quijote the humanist is made to learn new words, popular graphic expressions unknown to him—such as terms descriptive of *naturalia turpia* which the high-minded knight was wont to eschew in his conversation (1.48: *hacer aguas* "to urinate"; Sancho is triumphant: "Es posible que no entienda vuestra merced hacer aguas mayores o menores? [Is it possible that your worship does not understand how to make greater or lesser waters?]"), or low argot expressions (1.22: *gurapas, canario* [rogues, rascal], from the language of galley-slaves). And—the acme of shame for a humanist!—it may even happen that he has to be instructed in Latinisms by Sancho (with whom they appear, of course, in garbled form), as when he fails to understand his squire's remark: "quien infierno tiene [he who is in hell] *nula es retencia*" (1.25): it is significant that Sancho the Catholic Positivist is more familiar with ecclesiastical Latin terms than is his master, the idealistic humanist. Thus, Don Quijote is shown not only as a teacher but also as a student of language; his word-usage is by no means accepted as an ideal. And the reader is allowed to suppose that, to Cervantes himself, the language of the knight was not above reproach: when, in his solemn challenges or declarations of love, Quijote indulges in archaic phonetics (*f-* instead of *h-*) and morphology (uncontracted verb forms), this is not so different from the *a Dios prazca* [may it please God] of Sancho, or the *voacé* [thou] of one of the captives.

It seems to me that Cervantes means to present the problem of the Good Language in all its possibilities, without finally establishing an absolute: on the one hand, Sancho is allowed to state his ideal of linguistic tolerance (2.19): "Pues sabe que no me he criado en la corte ni he estudiado en Salamanca para saber si añado o quito alguna letra a mis vocablos, no hay para qué obligar al sayagués a que hable como el toledano, y toledanos puede haber que no las cortan en el aire en esto del hablar polido [You know I wasn't brought up at the Court, and never studied at Salamanca to learn whether I'm putting a letter too many or too few into my words. Good Lord! You mustn't expect a Sayagan to speak like a chap from Toledo, and there may be Toledans who aren't so slick at this business of speaking pretty either]." On the other, Don Quijote may assert his ideal of an "illustrated language" (in the sense of Du Bellay): when Sancho fails to understand the Latinism *erutar* (2.43), Don Quijote remarks: "*Erutar*, Sancho, quiere decir 'regoldar,' y este es uno de los mas torpes vocablos que tiene la lengua castellana, aunque cs mas significativo. La gente curiosa se ha acogido al latín, y al *regoldar* dice *erutar*, y a los *regüeldos, erutaciones*; y cuando algunos no entienden sus términos, importa poco, que el uso los irá introduciendo con el tiempo, que con facilidad se entiendan; y esto es enriquecer la lengua, sobre quien tiene poder el vulgo y el uso [*Erutar*, Sancho, means belch, and that is one of the coarsest words in the Castilian language, though it is very expressive; and so refined people have resorted to Latin, and instead of *belch* say *erutar* and for *belches, eructions*; and if some people do not understand these terms it is of little consequence, for they will come into use in time, and then they will be generally understood; for that is the way to enrich the language, which depends upon custom and the common people]." Thus, Don Quijote would create a more refined word-usage—though, at the same time, he realizes that the ultimate decision as to the enrichment of the language rests with the people; and he does not deny the expressivity of the popular expressions. Sancho's principle of linguistic expressivity, which is in line with his advocacy of the natural, of that which is inborn in man, must be seen *together* with Quijote's principle of linguistic refinement— which is a reflection of his consistent advocacy of the ideal: by positing the two points of view, the one problem in question is dialectically developed. It is obvious that in the passage on erutar we have a plea for a cultured language—though the ratification by the common people is urged. But this is not the same as saying that Cervantes himself is here pleading for linguistic refinement: rather, I believe, he takes no final stand but is mainly interested in a dialectical play, in bringing out the manifold facets of the problem involved. Sancho has a way of deciding problems trenchantly; Don Quijote is more aware of complexities; Cervantes stands above them both: to him, the two expressions regoldar and erutar serve to reveal so many perspectives of language.

Within the framework of linguistic perspectivism fits also Cervantes's attitude toward dialects and jargons. Whereas, to Dante, all dialects appeared as inferior (though inferior in different degrces) realizations of a Platonic-Christian ideal pattern of language, as embodied in the *vulgare illustre,*

Cervantes saw them as ways of speech which exist as individual realities and which have their justification in themselves. The basic Cervantine conception of perspectivism did not allow for the Platonic or Christian ideal of language: according to the creator of Don Quijote, dialects are simply the different reflections of reality (they are "styles," as the equally tolerant linguist of today would say), among which no one can take precedence over the other. Borgese, in "Il senso della letteratura italiana," speaks definitively of Dante's conception of the *vulgare illustre*: "Si veda nel *De vulgari eloquentia* com' egli si costruisca una lingua italiana che abbia carattere di perfezione divina, che sia, diremmo, una lingua celestiale e di angeli, di religione e di ragione; tanto che questa lingua, illustre, antica, cardinale, cortegiana, non si trova per natura in nessun luogo, e il parlare nativo di questo o di quel luogo, il dialetto di questa o quella città, è tanto più o meno nobile quanto più o meno s'avvicina a quell' ideale, così come un colore è più o meno cospicuo, più o meno luminoso, secondo che somigli al bianco o gli contrasti. Il bianco, il puro, il tutto-luce, l'astratto ... da Dante è considerato ... come tipo supremo del bello." Cervantes, on the contrary, delights in the different shades, in the particular gradations and nuances, in the gamut of colors between white and black, in the transitions between the abstract and the concrete. Hence we may explain the frequent excursions of Cervantes into what today we would call "dialectal geography" (1.2): "un pescado que en Castilla llaman *abadejo* y en Andalucía *bacallao* y en otras partes *curadillo*, y en otras *truchuela* [a fish that is called pollack in Castile and cod in Andalusia, in some parts ling and in others (sic) troutlet]" (in fact, a modern Catalonian linguist, Montoliu, has been able to base his study of the synonyms for "mackerel" on this passage); 1.41: "*Tagarinos* llaman en Berbería a los moros de Aragón, y a los de Granada *mudéjares*, y en el reino de Fez llaman a los mudéjares *elches* [In Barbary they call the Moors of Aragon *Tagarines*, and those of Granada *Mudejares*; and in the kingdom of Fez they call the Mudajares (sic) *Elches*]." In these lexicological variants, Cervantes must have seen not a striving toward the approximation of an ideal, but only the variegated phantasmagoria of human approaches to reality: each variant has its own justification, but all of them alike reflect no more than human "dreams." Don Quijote is allowed to expose the inadequacy of such chance designations, as appear in any one dialect, by punning on the word *truchuela* "mackerel": "Como hay muchas truchuelas, podrán servir de una trucha [As there are many troutlets they may serve me from one trout]," where he interprets (or pretends to interpret) truchuela as "little trout." What, ultimately, is offered here is a criticism of the arbitrariness of any fixed expression in human language (*Sprachkritik*): the criticism which underlies the unspoken question, "Why should a mackerel be called a small trout?" Again, when Don Quijote hears the expression *cantor* used in reference to the galley-slaves, he asks the candid question (1.22): "Por músicos y cantores van también a galeras? [Do men go to the galleys for being musicians and singers?]" Thus the literal interpretation of the expression serves to put into relief the macabre and ironic flavor of its metaphorical use [*cantar* = *cantar en el ansia* "to 'sing' under torture"]. Here we witness the bewilderment of Don Quijote, who tries to hold words to a strict account; we may, perhaps, sense a criticism of Quijote's too-literal approach toward language—but this, in itself, would amount to a criticism of the ambiguity of human speech. Cervantes is satisfied, however, merely to suggest the linguistic problem, without any didactic expansion.

A masterpiece of linguistic perspectivism is offered in the transposition, by Sancho, of the high-flown jargon of love contained in Don Quijote's letter to Dulcinea, of which the squire has remembered the spirit, if not the exact words. Sancho, like most primitive persons, has an excellent acoustic memory, "toma de memoria [learns by heart]" and "tiene en su memoria [has in his memory]" but, in attempting to cope with Don Quijote's florid language, he must necessarily "transpose," remembering what he *thinks* Quijote has said. In this way, "soberana y alta señora [supreme and great lady]" becomes "alta y sobajada señora [great and crumpled lady]"—which the barber corrects to ". . . sobrehumana o soberana [. . . superhuman or supreme]": for this single term of address we are presented with three versions, resulting in a polyonomasia, as in the case of the proper names. Again, "de punto de ausencia y el llagado de las telas del corazon [from the place of absence and the wound of the heart's tissues]" > "el llego y falto de sueño y el ferido [the arrival and lack of sleep and the wound]" (it is as though Sancho, while indulging in Isidorian etymologies, is shrewdly diagnosing his master). In such linguistic exchanges we have a parallel to the numerous dialogues between the knight and the squire which, as is well known, are inserted into the novel in order to show the different perspectives under which the same events must appear to two persons of such different backgrounds. This means that, in our novel, things are represented, not for what they are in themselves but only as things spoken about or thought about; and this involves breaking the narrative presentation into two points of view. There can be no certainty about the "unbroken" reality of the events; the only unquestionable truth on which the reader may depend is the will of the artist who chose to break up a multivalent reality into different perspectives. In other words: perspectivism suggests an Archimedean principle outside of the plot—and the Archimedes must be Cervantes himself.

In the second chapter, the nickname "los del rebuzno [the brayers]" is loaded with a double-entendre: the Spanish variants of Gothamites draw on the doubful art of braying for their proud war slogan: their banner bears the verse "no rebuznaron en balde / el uno y otro alcalde [they did not bray for naught / one mayor and another]" (the "regidores" have been promoted to "alcaldes" in the course of history and—evidently—thanks to the compulsion of rhyme). Here, Don Quijote is entrusted by Cervantes with exploding the vanity of such sectional patriotism: the humanistic knight, in a masterful speech which includes a series of Spanish ethnical nicknames (which take the modern philologian, Rodríguez Marín, over four full pages to explain): "los de la Reloja, los cazoleros, berenjeneros, ballenatos, jaboneros [the Relojas, the medlers, the eggplanters, whale calves, soapmakers]," shows the excessive vanity, originating in the flesh, not in the spirit, in the devil, not in true Catholicism, that is underlying the townspeople's attitude of resenting nicknames—i.e. of investing such trifling expressions of the language with disproportionate symbolic value. The Don Quijote who, on other occasions, is only too apt to introduce symbolism and general principles into everyday life, is here inspired by Cervantes to expose the vanity of misplaced symbolizing and generalization. The epithet "los del rebuzno" is thus made to shine with the double light of a stupidity—that wants to be taken seriously; of a local peculiarity—that aspires to "national" importance. The reader is free to go ahead and extend this criticism to other national slogans. That here Cervantes is endorsing Don Quijote seems beyond doubt since, when the novelist introduces this incident, he, speaking in his own right, attributes the adoption of the communal slogan to the activity of "the devil who never sleeps" and who is forever building "quimeras de no nada [chimeras from nothing at all]"—we might say: to a baroque devil who delights in deluding man. The chimeric and self-deluding quality of human vanity could hardly be illustrated more effectively than in this story, where the art of braying is first inflated and then deflated before our eyes, appearing as a "special language of human vanity." And we may see in Cervantes's twofold treatment of the problem of nicknames another example of his baroque attitude (what is true, what is dream?)—this time, toward language. Is not human language, also *vanitas vanitatum*, is it not sometimes a "braying" of a sort? Cervantes does not outspokenly say so.

The double point of view into which Cervantes is wont to break up the reality he describes may also appear in connection with one key-word, recurring throughout a given episode, upon which Cervantes casts two different lighting effects. We have a most successful example of this in two chapters [part 2, 25 and 27] where our interest is focused on the motif "braying like an ass." The connecting link between the two chapters is evidently "vanity": it is vanity that prompts the two *regidores* of the Mancha de Aragón to try to out-bray each other, as they search for the lost animal which they want to decoy and whose answering bray each seems to hear—only to learn, at the end, that the braying he heard was that of the other *regidor* (the ass, meanwhile, having died). It is vanity, again, that induces the townspeople—who, after this adventure, were called "los del rebuzno" by the inhabitants of neighboring villages—to sally forth to do battle with their deriders. And it is also due to vanity, on Sancho's part, that he, while deprecating, along with Don Quijote, the gift of imitating an ass, cannot refrain from showing off his own prowess in this regard before the townspeople—who straightway turn upon him in anger and beat him.

The vanity of "braying" shares with all other vanities the one characteristic that an inconsequential feature is invested with a symbolic value which it cannot, in the light of reason, deserve. Thus a duality (sham value vs. real value) offers itself to the artist for exploitation. In the first chapter, Cervantes has the two regidores address each other with doubtful compliments: "de vos a un asno, compadre, no hay alguna diferencia en cuanto toca al rebuznar [between you and an ass, friend, there is no difference when it comes to braying]" or "[you are the] más perito rebuznador del mundo [best brayer in all the world]." In the word *rebuznador,* there is a striving after the noble ring of *campeador, emperador* [great warrior, emperor]—which is drowned out by the blatant voice of the unregenerate animal: an ambivalence which exposes the hollow pretense.

There is one case in which Cervantes's perspectivism has crystallized into a bifocal word-formation; in Don Quijote's remark: "eso que a ti te parece bacía de barbero me parece a mí el yelmo de Mambrino, y a otro le parecerá otra cosa [so what seems to you to be a barber's basin appears to me to be Mambrino's helmet, and to another as something else]" (1.25), there is contained a Weltanschauung which Américo Castro has, in a masterly fashion, recognized as a philosophical criticism (typical of the Renaissance) of the senses ("el engaño a los ojos [deception of the eyes]"); and this vision finds its linguistic expression, highly daring for Cervantes's time, in the coinage *baciyelmo,* with which the tolerant Sancho concludes the debate about the identity of the shining object—as if he were reasoning: "if a thing appears to me as *a*, to you as *b*, it may be, in reality, neither *a* nor *b*, but *a* + *b*" (a similar tolerance is shown by Don Quijote a little later in the same episode, when he remarks, in the argument about the hypothetical nature of the hypothetical Mambrino: "Asi que, Sancho, deja ese caballo, o asno, o lo que quisieras que sea [So Sancho leave that horse, or ass, or whatever you want to call it]"; Quijote, however, does not go so far as to coin a *caballi-asno*). Now, it is evident to any linguist that, when shaping baciyelmo, Cervantes must have had in mind an existing formation of the same type; and his pattern must have been that which furnished designations of hybrid animals—i.e. of a fantastic deviation from Nature—so that this quality of the fantastic and the grotesque is automatically transferred to the coinage baciyelmo; such a form does not guarantee the "actual" existence of any such entity $a + b$. In most cases, Cervantes must obey language, though he questions it: a basin he can only call "bacía," a helmet, only "yelmo"; with the creation of baciyelmo, however, he frees himself from linguistic limitations. Here, as elsewhere, I would emphasize, more than Castro (whose task it was to show us the conformity to Renaissance thinking of what Cervantes himself has called his "espíritu lego [layman's spirit]"), the artistic freedom conquered by Cervantes. In the predicament indicated by (the paradigmatic) ". . . o lo que quisieras que sea," the artist has asserted his own free will.

Now, from what has been said it would appear that the artist Cervantes uses linguistic perspectivism only in order to assert his own creative freedom; and this linguistic perspectivism, as I have already suggested, is only one facet of the general spirit of relativism which has been recognized by most critics as characteristic of our novel. Such perspectivism, however, had, in the age of Cervantes, to acknowledge ultimately a realm of the absolute—which was, in his case, that of Spanish Catholicism. Cervantes, while glorying in his role of the artist who can stay aloof from the "engaños a los ojos," the "sueños" of this world, and create his own, always sees himself as over-shadowed by supernal forces: the artist Cervantes never denies God, or His institutions, the King and the State. God, then, cannot be attracted into the artist's linguistic perspectivism; rather is Cervantes's God placed above the perspectives of language, he is said to be, as we have seen, the supreme "Entendedor" of the language He has created—just as Cervantes, from his lower vantage-point, seeks to be. Perhaps we may assume with Cervantes the old Neo-platonic belief in an artistic Maker who is enthroned above the manifold facets and perspectives of the world.

The story of the *Cautivo* (1.37 *seq*), one of the many tales interpolated into the main plot, exemplifies linguistic perspectivism made subservient to the divine. The maiden betrothed to the ex-captive, who enters the stage dressed and veiled in Moorish fashion and who, without speaking a word, bows to the company in Moorish fashion, gives from the beginning the impression "que . . . devia de ser mora y que no sabía hablar cristiano [that . . . she had to be a Moor and did not know how to talk like a Christian]" (note the expression *hablar cristiano* [instead of *hablar castellano*] which, with its identification of "Spanish" and "Christian," anticipates the religious motif basic to the story). Dorotea is the one to ask the all-important question: "esta señora es mora o cristiana? [is this woman a Moor or a Christian?]"— to which the Cautivo answers that she is a Moor in her costume and in her body, but in her soul, a great Christian, although not yet baptized—but "Dios será servido que presto se bautice [God will be well served as she will soon be baptized]" (again, we may see in this mention of God not only a conventional form but a suggestion of the main problem, which is the working of Divine Grace). The Cautivo, speaking in Arabic, asks his betrothed to lift her veil in order to show forth her enchanting beauty; when asked about her name, he gives it in the Arabic form: *lela Zoraida.* And now the Moorish girl herself speaks for the first time: "No, no Zoraida: María, María"—repeating this statement twice more (the last time half in Arabic, half in Spanish: "Sí, sí, María: Zoraida *macange* [not at all]." The change of name which she claims—evidently in anticipation of the change of name which will accompany her baptism—is of deep significance; it is a profession of faith, of conversion. We will learn later that she must become a María because, since her early childhood, she had been taken under the mantle of the Virgin.

After this first appearance of "Zoraida-María," whose two names are nothing but the linguistic reflection of her double nature, the episode is interrupted by Don Quijote's speech on *armas y letras* [arms and letters]; thus, after the briefest of introductions, we must lose sight for a while of Zoraida-María, the puzzle of whose twofold name and Januslike personality remains suspended in midair. The interruption is significant: Cervantes, in the episodic short stories, follows for the most part a technique opposed to that of the main plot: in the latter we are always shown first the objective reality of events, so that when they later become distorted after having passed through the alembic of Don Quijote's mind (Sancho, in general, remains more true to the reality he has experienced) we, from the knowledge we have previously gained, are proof against the knight's folly. But, in the short stories, on the contrary, Cervantes's technique is to tantalize us with glimpses into what seems an incredible situation, worthy of Quijote's own imagination (in our own story there suddenly appears before the group of Don Quijote's friends assembled in an inn, an exotic-looking woman, dressed in outlandish gear, with her companion who has to talk for her) and with all the connotations of the unreal; and the author is careful to protract our suspense to the utmost before giving us the solution of the initial puzzle. Thus the interpolations of these episodic short stories, whose reality is at least as fantastic as the most daring dreams of the mad knight, offer another revelation of the perspectivism of Cervantes; we have to do not only with the opposition between prosaic reality and fantastic dreams: reality itself can be both prosaic and fantastic. If, in the main plot, Cervantes has carried out his program of "derribar la máquina mal fundada [toppling the ill-founded machinery]" of the fantastic, he has taken care to rebuild this machinery in the by-stories. And our tale of the *Captive* is an excellent illustration of this rule.

When, after Don Quijote's speech, the Captive tells his story *ab ovo*, explaining how the startling fact of a "Zoraida-María" came to pass, we are allowed a glimpse into the historic reality of that hybrid world of Mohammedans and Christians, which was the equivalent in Cervantes's time of the *fronterizo* milieu of the romances—only, a more complicated variant because of the two different groups representative of the Mohammedan faith then facing the Spaniards: the Turks and the Arabs, the former the more ruthless type, the latter (to which Lela Marién and her father belong) the type more amenable to the Christian way of life. Indeed, the Arabs themselves seem to feel more akin to the Christian civilization than to the Turkish (the girl's father calls the Turks *canes* [canines]; it is ironic that later, after he has been deeply wronged by the Christians, he must call them *perros* [dogs]).

As the Captive tells the story of the tragic events that took place against the background of the warring Turkish Empire, he embellishes his (Spanish-language) narrative with words from Turkish and Arabic, offering a linguistic mosaic that adds to the local color of his story. If we compare the Turkish words with the Arabic, we will note the sharpest of contrasts: the former are of a factual reference, narrowly descriptive, with no transcendental connotations (for the Turks are excluded from the possibility of Enlightenment by Grace): *leventes, bagarinos, baño* [Turkish sailors, Bagarine oarsmen, prison-house], *pasamaques, zoltanís, gilecuelco* [shoes, coins, jacket]; we find also the pejorative epithet *Uchalí Fartax* "que quiere decir en lengua turquesca el renegado tiñoso, porque lo era [which means in Turkish "the scabby renegade," which he was]" (again, the *convenientia* between names and objects!). The Arabic words, on the contrary, are nearly always connected with things religious and, more specifically, with things Christian— so that a kind of transposition (or perspectivism) is achieved: "Lela Marién" instead of "Nuestra Señora la Vírgen María"; "Alá," for the Christian God, and also the interjection "quelá" in the same reference; *nizarani* for "Christians"; *la zalá cristianesca* for "the Christian prayer," in which the adjective *cristianesco* (instead of *cristiano*), formed after *morisco, turquesco*, has something of the same transposed character, as if the Christian rites were seen from the outside. And, in addition to the linguistic medley offered the reader directly, there is a reference to the polyglot habits among the protagonists of the story. Zoraida, for example, chooses Arabic as the private language in which to talk and write to the Captive, but converses with the Christians (as also does her father) in the *lingua franca*—which language is characterized by the Captive as "lengua que en toda la Berberia, y aun en Constantinopla se habla entre cautivos y moros, que ni es morisca ni castellana ni de otra nacion alguna, sino una mezcla de todas las lenguas, con la cual todos nos entendemos [a language spoken by captives and Moors throughout Barbary and even in Constantinople, which is neither Morisco nor Castillian nor of any other nation, but, rather, is a mixture of all languages, and with it we all understand each other]," or "la bastarda lengua que . . . allí se usa [the bastard language . . . used there]": a characterization, it may be noted, which is not basically different from that offered in our times by Schuchardt ("Mischsprache," "Verkehrssprache"), the student of lingua franca, of the Creole languages etc., and the advocate of an international artificial language. Castilian, Turkish, Arabic, with reminiscences of lingua franca: why this Babelic confusion of tongues in our story? It does not suffice to appeal to the historical fact that these languages were actually spoken at the time in the Ottoman Empire, where Cervantes himself had lived as a captive: for, in addition to the foreign phrases that might serve simply for local color, we have to do evidently with an express concern for each individual language as such—to the extent that we are always informed in which language a certain speech, letter or dialogue was couched. It seems to me that Cervantes would point out that differences of language do not, by principle, hinder the working of Christian Grace—though he evidently grades the languages according to their penetrability by things Christian: Turkish is presented as on a lower level than Arabic—which lends itself so easily to the transposition of Christian concepts. And this linguistic transposition of things Christian into things Moorish reflects only the transposed situation of a Moor who becomes a Christian; the story of the Captive and of Zoraida María shows Grace working toward the salvation of a disbeliever and toward the sacramental union, by a Christian marriage, of two beings of different races: above the divergence of race and language God understands the Christian longing of Zoraida for the *Alá cristiano*. It was the Virgin Mary, of whom she had learned from a Christian nurse, who inspired her to rescue the Christian solider and to flee with him to a Christian country in order there to be baptized and married. When Zoraida speaks of Alá, every one knows that the Christian God is meant—whose true nature shines through the linguistic disguise. The same symbol is carried out on another plane: when, from her window, Zoraida's white hand is seen, adorned with

Moorish jewels (*ajorcas*), waving a Christian cross, the ajorcas are naturally overshadowed by the cross. Again, in the case of Zoraida's letters to the prisoners, written in Arabic but adorned with the sign of the Cross, it is clear that these indications of different cultural climates clearly express only one thing: her will to be a Christian. It is not the language, the gesture, the costume, or the body that matter to Him, but the meaning behind all the exterior manifestations: the soul. God, Cervantes is telling us, can recognize behind the "perspective" of a disbeliever, His true faithful follower.

I cannot quite agree with Castro, whom seems to see mainly the human side of the episode, when he says: "Amor y religión (ésta como envoltura de aquél) llevan a Zoraida tras su cautivo [Love and religion (the latter acting as a cover for the former) bring Zoraida after her captive]," and considers the story to be one of "armonía entre seres concordados [harmony among reconciled beings]." Rather, I should say that religion is the kernel, love the envelopment; we have here a drama of Divine Grace working against all possible handicaps and using the love between Moor and Christian as a means to an end: the conversion of Zoraida (and, incidentally, the return of a renegade to the bosom of the Church); therefore Cervantes has devised his story against the background of the Spanish-Turkish wars, which ended with the victory of the Spaniards at Lepanto and in which, as Titian has represented it, Spain succors Christian faith. I concur absolutely with Castro, however, when he goes on to say that this story of abduction is the most violent and the most tragic of all the episodes in the novel: Zoraida, in her zeal to receive holy baptism and the sacrament of Christian marriage, must cheat her father, must see him subjected by her doings to the violence of the Christians who truss him up and finally leave him marooned on a desert island, where he cries out to his daughter, alternately cursing and beseeching her. Here is a good Arab, meek and truthful to Christians, who is thrown back to the Mohammedan god by the ruthless deed of his Christian daughter. That such sins may be committed for the rescue of a soul can only be explained, Cervantes seems to tell us, by the incalculable will of Providence. Why should these sins be made corollary to the salvation of the particular soul of Zoraida—while the soul of her father becomes thereby utterly lost to salvation? What whimsicality of God! I should say that this scene exhibits not so much the "abismos de lo humano [human abysses]," as Castro has it, but rather "abismos de lo divino [divine abysses]." No harmonious earthly marriage could be concluded on the basis of such a terrifying violation of the Fourth Commandment; but God is able to put the laws of morality out of function in order to reach His own goal.

In our story, which is the story of a great deceit, the words referring to "deceit" take on a particularly subtle double-entendre. When, for example, Zoraida, in one of her letters to the Captive, says: "no te fíes de ningun moro, porque son todos *marfuzes* [do not trust any Moor; they are all deceitful]" of her Moslem coreligionists, she is using an originally Arabic word for "treacherous" which had come to be borrowed by the Spaniards probably to refer, primarily, to the treachery of the Mohammedans (meaning something like "false as a Moor"); the choice of this word, which sounds rather strange when used by an Arab, must mean that Zoraida is judging the Arabs according to Christian prejudices (it is ironical that, in this story, it is the Arabs who are faithful and kind, and the Christians who are "marfuzes"—although working toward a goal presumably willed by Providence). Again, the accusation of cheating is reversed when Zoraida, speaking as a Moor to the Christian captive, in the presence of her father, remarks: ". . . vosotros cristianos siempre mentís en cuanto decís, y os hacéis pobres por engañar a los moros [You Christians always lie, and you impoverish yourselves by deceiving the Moors]"; here, where her judgment is, indeed, factually justified, she is actually speaking disingenuously—in order to further the stratagem planned by the Christians. The discrepancy between words and meaning, between judgment and behavior, has reached such proportions that we can view only with perplexity the "abismo del divino" which makes it possible that such evil means are accepted to further a noble purpose; the story offers us no way out but to try to share Zoraida's belief in the beneficent intervention of Lela Marién, who has prompted the good-wicked enterprise ("plega a Alá, padre mio, que Lela Marién, que ha sido la causa de que yo sea cristiana, ella te consuele en tu tristeza [may it please Allah, my father, that Lela Marién, who caused me to be Christian, console you in your sadness]"). When Zoraida, speaking to her father, states of her deed "que parece tan buena como tú, padre amado, la juzgas por mala [it seems as good as you, beloved father, yet you hold it to be evil]," we are offered basically the same perspectivistic pattern that we have noted in the case of baciyelmo: it is implied, evidently, that Lela Marién knows of no perspectivism. There can be no doubt that what Cervantes is dealing with here is the tortuous and Jesuitic divinity that he was able to see in his time—whose decisions he accepts, while bringing out all the complications involved. Along with the submission to the divine there is instituted a tragic trial against it, a trial on moral grounds, and, on these grounds, the condemnation is unmitigated; the sacramental force of a father's curse is not entirely counterbalanced by the sacramental force of the Christian rites, the desire for which on Zoraida's part brought about the father's plight. Perhaps no writer, remaining within the boundaries of orthodox religion, has revealed more of the perplexities inherent in the theocratic order (a Nietzsche might have called this story an example of the immorality of God and have advocated the overthrow of such a God—whereas Cervantes quietly stays within the boundaries of the Christian fold). And this acme of submissive daring has been achieved by placing the divine beyond the perspectives which appear to the human eye.

Zoraida herself, for all her religious fervor, innocence, and supernatural beauty is, at the same time, capable of great wickedness. And again linguistic perspectivism is invoked in order to bring this side of her nature into relief. There is a moment when the band of fugitives pass the promontory called, after the mistress of Roderick, the last of the Gothic Kings, *cabo de la Cava Rumia* ". . . de la mala mujer cristiana [. . . of the evil Christian woman]"; they insist, however, that to them it is not the "abrigo de mala mujer, sino puerto seguro de nuestro remedio [shelter of the evil woman, but the safe port of our remedy]." Now, when the name of this infamous woman, who sinned for love, is brought before the reader, he cannot fail to think of Zoraida—though, in the comparison with the Arabic prostitute "por quien se perdió España [for whom Spain was lost]," the betrothed of the Captive must appear as a pure woman, who refused to live in a state of sin before her marriage. At the same time, however, Cervantes may wish us to realize how close was Zoraida to the abyss, and to see the ward of the Virgin, for a moment, under the perspective of la Cava.

If we look back now over the development of this essay, we will see that we have been led from a plethora of names, words, languages, from polynomasia, polyetymologia and polyglottism, to the linguistic perspectivism of the artist Cervantes who knows that the transparence of language is a fact for God alone. And, at this point, I may be allowed to repeat, as a kind of epitomizing epilogue, the final passages of a lecture on the *Quijote* which I have given at several universities—which, I trust, will serve to round out the linguistic details I have pointed out earlier and to put them into relationship with the whole of the novel: a relationship which, in the course of our linguistic discussion, has already been tentatively indicated. After explaining that the *Quijote* appeals as well to children as to adults because of its combination of imagination and criticism, and that the modern genre of the critical novel, which started with a criticism of books and of a bookish culture (a criticism of the romances of chivalry) and came to be expanded to a new integration of the critical and the imaginative, was the discovery of Cervantes, I continued thus:

It is one of the great miracles of history (which is generally regarded deterministically by professional historians, who present individual phenomena as enclosed within tight compartments), that the greatest deeds sometimes occur at a place and a time when the historian would least expect them. It is a historical miracle that, in the Spain of the Counter-Reformation, when the trend was toward the reestablishment of authoritarian discipline, an artist should have arisen who, thirty-two years before Descartes's *Discours de la méthode* (that autobiography of an independent philosophical thought, as Lanson has called it), was to give us a narrative which is simply one exaltation of the independent mind of man—and of a particularly powerful type of man: of the artist. It is not Italy, with its Ariosto and Tasso, not France with its Rabelais and Ronsard, but Spain that gave us a narrative which is a monument to the narrator qua narrator, qua artist. For, let us not be mistaken: the real protagonist of this novel is not Quijote, with his continual misrepresentation of reality, or Sancho with his skeptical half-endorsement of quixotism—and surely not any of the central figures of the illusionistic by-stories: the hero is Cervantes, the artist himself, who combines a critical and illusionistic art according to his free will. From the moment we open the book to the moment we put it down, we are given to understand that an almighty overlord is directing us, who leads us where he pleases. The prologue of the whole work shows us Cervantes in the perplexity of an author putting the final touches to his work, and we understand that the "friend" who seemingly came to his aid with a solution was only one voice within the freely fabricating poet. And, on the last page of the book when, after Quijote's Christian death, Cervantes has that Arabian historian Cide Hamete Benegeli lay away his pen, to rest forever, on the top of the cupboard in order to forestall any further spurious continuation (after the manner of Avellaneda) of the novel, we know that the reference to the Arabian pseudo-historian is only a pretext for Cervantes to reclaim for himself the relationship of real father (no longer the "step-father," as in the prologue) to his book. Then the pen delivers itself of a long speech, culminating in the words: "For me alone Don Quijote was born and I for him; his task was to act, mine to write. For we alone are made for each other" ("Para mí solo nació Don Quijote, y yo para él; él supo obrar, y yo escribir; solos los dos somos para en uno"). An imperious *alone* (*solo*[*s*]) which only Cervantes could have said and in which all the Renaissance pride of the poet asserts itself: the poet who was the traditional immortalizer of the great deeds of historical heroes and princes. An Ariosto could have said the same words about the Duke of Ferrara.

The function of eulogizing princes was, as is well known, the basis of the economical situation of the Renaissance artist: he was given sustenance by the prince in return for the immortal glory which he bestowed upon his benefactor. But Don Quijote is no prince from whom Cervantes could expect to receive a pension, no doer of great deeds in the outer world (his greatness lay only in his warm heart), and not even a being who could be attested in any historical source—however much Cervantes might pretend to such sources. Don Quijote acquired his immortality exclusively at the hands of Cervantes—as the latter well knows and admits. Obviously, Quijote wrought only what Cervantes wrote, and he was born for Cervantes as much as Cervantes was born for him! In the speech of the pen of the pseudo-chronicler we have the most discreet and the most powerful self-glorification of the artist which has ever been written. The artist Cervantes grows by the glory which his characters have attained; and in the novel we see the process by which the figures of Don Quijote and Sancho become living persons, stepping out of the novel, so to speak, to take their places in real life—finally to become immortal historical figures. Thomas Mann, in a recent essay on the *Quijote* (in "Leiden und Grösse der Meister"), has said: "This is quite unique. I know of no other hero of a novel in world literature who would equally, so to speak, live off the glory of his own glorification ("ein Held, der von seinem Ruhm, von seiner Besungenheit lebte"). In the second part of the novel, when the Duke and Duchess ask to see the by now historical figures of Quijote and Panza, the latter says to the Duchess: "I am Don Quijote's squire who is to be found also *in the story* and who is called Sancho Panza—unless they have changed me in the cradle—I mean to say, at the printer's." In such passages, Cervantes willingly destroys the artistic illusion: he, the puppeteer, lets us see the strings of his puppet-show: "see, reader, this is not life, but a stage, a book: art; recognize the life-giving power of the artist as a thing distinct from life!" By multiplying his masks (the friend of the prologue, the Arabian historian, sometimes the characters who serve as his mouthpiece), Cervantes seems to strengthen his grip on that whole artistic cosmos. And the strength of the grip is enhanced by the very nature of the protagonists: Quijote is what we would call today a split personality, sometimes rational, sometimes foolish; Sancho, too, at times no less quixotic than his master, is at other times incalculably rational. In this way, the author makes it possible for himself to decide when his characters will act reasonably, when foolishly (no one is more unpredictable than a fool who pretends to wisdom). At the start of his journey with Sancho, Don Quijote promises his squire an island kingdom to be ruled over by him, just as was done in the case of numerous squires in literature. But, acting on his critical judgment (of which he is not devoid), Don Quijote promises to give it to him immediately after their conquest—instead of waiting until the squire has reached old age, as is the custom in the books of chivalry. The quixotic side of Sancho accepts this prospective kingship without questioning its possibility, but his more earthly nature visualizes—and criticizes—the actual scene of the coronation: how would his rustic spouse Juana Gutiérrez look with a crown on her head? Two examples of foolishness, two critical attitudes: none of them is the attitude of the writer, who remains above the two split personalities and the four attitudes.

With the Machiavellian principle "divide and conquer" applied to his characters, the author succeeds in making himself indispensable to the reader: while, in his Prologue, Cervantes calls for a critical attitude on our part, he makes us depend all the more on his guidance through the psychological intricacies of the narrative: here, at least, he leaves us no free will. We may even infer that Cervantes rules imperiously over his own self: it was he who felt this self to be split into a critical and an illusionistic part (*desengaño* [disillusion] and *engaño* [deceit]); but in this baroque Ego he made order, a precarious order, it is true, which was reached only once by Cervantes in all his works—and which was reached in Spain only by Cervantes (for Calderón, Lope, Quevedo, Gracián decided that the world is only illusion and dreams, "que los sueños sueño son"). And indeed only once in world literature has this precarious order come into being: later thinkers and artists did not stop at proclaiming the inanity of the world: they went so far as to doubt the existence of any universal order and to deny a Creator, or at least, when imitating Cervantes's perspectivism (Gide, Proust, Conrad, Joyce, Virginia Woolf, Pirandello), they have failed to sense the unity behind perspectivism—so that, in their hands, the personality of the author is allowed to disintegrate. Cervantes stands at the other pole from that modern dissolution of the personality of the narrator: what grandeur there is in his attempt—made in the last moment before the unified Christian vision of the world was to fall asunder—to restore this vision on the artistic plane, to hold before our eyes a cosmos split into two separate halves: disenchantment and illusion, which, nevertheless, by a miracle, do not fall apart! Modern anarchy checked by a classical will to equipoise (the baroque attitude)! We recognize now that it is not so much that Cervantes's nature is split in two (critic and narrator) because this is required by the nature of Don Quijote, but rather that Don Quijote is a split character because his creator was a critic-poet who felt with almost equal strength the urge of illusionary beauty and of pellucid clarity.

To modern readers the "schizophrenic" Don Quijote might seem to be a typical case of social frustration: a person whose madness is conditioned

by the social insignificance into which the caste of the knights had
with the beginnings of modern warfare—just as, in Flaubert's *Un
simple,* we are meant to see as socially conditioned the frustrations of Félicité,
the domestic servant, which lead to the aberration of her imagination. I
would, however, warn the reader against interpreting Cervantes in terms of
Flaubert, since Cervantes himself has done nothing to encourage such a
sociological approach. Don Quijote is able to recover his sanity, if only on
his death-bed; and his erstwhile madness is but one reflection of that generally human lack of reason—above which the author has chosen to take his
stand.

High above this worldwide cosmos of his making, in which hundreds
of characters, situations, vistas, themes, plots and subplots are merged, Cervantes's artistic self is enthroned, an all-embracing creative self, Naturelike,
Godlike, almightly, all-wise, all-good—and benign: this visibly omnipresent
Maker reveals to us the secrets of his creation, he shows us the work of art
in the making, and the laws to which it is necessarily subjected. For this
artist is Godlike but not deified; far be it from us to conceive of Cervantes
as attempting to dethrone God, replacing Him by the artist as a superman.
On the contrary, Cervantes always bows before the supernal wisdom of God,
as embodied in the teaching of the Catholic Church and the established order
of the state and of society. *Qua* moralist, Cervantes is not at all "perspectivistic." Nor can we expect to find in Cervantes any of that romantic revolt
of the artist against society. But, on the other hand, the artist Cervantes has
extended, by the mere art of his narrative, the Demiurge-like, almost cosmic
independence of the artist. His humor, which admits of many strata, perspectives, masks—of relativization and dialectics—bears testimony to his
high position above the world. His humor is the freedom of the heights, no
fate-bound dionysiac dissolution of the individual into nothingness and
night, as with Schopenhauer and Wagner, but a freedom beneath the dome
of that religion which affirms the freedom of the will. There is, in the world
of his creation, the bracing air with which we may fill our lungs and by
which our individual senses and judgment are sharpened; and the crystalline
lucidity of an artistic Maker in its manifold reflections and refractions.

ERICH AUERBACH

The Enchanted Dulcinea

—Yo no veo, Sancho, dijo Don Quijote, sino a tres labradoras sobre tres borricos.

—Ahora me libre Dios del diablo, respondió Sancho; ¿y es posible que tres hacaneas, o como se llaman, blancas como el ampo de la nieve, le parezcan a vuesa merced borricos? Vive el Señor, que me pele estas barbas si tal fuese verdad.

—Pues yo te digo, Sancho amigo, dijo Don Quijote, que es tan verdad que son borricos o borricas, como yo soy Don Quijote, y tú Sancho Panza: a lo menos a mí tales me parecen.

—Calle, señor, dijo Sancho, no diga la tal palabra, sino despabile esos ojos, y venga a hacer reverencia a la señora de sus pensamientos, que ya llega cerca: y diciendo esto se adelantó a recebir a las tres aldeanas, y apeándose del rucio tuvo del cabestro al jumento de una de las tres labradoras, y hincando ambas rodillas en el suelo, dijo:

—Reina y princesa y duquesa de la hermosura, vuestra altivez y grandeza sea servida de recebir en su gracia y buen talante al cautivo caballero vuestro, que allí está hecho piedra mármol, todo turbado y sin pulsos de verse ante vuesa magnífica presencia. Yo soy Sancho su escudero, y él es el asendereado caballero Don Quijote de la Mancha, llamado por otro nombre el Caballero de la Triste Figura.

A esta sazón ya se había puesto Don Quijote de hinojos junto a Sancho, y miraba con ojos desencajados y vista turbada a la que Sancho llamaba reina y señora; y como no descubría en ella sino una moza aldeana y no muy buen rostro, porque era carirredonda y chata, estaba suspenso y admirabo, sin osar desplegar los labios. Las labradoras estaban asimismo atónitas viendo a aquellos dos hombres tan diferentes hincados de rodillas, que no dejaban pasar adelante a su compañera; pero rompiendo el silencio la detenida, toda desgradiada y mohína, dijo:

—Apártense nora en tal del camino, y dejenmos pasar, que vamos de priesa.

A lo que respondió Sancho:

—Oh princesa y señora universal del Toboso, ¿cómo vuestro magnífico corazón no se enternece viendo arrodillado ante vuestra sublimada precensia a la coluna y sustento de la andante caballería?

Oyendo lo cual otra de las dos dijo:

—Mas yo que te estrego burra de mi suegro: mirad con qué se vienen los señoritos ahora a hacer burlas de las aldeanas, como si aquí no supiésemos echar pullos como ellos: vayan su camino, y déjenmos hacer el nueso, y serles ha sano.

—Levántate, Sancho, dijo a este punto Don Quijote, que ya veo que la fortuna, de mi mal no harta, tiene tomados los caminos todos por donde pueda venir algún contento a esta ánima mezquina que tengo en las carnes. Y tú, oh extremo valor que puede desearse, término de la humana gentileza, único remedio de este afligido corazón que te adora, ya que el maligno encantador me persigue, y ha puesto nubes y cataratas en mis ojos, y para sólo ellos y no para otros ha mudado y transformando tu sin igual hermosura y rostro en el de una labradora pobre, si ya también el mío no le ha cambiado en el de algún vestiglo para hacerle aborrecible a tus ojos, no dejes de mirarme blanda y amorosamente, echando de ver en esta sumisión y arrodillamiento que a tu contrahecha hermosura hago, la humildad con que mi alma te adora.

—Toma que me agüelo, respondió la aldeana, amiguita soy yo de oír resquebrajos. Apártense y déjenmos ir, y agradecérselo hemos.

Apartóse Sancho y déjola ir, contentísimo de haber salido bien de su enredo. Apenas se vió libre la aldeana que había hecho la figura de Dulcinea cuando picando a su hacanea con un aguijón que en un palo traía, dió a correr por el prado adelante; y como la borrica sentía la punta del aguijón, que le fatigaba más de lo ordinario, comenzó a dar corcovos, de manera que dió con la señora Dulcinea en tierra: lo cual visto por Don Quijote, acudió a levantarla, y Sancho a componer y cinchar el albarda, que también vino a la barriga de la pollina. Acomodada pues el albarda, y queriendo Don Quijote levantar a su encantada señora en los brazos sobre la jumenta, la señora levantándose del suelo le quitó de aquel trabajo, porque haciéndose algún tanto atrás tomó una corridica, y puestas ambas manos sobre las ancas de la pollina dió con su cuerpo más ligero que un halcón sobre la albarda, y quedó a horcajadas como si fuera hombre, y entonces dijo Sancho:

—¡Vive Roque, que es la señora nuestra ama más ligera que un alcotán, y que puede enseñar a subir de la jineta al más diestro cordobés o mejicano; el arzón trasero de la silla pasó de un salto, y sin espuelas hace correr la hacanea como una cebra, y no le van en zaga sus doncellas, que todas corren como el viento!

Y así era la verdad, porque en viéndose a caballo Dulcinea todas picaron tras ella y dispararon a correr, sin volver la cabeza atrás por espacio de más de media legua. Siguiólas Don Quijote con las vista, y cuando vió que no parecían, volviéndose a Sancho le dijo:

—Sancho, ¿qué te parece, cuán mal quisto soy de encantadores? . . .

("I see nothing," declared Don Quixote, "except three farm girls on three jackasses."

"Then God deliver me from the devil!" exclaimed Sancho. "Is it possible that those three hackneys, or whatever you call them, white as the driven snow, look like jackasses to your Grace? By the living God, I would tear out this beard of mine if that were true!"

"But I tell you, friend Sancho, it is as true that those are jackasses, or she-asses, as it is that I am Don Quixote and you Sancho Panza. At least, that is the way they look to me."

"Be quiet, sir," Sancho admonished him, "you must not say such a thing as that. Open those eyes of yours and come do reverence to the lady of your affections, for she draws near."

Saying this, he rode on to meet the village maids and, slipping
down off his donkey, seized one of their beasts by the halter and
fell on his knees in front of its rider.

"O queen and princess and duchess of beauty," he said, "may
your Highness and Majesty be pleased to receive and show favor
to your captive knight, who stands there as if turned to marble,
overwhelmed and breathless at finding himself in your magnificent presence. I am Sancho Panza, his squire, and he is the world-
weary knight Don Quixote, otherwise known as the Knight of
the Mournful Countenance."

By this time Don Quixote was down on his knees beside Sancho. His eyes were fairly starting from their sockets and there
was a deeply troubled look in them as he stared up at the one
whom Sancho had called queen and lady; all that he could see in
her was a village wench, and not a very pretty one at that, for
she was round-faced and snub-nosed. He was astounded and per-
plexed and did not dare open his mouth. The girls were also very
much astonished to behold these two men, so different in appearance, kneeling in front of one of them so that she could not
pass. It was this one who most ungraciously broke the silence.

"Get out of my way," she said peevishly, "and let me pass.
And bad luck go with you. For we are in a hurry."

"O princess and universal lady of El Toboso!" cried Sancho.
"How can your magnanimous heart fail to melt as you behold
kneeling before your sublimated presence the one who is the very
pillar and support of knight-errantry?"

Hearing this, one of the others spoke up. "Whoa, there, she-
ass of my father!" she said. "Wait until I curry you down. Just
look at the small-fry gentry, will you, who've come to make sport
of us country girls! Just as if we couldn't give them tit for tat.
Be on your way and get out of ours, if you know what's good
for you."

"Arise, Sancho," said Don Quixote, "for I perceive that fortune
has not had her fill of evil done to me but has taken possession
of all the roads by which some happiness may come to what little
soul is left within me. And thou, who art all that could be desired,
the sum of human gentleness and sole remedy for this afflicted
heart that doth adore thee! The malign enchanter who doth persecute me hath placed clouds and cataracts upon my eyes, and
for them and them alone hath transformed thy peerless beauty
into the face of a lowly peasant maid; and I can only hope that

he has not likewise changed my face into that of some monster by way of rendering it abhorrent in thy sight. But for all of that, hesitate not to gaze upon me tenderly and lovingly, beholding in this act of submission as I kneel before thee a tribute to thy metamorphosed beauty from this humbly worshiping heart of mine."

"Just listen to him run on, will you? My grandmother!" cried the lass. "Enough of such gibberish. We'll thank you to let us go our way."

Sancho fell back and let her pass, being very thankful to get out of it so easily.

No sooner did she find herself free than the girl who was supposed to have Dulcinea's face began spurring her "cackney" with a spike on the end of a long stick that she carried with her, whereupon the beast set off at top speed across the meadow. Feeling the prick, which appeared to annoy it more than was ordinarily the case, the ass started cutting such capers that the lady Dulcinea was thrown to the ground. When he saw this, Don Quixote hastened to lift her up while Sancho busied himself with tightening the girths and adjusting the packsaddle, which had slipped down under the animal's belly. This having been accomplished, Don Quixote was about to take his enchanted lady in his arms to place her upon the she-ass when the girl saved him the trouble by jumping up from the ground, stepping back a few paces, and taking a run for it. Placing both hands upon the crupper of the ass, she landed more lightly than a falcon upon the packsaddle and remained sitting there astride it like a man.

"In the name of Roque!" exclaimed Sancho, "our lady is like a lanner, only lighter, and can teach the cleverest Cordovan or Mexican how to mount. She cleared the back of the saddle in one jump, and without any spurs she makes her hackney run like a zebra, and her damsels are not far behind, for they all of them go like the wind."

This was the truth. Seeing Dulcinea in the saddle, the other two prodded their beasts and followed her on the run, without so much as turning their heads to look back for a distance of half a league. Don Quixote stood gazing after them, and when they were no longer visible he turned to Sancho and spoke.

"Sancho," he said, "you can see now, can you not, how the enchanters hate me?")

(trans. Samuel Putnam)

This is a passage from chapter 10 of part 2 of Cervantes's *Don Quijote*. The knight has sent Sancho Panza to the hamlet of El Toboso to call on Dulcinea and announce his intention of paying her a visit. Sancho, entangled in his earlier lies, and not knowing how to find the imaginary lady, decides to deceive his master. He waits outside the hamlet for a time, long enough to make Don Quijote believe that he has done his errand. Then, seeing three peasant women on donkeys riding toward him, he hurries back and tells his master that Dulcinea and two of her ladies are coming to greet him. The knight is overwhelmed with surprise and joy, and Sancho leads him toward the peasant women, describing their beauty and splendid gear in glowing colors. But for once Don Quijote sees nothing except the actual reality, that is, three peasant women on donkeys—and this leads to the scene we have quoted.

Among the many episodes which represent a clash between Don Quijote's illusion and an ordinary reality which contradicts it, this one holds a special place. First because it is concerned with Dulcinea herself, the ideal and incomparable mistress of his heart. This is the climax of his illusion and disillusionment: and although this time too he manages to find a solution, a way to save his illusion, the solution (Dulcinea is under an enchantment) is so intolerable that henceforth all his thoughts are concentrated upon one goal: to save her and break the enchantment. In the last chapters of the book, his recognition or foreboding that he will never achieve this is the direct preparation for his illness, his deliverance from his illusion, and his death. In the second place the scene is distinguished by the fact that here for the first time the roles appear exchanged. Until now it had been Don Quijote who, encountering everyday phenomena, spontaneously saw and transformed them in terms of the romances of chivalry, while Sancho was generally in doubt and often tried to contradict and prevent his master's absurdities. Now it is the other way round. Sancho improvises a scene after the fashion of the romances of chivalry, while Don Quijote's ability to transform events to harmonize with his illusion breaks down before the crude vulgarity of the sight of the peasant women. All this seems most significant. As we have here (intentionally) presented it, it sounds sad, bitter, and almost tragic.

But if we merely read Cervantes's text, we have a farce, and a farce which is overwhelmingly comic. Many illustrators have rendered the scene: Don Quijote on his knees beside Sancho, staring in wide-eyed bewilderment at the repellent spectacle before him. But only the stylistic contrast in the speeches, and the grotesque movement at the end (Dulcinea's fall and remounting), afford the fullest enjoyment of what is going on. The stylistic contrast in the speeches develops only slowly, because at first the peasant women are much too astonished. Dulcinea's first utterance (her request to be allowed to pass) is still moderate. It is only in their later speeches that the peasant women display the pearls of their eloquence. The first representative of the chivalric style is Sancho, and it is amusing and surprising to see how well he plays his part. He jumps off his donkey, throws himself at the women's feet, and speaks as though he had never heard anything in all his life but the jargon of romances of chivalry. Forms of address, syntax, metaphors, epithets, the description of his master's posture, and his supplication to be heard—it all comes out most successfully, although Sancho cannot read and owes his education wholly to the example set him by Don Quijote. His performance is successful, at least insofar as he gets his master to follow suit: Don Quijote kneels down beside him.

It might be supposed that all this would bring on a terrible crisis. Dulcinea is really "la señora de sus pensamientos," the paragon of beauty, the goal and meaning of his life. Arousing his expectations in this way, and then disappointing them so greatly, is no harmless experiment. It could produce a shock which in turn could bring on much deeper insanity. But there is also the possibility that the shock might bring about a cure, instantaneous liberation from his idée fixe. Neither of these things happens. Don Quijote surmounts the shock. In his idée fixe itself he finds a solution which prevents him both from falling into despair and from recovering his sanity: Dulcinea is enchanted. This solution appears each time the exterior situation establishes itself as in insuperable contrast to the illusion. It makes it possible for Don Quijote to persist in the attitude of the noble and invincible hero persecuted by a powerful magician who envies his glory. In this particular case— the case of Dulcinea—the idea of so repellent and base an enchantment is certainly hard to endure. Still, it is possible to meet the situation by means available within the realm of the illusion itself, that is, by means of the knightly virtues of unalterable loyalty, devoted self-sacrifice, and unhesitating courage. And then there is the established fact that virtue will win in the end. The happy ending is a foregone conclusion. Thus both tragedy and cure are circumvented. And so, after a brief pause of disconcerted silence, Don Quijote begins to speak. He turns to Sancho first. His words show that he has recovered his bearings, that he has interpreted the situation in terms of his illusion. This interpretation has become so firmly crystallized in him that even the earthy colloquialisms in the directly preceding speech of one of the peasant women—however sharply they may contrast with the elevated style of knightly refinement—can no longer make him doubtful of his attitude.

Sancho's stratagem has succeeded. Don Quijote's second sentence is addressed to Dulcinea.

It is a very beautiful sentence. A moment ago we pointed out how cleverly and amusingly Sancho handles the style of the romances of chivalry which he has picked up from his master. Now we see what sort of a master he had. The sentence begins, like a prayer, with an imploring apostrophe ("invocatio"). This has three gradations ("*extremo del valor...*, *término...*, *único remedio...*"), and they are very carefully considered and arranged, for it first emphasizes an absolute perfection, then a perfection in human terms, and finally the special personal devotion of the speaker. The threefold structure is held together by the initial words "y tú," and ends, in its third, sweepingly constructed division, with the rhythmically conventional but magnificently integrated "corazón que te adora." Here, in content, choice of words, and rhythm, the theme which appears at the end is already alluded to. Thus a transition is established from the invocatio to its obligatory complement, the "supplicatio," for which the optative principal clause is reserved ("no dejes de mirarme..."), although it is still some time before we are allowed to reach it. First we have the multiple gradation—dramatically contrasting with both invocatio and supplicatio—of the concessive complex, "ya que..., y..., y..., si ya también...." Its sense is "and even though," and its rhythmic climax is reached in the middle of the first (ya que) part, in the strongly emphasized words "y para sólo ellos." Only after this entire wonderful and dramatic melody of the concessive clause has run its course, is the long-restrained principal clause of the supplicatio allowed to appear, but it too holds back and piles up paraphrases and pleonasms until finally the main motif, which constitutes the goal and purpose of the entire period, is sounded: the words which are to symbolize Don Quijote's present attitude and his entire life, "la humildad con que mi alma te adora." This is the style so greatly admired by Sancho in part 1, chapter 25, where Don Quijote reads his letter to Dulcinea aloud to him: "¡y como que le dice vuestra merced ahí todo cuanto quiere, y qué bien que encaja en la firma El Caballero de la Triste Figura! [How your worship says everything he wants to there, and how well the knight of the Mournful Countenance fits into the signature.]" But the present speech is incomparably more beautiful; with all its art it shows less pedantic preciosity than the letter. Cervantes is very fond of such rhythmically and pictorially rich, such beautifully articulated and musical bravura pieces of chivalric rhetoric (which are nevertheless rooted in the tradition of antiquity). And he is a master in the field. Here again he is not merely a destructive critic but a continuer and consummator of the great epico-rhetorical tradition for which prose too is an art. As soon as great emotions and passions or sublime events are involved, this elevated style with all its devices appears. To be sure, its being so long a convention has shifted it slightly from the sphere of high tragedy toward that of the smoothly pleasant, which is capable of at least a trace of self-irony. Yet it is still dominant in the serious sphere. One has only to read Dorotea's speech to her unfaithful lover (part 1, chap. 36), with its numerous figures, similes, and rhythmic clauses, in order to sense that this style is still alive even in the serious and the tragic.

Here, however, in Dulcinea's presence, it simply serves the effect of contrast. The peasant girl's crude, contemptuous reply gives it its real significance; we are in the realm of the low style, and Don Quijote's elevated rhetoric only serves to make the comedy of the stylistic anticlimax fully effective. But even this is not enough to satisfy Cervantes. To the stylistic anticlimax he adds an extreme anticlimax in the action by having Dulcinea fall off her donkey and jump on again with grotesque dexterity, while Don Quijote still tries to maintain the chivalric style. His being so firmly fixed in his illusion that neither Dulcinea's reply nor the scene with the donkey can shake him is the acme of farce. Even Sancho's exuberant gaiety (*Vive Roque*), which after all is nothing short of impertinent, cannot make him lose his bearings. He looks after the peasant women as they ride away, and when they have disappeared he turns to Sancho with words expressive much less of sadness or despair than of a sort of triumphant satisfaction over the fact that he has become the target of the evil magician's darkest arts. This makes it possible for him to feel that he is elect, unique, and in a way which tallies perfectly with the conventions of the knight-errant: "yo nací para ejemplo de desdichados, y para ser blanco y terrero donde tomen la mira y asesten las flechas de la mala fortuna [I was born to be an example to the unfortunate, and to be a target and mark wherever Bad Fortune aims its arrows]." And the observation he now makes, to the effect that the evil enchantment affects even Dulcinea's aura—for her breath had not been pleasant—can disturb his illusion as little as Sancho's grotesque description of details of her beauty. Encouraged by the complete success of his trick, Sancho has now really warmed up and begins to play with his master's madness purely for his own amusement.

In our study we are looking for representations of everyday life in which that life is treated seriously, in terms of its human and social problems or even of its tragic complications. The scene from Don Quijote with which we are dealing is certainly realistic. All the participants are presented in their true reality, their living everyday existence. Not only the peasant women but Sancho too, not only Sancho but also Don Quijote, appear as persons rep-

resentative of contemporary Spanish life. For the fact that Sancho is playing
a rogue's game and that Don Quijote is enmeshed in his illusion does not
raise either of them out of his everyday existence. Sancho is a peasant from
La Mancha, and Don Quijote is no Amadis or Roland, but a little country
squire who has lost his mind. At best we might say that the hidalgo's madness
translates him into another, imaginary sphere of life; but even so the everyday
character of our scene and others similar to it remains unharmed, because
the persons and events of everyday life are constantly colliding with his
madness and come out in stronger relief through the contrast.

It is much more difficult to determine the position of the scene, and of
the novel as a whole, on the scale of levels between tragic and comic. As
presented, the story of the encounter with the three peasant women is nothing if not comic. The idea of having Don Quijote encounter a concrete
Dulcinea must certainly have come to Cervantes even when he was writing
the first part of the novel. The idea of building up such a scene on the basis
of a deceitful trick played by Sancho, so that the roles appear interchanged,
is a stroke of genius, and it is so magnificently carried out that the farce
presents itself to the reader as something perfectly natural and even bound
to take place, despite the complex absurdity of all its presuppositions and
relations. But it remains pure farce. We have tried to show above that, in
the case of the only one of the participants with whom the possibility of a
shift into the tragic and problematic exists, that is, in the case of Don Quijote,
such a shift is definitely avoided. The fact that he almost instantaneously and
as it were automatically takes refuge in the interpretation that Dulcinea is
under an enchantment excludes everything tragic. He is taken in, and this
time even by Sancho; he kneels down and orates in a lofty emotional style
before a group of ugly peasant women; and then he takes pride in his sublime
misfortune.

But Don Quijote's feelings are genuine and profound. Dulcinea is really
the mistress of his thoughts; he is truly filled with the spirit of a mission
which he regards as man's highest duty. He is really true, brave, and ready
to sacrifice everything. So unconditional a feeling and so unconditional a
determination impose admiration even though they are based on a foolish
illusion, and this admiration has been accorded to Don Quijote by almost
all readers. There are probably few lovers of literature who do not associate
the concept of ideal greatness with Don Quijote. It may be absurd, fantastic,
grotesque; but it is still ideal, unconditional, heroic. It is especially since the
Romantic period that this conception has become almost universal, and it
withstands all attempts on the part of philological criticism to show that
Cervantes's intention was not to produce such an impression.

The difficulty lies in the fact that in Don Quijote's idée fixe we have a combination of the noble, immaculate, and redeeming with absolute nonsense. A tragic struggle for the ideal and desirable cannot at first blush be imagined in any way but as intervening meaningfully in the actual state of things, stirring it up, pressing it hard; with the result that the meaningful ideal encounters an equally meaningful resistance which proceeds either from inertia, petty malice, and envy, or possibly from a more conservative view. The will working for an ideal must accord with existing reality at least to such an extent that it meets it, so that the two interlock and a real conflict arises. Don Quijote's idealism is not of this kind. It is not based on an understanding of actual conditions in this world. Don Quijote does have such an understanding but it deserts him as soon as the idealism of his idée fixe takes hold of him. Everything he does in that state is completely senseless and so incompatible with the existing world that it produces only comic confusion there. It not only has no chance of success, it actually has no point of contact with reality; it expends itself in a vacuum.

The same idea can be developed in another way, so that further consequences become clear. The theme of the noble and brave fool who sets forth to realize his ideal and improve the world, might be treated in such a way that the problems and conflicts in the world are presented and worked out in the process. Indeed, the purity and ingenuousness of the fool could be such that, even in the absence of any concrete purpose to produce effects, wherever he appears he unwittingly goes to the heart of things, so that the conflicts which are pending and hidden are rendered acute. One might think here of Dostoyevski's *Idiot*. Thus the fool could be involved in responsibility and guilt and assume the role of a tragic figure. Nothing of the sort takes place in Cervantes's novel.

Don Quijote's encounter with Dulcinea is not a good illustration of his relationship to concrete reality, inasmuch as here he does not, as elsewhere, impose his ideal will in conflict with that reality; here he beholds and worships the incarnation of his ideal. Yet this encounter too is symbolic of the mad knight's relationship to the phenomena of this world. The reader should recall what traditional concepts were contained in the Dulcinea motif and how they are echoed in Sancho's and Don Quijote's grotesquely sublime words. "La señora de sus pensamientos, extremo del valor que puede desearse, término de la humana gentileza," and so forth—alive in all this are Plato's idea of beauty, courtly love, the "donna gentile" of the "dolce stil nuovo," Beatrice, "la gloriosa donna della mia mente." And all this ammunition is expended on three ugly and vulgar peasant women. It is poured into a void. Don Quijote can neither be graciously received nor graciously

rejected. There is nothing but amusingly senseless confusion. To find anything serious, or a concealed deeper meaning in this scene, one must violently
overinterpret it.

The three women are flabbergasted; they get away as fast as they can.
This is an effect frequently produced by Don Quijote's appearance. Often
disputes result and the participants come to blows. People are apt to lose
their temper when Don Quijote interferes in their business with his nonsense.
Very often too they humor him in his idée fixe in order to get some fun from
it. The innkeeper and the whores at the time of his first departure react in
this way. The same thing happens again later with the company at the second
inn, with the priest and the barber, Dorotea and Don Fernando, and even
with Maritornes. Some of these, it is true, mean to use their game as a way
of getting the knight safely back home, but they carry it much further than
their practical purpose would require. In part 2 the "bachiller" Sansón Carrasco bases his therapeutic plan on playing along with Don Quijote's idée
fixe; later, at the duke's palace and in Barcelona, his madness is methodically
exploited as a pastime, so that hardly any of his adventures are genuine; they
are simply staged, that is, they have been especially prepared to suit the
hidalgo's madness, for the amusement of those who get them up. Among all
these reactions, both in part 1 and part 2, one thing is completely lacking:
tragic complications and serious consequences. Even the element of contemporary satire and criticism is very weak. If we leave out of consideration the
purely literary criticism, there is almost none at all. It is limited to brief
remarks or occasional caricatures of types (for example the priest at the
duke's court). It never goes to the roots of things and is moderate in attitude.
Above all, Don Quijote's adventures never reveal any of the basic problems
of the society of the time. His activity reveals nothing at all. It affords an
opportunity to present Spanish life in its color and fullness. In the resulting
clashes between Don Quijote and reality no situation ever results which puts
in question that reality's right to be what it is. It is always right and he
wrong; and after a bit of amusing confusion it flows calmly on, untouched.
There is one scene where this might seem doubtful. It is the freeing of the
galley slaves in part 1, chapter 22. Here Don Quijote intervenes in the established legal order, and some critics will be found to uphold the opinion
that he does so in the name of a higher morality. This view is natural, for
what Don Quijote says: "allá se lo haya cada uno con su pecado; Dios hay
en el cielo que no se descuida de castigar al malo ni de premiar al bueno, y
no es bien que los hombres honrados sean verdugos do los otros hombres,
no yéndoles nada en ello [up there every one answers for his sins; there is a
God in Heaven who does not neglect to punish the evil and to reward the

good, and it is not right for honorable men to be the executioners of other men in something that is none of their concern]"—such a statement is certainly on a higher level than any positive law. But a "higher morality" of the kind here envisaged must be consistent and methodical if it is to be taken seriously. We know, however, that Don Quijote has no idea of making a basic attack on the established legal order. He is neither an anarchist nor a prophet of the Kingdom of God. On the contrary, it is apparent again and again that whenever his idée fixe happens not to be involved he is willing to conform, that it is only through his idée fixe that he claims a special position for the knight-errant. The beautiful words, "alla se lo haya," etc., are deeply rooted, to be sure, in the kindly wisdom of his real nature (this is a point to which we shall return), but in their context they are still merely an improvisation. It is his idée fixe which determines him to free the prisoners. It alone forces him to conceive of everything he encounters as the subject of a knightly adventure. It supplies him with the motifs "help the distressed" or "free the victims of force," and he acts accordingly. I think it wholly erroneous to look for a matter of principle here, for anything like a conflict between natural Christian and positive law. For such a conflict, moreover, an opponent would have to appear, someone like the Grand Inquisitor in Dostoyevski, who would be authorized and willing to represent the cause of positive law against Don Quijote. His Majesty's commissary who is in charge of the convoy of prisoners is neither suited for the role nor prepared to play it. Personally he may very well be ready to accept the argument, "judge not that ye be not judged." But he has passed no judgment; he is no representative of positive law. He has his instructions and is quite justified in appealing to them.

Everything comes out all right, and time and again the damage done or suffered by Don Quijote is treated with stoic humor as a matter of comic confusion. Even the bachiller Alonso Lopez, as he lies on the ground, badly mauled and with one leg pinned under his mule, consoles himself with mocking puns. This scene occurs in chapter 19 of book 1. It also shows that Don Quijote's idée fixe saves him from feeling responsible for the harm he does, so that in his conscience too every form of tragic conflict and somber seriousness is obviated. He has acted in accordance with the rules of knight-errantry, and so he is justified. To be sure, he hastens to assist the bachiller, for he is a kind and helpful soul; but it does not occur to him to feel guilty. Nor does he feel any guiltier when at the beginning of chapter 30 the priest puts him to the test by telling him what evil effects his freeing of the prisoners had produced. He angrily exclaims that it is the duty of a knight-errant to help those in distress but not to judge whether their plight is deserved or not. And that settles the question as far as he is concerned. In part 2, where the gaiety is even more relaxed and elegant, such complications no longer occur at all.

There is, then, very little of problem and tragedy in Cervantes's book—and yet it belongs among the literary masterpieces of an epoch during which the modern problematic and tragic conception of things arose in the European mind. Don Quijote's madness reveals nothing of the sort. The whole book is a comedy in which well-founded reality holds madness up to ridicule.

And yet Don Quijote is not only ridiculous. He is not like the bragging soldier or the comic old man or the pedantic and ignorant doctor. In our scene Don Quijote is taken in by Sancho. But does Sancho despise him and deceive him all the way through? Not at all. He deceives him only because he sees no other way out. He loves and reveres him, although he is half conscious (and sometimes fully conscious) of his madness. He learns from him and refuses to part with him. In Don Quijote's company he becomes cleverer and better than he was before. With all his madness, Don Quijote preserves a natural dignity and superiority which his many miserable failures cannot harm. He is not vulgar, as the above-mentioned comic types normally are. Actually he is not a "type" at all in this sense, for on the whole he is no automaton producing comic effects. He even develops, and grows kinder and wiser while his madness persists. But would it be true to say that his is a wise madness in the ironical sense of the romanticists? Does wisdom come to him through his madness? Does his madness give him an understanding he could not have attained in soundness of mind, and do we hear wisdom speak through madness in his case as we do with Shakespeare's fools or with Charlie Chaplin? No, that is not it either. As soon as his madness, that is, the idée fixe of knight-errantry, takes hold of him, he acts unwisely, he acts like an automaton in the manner of the comic types mentioned above. He is wise and kind independently of his madness. A madness like this, it is true, can arise only in a pure and noble soul, and it is also true that wisdom, kindness, and decency shine through his madness and make it appear lovable. Yet his wisdom and his madness are clearly separated—in direct contrast to what we find in Shakespeare, the fools of Romanticism, and Charlie Chaplin. The priest says it as early as chapter 30 of part 1, and later it comes out again and again: he is mad only when his idée fixe comes into play; otherwise he is a perfectly normal and very intelligent individual. His madness is not such that it represents his whole nature and is completely identical with it. At a specific moment an idée fixe laid hold on him; but even so it leaves parts of his being unaffected, so that in many instances he acts and speaks like a person of sound mind; and one day, shortly before his death, it leaves

him again. He was some fifty years of age when, under the influence of his
excessive reading of romances of chivalry, he conceived his absurd plan. This
is strange. An overwrought state of mind resulting from solitary reading
might rather be expected in a youthful person (Julien Sorel, Madame Bo-
vary), and one is tempted to look for a specific psychological explanation.
How is it possible that a man in his fifties who leads a normal life and whose
intelligence is well developed in many ways and not at all unbalanced, should
embark upon so absurd a venture? In the opening sentences of his novel
Cervantes supplies some details of his hero's social position. From them we
may at best infer that it was burdensome to him, for it offered no possibility
of an active life commensurate with his abilities. He was as it were paralyzed
by the limitations imposed upon him on the one hand by his class and on
the other by his poverty. Thus one might suppose that his mad decision
represents a flight from a situation which has become unbearable, a violent
attempt to emancipate himself from it. This sociological and psychological
interpretation has been advocated by various writers on the subject. I myself
advanced it in an earlier passage of [*Mimesis*], and I leave it there because
in the context of that passage it is justified. But as an interpretation of
Cervantes's artistic purpose it is unsatisfactory, for it is not likely that he
intended his brief observations on Don Quijote's social position and habits
of life to imply anything like a psychological motivation of the knight's idée
fixe. He would have had to state it more clearly and elaborate it in greater
detail. A modern psychologist might find still other explanations of Don
Quijote's strange madness. But this sort of approach to the problem has no
place in Cervantes's thinking. Confronted with the question of the causes of
Don Quijote's madness, he has only one answer: Don Quijote read too many
romances of chivalry and they deranged his mind. That this should happen
to a man in his fifties can be explained—from within the work—only in
aesthetic terms, that is, through the comic vision which came to Cervantes
when he conceived the novel: a tall, elderly man, dressed in old-fashioned
and shabby armor, a picture which is beautifully expressive not only of
madness but also of asceticism and the fanatic pursuit of an ideal. We simply
have to accept the fact that this cultured and intelligent country gentleman
goes suddenly mad—not, like Ajax or Hamlet, because of a terrible shock—
but simply because he has read too many romances of chivalry. Here again
there is nothing tragic. In the analysis of his madness we have to do without
the concept of the tragic, just as we have to do without the specifically
Shakespearean and romantic combination of wisdom and madness in which
one cannot be conceived without the other.

Don Quijote's wisdom is not the wisdom of a fool. It is the intelligence,

the nobility, the civility, and the dignity of a gifted and well-balanced man—
a man neither demonic nor paradoxical, not beset by doubt and indecision
nor by any feeling of not being at home in this world, but even-tempered,
able to weigh and ponder, receptive, and lovable and modest even in his
irony. Furthermore he is a conservative, or at least essentially in accord with
the order of things as it is. This comes out wherever and whenever he deals
with people—especially with Sancho Panza—in the longer or shorter inter-
vals during which his idée fixe is quiescent. From the very beginning—although more in part 2 than in part 1—the kindly, intelligent, and amiable
figure, Alsonso Quijano el bueno, whose most distinguishing characteristic
is his naturally superior dignity, coexists with the mad adventurer. We need
only read with what kindly and merry irony he treats Sancho in part 2,
chapter 7, when the latter, on the advice of his wife Teresa, begins to present
his request for a fixed salary. His madness intervenes only when he justifies
his refusal by referring to the customs of knights-errant. Passages of this
kind abound. There is evidence everywhere that we have to do with an
intelligent Don Quijote and a mad one, side by side, and that his intelligence
is in no way dialectically inspired by his madness but is a normal and, as it
were, average intelligence.

That in itself yields an unusual combination. There are levels of tone
represented here which one is not accustomed to finding in purely comic
contexts. A fool is a fool. We are used to seeing him represented on a single
plane, that of the comic and foolish, with which, at least in earlier literature,
baseness and stupidity, and at times underhanded malice, were connected as
well. But what are we to say of a fool who is at the same time wise, with
that wisdom which seems the least compatible with folly, that is, the wisdom
of intelligent moderation? This very fact, this combination of intelligent moderation with absurd excesses results in a multiplicity which cannot be made
to accord altogether with the purely comic. But that is by no means all. It is
on the very wings of his madness that his wisdom soars upward, that it
roams the world and becomes richer there. For if Don Quijote had not gone
mad, he would not have left his house. And then Sancho too would have
stayed home, and he could never have drawn from his innate being the things
which—as we find in delighted amazement—were potentially contained in
it. The multifarious play of action and reaction between the two and their
joint play in the world would not have taken place.

This play, as we think we have been able to show, is never tragic; and
never are human problems, whether personal or social, represented in such
a way that we tremble and are moved to compassion. We always remain in
the realm of gaiety. But the levels of gaiety are multiplied as never before. Let

us return once more to the text from which we set out. Don Quijote speaks
to the peasant women in a style which is genuinely the elevated style of courtly
love and which in itself is by no means grotesque. His sentences are not at
all ridiculous (though they may seem so to many readers in our day), they
are in the tradition of the period and represent a masterpiece of elevated
expression in the form in which it was then alive. If it was Cervantes's
purpose to attack the romances of chivalry (and there can be no doubt that
it was), he nevertheless did not attack the elevated style of chivalric expression. On the contrary, he reproaches the romances of chivalry with not
mastering the style, with being stylistically wooden and dry. And so it comes
about that in the middle of a parody against the knightly ideology of love
we find one of the most beautiful prose passages which the late form of the
tradition of courtly love produced. The peasant women answer with characteristic coarseness. Such a rustically boorish style had long been employed
in comic literature (although possibly never with the same balance between
moderation and verve), but what had certainly never happened before was
that it should follow directly upon a speech like Don Quijote's—a speech
which, taken by itself, could never make us suspect that it occurs in a grotesque context. The motif of a knight begging a peasant woman to hear his
love—a motif which produces a comparable situation—is age old. It is the
motif of the *pastourelle*; it was in favor with the early Provençal poets, and,
as we shall see when we come to Voltaire, it was remarkably long-lived.
However, in the pastourelle the two partners have adapted themselves to each
other; they understand each other; and the result is a homogeneous level of
style on the borderline between the idyllic and the everyday. In Cervantes's
case, the two realms of life and style clash by reason of Don Quijote's
madness. There is no possibility of a transition; each is closed in itself; and
the only link that holds them together is the merry neutrality of the playful
scheme of puppet-master Sancho—the awkward bumpkin, who but a short
time before believed almost everything his master said, who will never get
over believing some of it, and who always acts in accordance with the momentary situation. In our passage the dilemma of the moment has inspired
him to deceive his master; and he adapts himself to the position of puppet-
master with as much gusto and elasticity as he later will to the position of
governor of an island. He starts the play in the elevated style, then switches
to the low—not, however, in the manner of the peasant women. He maintains
his superiority and remains master of the situation which he has himself
created under the pressure of necessity but which he now enjoys to the full.

What Sancho does in this case—assuming a role, transforming himself,
and playing with his master's madness—other characters in the book are

perpetually doing. Don Quijote's madness gives rise to an inexhaustible series
of disguises and histrionics: Dorotea in the role of Princess Micomicona, the
barber as her page, Sansón Carrasco as knight-errant, Ginés de Pasamonte
as puppet-master—these are but a few examples. Such metamorphoses make
reality become a perpetual stage without ever ceasing to be reality. And when
the characters do not submit to the metamorphosis of their own free will,
Don Quijote's madness forces them into their roles—as happens time and
again, beginning with the innkeeper and the whores in the first tavern. Reality willingly cooperates with a play which dresses it up differently every
moment. It never spoils the gaiety of the play by bringing in the serious
weight of its troubles, cares, and passions. All that is resolved in Don Quijote's madness; it transforms the real everyday world into a gay stage. Here
one should recall the various adventures with women which occur in the
course of the narrative in addition to the encounter with Dulcinea: Maritornes struggling in Don Quijote's arms, Dorotea as Princess Micomicona,
the lovelorn Altisidora's serenade, the nocturnal encounter with Doña Rodriguez (a scene which Cide Hamete Benengeli says that he would have given
his best coat to see)—each of these stories is in a different style; each contains
a shift in stylistic level; all of them are resolved by Don Quijote's madness,
and all of them remain within the realm of gaiety. And yet there are several
which need not necessarily have been thus restricted. The description of
Maritornes and her muleteer is coarsely realistic; Dorotea is unhappy; and
Doña Rodriguez is in great distress of mind because her daughter has been
seduced. Don Quijote's intervention changes nothing of this—neither Maritornes's loose life nor the sad plight of Doña Rodriguez's daughter. But
what happens is that we are not concerned over these things, that we see
the lot and the life of these women through the prism of gaiety, and that our
consciences do not feel troubled over them. As God lets the sun shine and
the rain fall on the just and the unjust alike, so Don Quijote's madness, in
its bright equanimity, illumines everything that crosses his path and leaves
it in a state of gay confusion.

The most varied suspense and wisest gaiety of the book are revealed in
a relationship which Don Quijote maintains throughout: his relationship
with Sancho Panza. It is not at all as easy to describe in unambiguous terms
as the relationship between Rocinante and Sancho's donkey or that between
the donkey and Sancho himself. They are not always united in unfailing
loyalty and love. It frequently happens that Don Quijote becomes so angry
with Sancho that he abuses and maltreats him; at times he is ashamed of
him; and once—in part 2, chapter 27—he actually deserts him in danger.
Sancho, for his part, originally accompanies Don Quijote because he is stupid

and for the selfishly materialistic reason that he expects fantastic advantages from the venture, and also because, despite all its hardships, he prefers a vagabond life to the regular working hours and monotony of life at home. Before long he begins to sense that something must be wrong with Don Quijote's mind, and then he sometimes deceives him, makes fun of him, and speaks of him disrespectfully. At times, even in part 2, he is so disgusted and disillusioned that he is all but ready to leave Don Quijote. Again and again the reader is made to see how variable and composite our human relationships are, how capricious and dependent on the moment even the most intimate of them. In the passage which was our point of departure Sancho deceives his master and plays almost cruelly on his madness. But what painstaking humoring of Don Quijote's madness, what sympathetic penetration of his world, must have preceded Sancho's conceiving such a plan and his being able to act his role so well! Only a few months earlier he had not the slightest inkling of all this. Now he lives, after his own fashion, in the world of knightly adventure; he is fascinated by it. He has fallen in love with his master's madness and with his own role. His development is most amazing. Yet withal, he is and remains Sancho, of the Panza family, a Christian of the old stock, well known in his village. He remains all that even in the role of a wise governor and also—and indeed especially—when he insists on Sanchica's marrying nothing less than a count. He remains Sancho; and all that happens to him could happen only to Sancho. But the fact that these things do happen, that his body and his mind are put in such violent commotion and emerge from the ordeal in all their unshakable and idiosyncratic genuineness—this he owes to Don Quijote, *su amo y natural señor* [his master and natural lord]. The experience of Don Quijote's personality is not received by anyone as completely as it is by Sancho; it is not assimilated pure and whole by anyone as it is by him. The others all wonder about him, are amused or angered by him, or try to cure him. Sancho lives himself into Don Quijote, whose madness and wisdom become productive in him. Although he has far too little critical reasoning power to form and express a synthetic judgment upon him, it still is he, in all his reactions, through whom we best understand Don Quijote. And this in turn binds Don Quijote to him. Sancho is his consolation and his direct opposite, his creature and yet an independent fellow being who holds out against him and prevents his madness from locking him up as though in solitary confinement. Two partners who appear together as contrasting comic or semi-comic figures represent a very old motif which has retained its effectiveness even today in farce, caricature, the circus, and the film: the tall thin man and the short fat one; the clever man and his stupid companion; master and servant; the

refined aristocrat and the simple-minded peasants; and whatever other combinations and variants there may be in different countries and under different
cultural conditions. What Cervantes made of it is magnificent and unique.

Perhaps it is not quite correct to speak of what Cervantes made of it. It
may be more exact to say "what became of the motif in his hands." For
centuries—and especially since the romanticists—many things have been read
into him which he hardly foreboded, let alone intended. Such transforming
and transcendent interpretations are often fertile. A book like *Don Quijote*
dissociates itself from its author's intention and leads a life of its own. Don
Quijote shows a new face to every age which enjoys him. Yet the historian—
whose task it is to define the place of a given work in a historical continuity—
must endeavor insofar as that is still possible, to attain a clear understanding
of what the work meant to its author and his contemporaries. I have tried
to interpret as little as possible. In particular, I have pointed out time and
again how little there is in the text which can be called tragic and problematic. I take it as merry play on many levels, including in particular the level
of everyday realism. The latter differentiates it from the equally unproblem-
atic gaiety of let us say Ariosto; but even so it remains play. This means that
no matter how painstakingly I have tried to do as little interpreting as possible, I yet cannot help feeling that my thoughts about the book often go far
beyond Cervantes's aesthetic intention. Whatever that intention may have
been (we shall not here take up the problems presented by the aesthetics of
his time), it most certainly did not consciously and from the beginning propose to create a relationship like that between Don Quijote and Sancho Panza
as we see it after having read the novel. Rather, the two figures were first a
single vision, and what finally developed from them—singly and together—
arose gradually, as the result of hundreds of individual ideas, as the result
of hundreds of situations in which Cervantes puts them and to which they
react on the spur of the moment, as the result of the inexhaustible, ever-
fresh power of the poetic imagination. Now and again there are actual in-
congruities and contradictions, not only in matters of fact (which has often
been noted) but also in psychology: developments which do not fit into the
total picture of the two heroes—which indicates how much Cervantes allowed himself to be guided by the momentary situation, by the demands of
the adventure in hand. This is still the case—more frequently even—in part 2.
Gradually and without any preconceived plan, the two personages evolve,
each in himself and also in their relation to each other. To be sure, this is
the very thing which allows what is peculiarly Cervantean, the sum of Cervantes's experience of life and the wealth of his imagination, to enter the
episodes and speeches all the more richly and spontaneously. The "peculiarly

Cervantean" cannot be described in words. And yet I shall attempt to say something *about* it in order to clarify its power and its limits. First of all it is something spontaneously sensory: a vigorous capacity for the vivid visualization of very different people in very varied situations, for the vivid realization and expression of what thoughts enter their minds, what emotions fill their hearts, and what words come to their lips. This capacity he possesses so directly and strongly, and in a manner so independent of any sort of ulterior motive, that almost everything realistic written before him appears limited, conventional, or propagandistic in comparison. And just as sensory is his capacity to think up or hit upon ever new combinations of people and events. Here, to be sure, we have to consider the older tradition of the romance of adventure and its renewal through Boiardo and Ariosto, but no one before him had infused the element of genuine everyday reality into that brilliant and purposeless play of combinations. And finally he has a "something" which organizes the whole and makes it appear in a definite "Cervantean" light. Here things begin to be very difficult. One might avoid the difficulty and say that this "something" is merely contained in the subject matter, in the idea of the country gentleman who loses his mind and convinces himself that it is his duty to revive knight-errantry, that it is this theme which gives the book its unity and its attitude. But the theme (which Cervantes, by the way, took over from the minor and in itself totally uninteresting contemporary work, the *Entremés de los romances* [Interlude of Romances]) could have been treated quite differently too. The hero might have looked very different; it was not necessary that there should be a Dulcinea and particularly a Sancho. But above all, what was it that so attracted Cervantes in the idea? What attracted him was the possibilities it offered for multifariousness and effects of perspective, the mixture of fanciful and everyday elements in the subject, its malleability, elasticity, adaptability. It was ready to absorb all forms of style and art. It permitted the presentation of the most variegated picture of the world in a light congenial to his own nature. And here we have come back to the difficult question we asked before: what is the "something" which orders the whole and makes it appear in a definite, "Cervantean" light?

It is not a philosophy; it is no didactic purpose; it is not even a being stirred by the uncertainty of human existence or by the power of destiny, as in the case of Montaigne and Shakespeare. It is an attitude—an attitude toward the world, and hence also toward the subject matter of his art—in which bravery and equanimity play a major part. Together with the delight he takes in the multifariousness of his sensory play there is in him a certain Southern reticence and pride. This prevents him from taking the play very seriously. He looks at it; he shapes it; he finds it diverting; it is also intended to afford the reader refined intellectual diversion.

But he does not take sides (except against badly written books); he remains neutral. It is not enough to say that he does not judge and draws no conclusions: the case is not even called, the questions are not even asked. No one and nothing (except bad books and plays) is condemned in the book: neither Ginés de Pasamonte nor Roque Guinart, neither Maritornes nor Zoraida. For us Zoraida's behavior toward her father becomes a moral problem which we cannot help pondering, but Cervantes tells the story without giving a hint of his thoughts on the subject. Or rather, it is not Cervantes himself who tells the story, but the prisoner—who naturally finds Zoraida's behavior commendable. And that settles the matter. There are a few caricatures in the book—the Biscayan, the priest at the duke's castle, Doña Rodriguez; but these raise no ethical problems and imply no basic judgments.

On the other hand no one is praised as exemplary either. Here one might think of the Knight of the Green Caftan, Don Diego de Miranda, who in part 2, chapter 16, gives a description of his temperate style of life and thereby makes such a profound impression upon Sancho. He is temperate and inclined to rational deliberation; in dealing with both Don Quijote and Sancho he finds the right tone of benevolent, modest, and yet self-assured politeness. His attempts to confute or mitigate Don Quijote's madness are friendly and understanding. He must not be put with the narrow-minded and intolerant priest at the duke's court (as has been done by the distinguished Spanish scholar, Américo Castro). Don Diego is a paragon of his class, the Spanish variety of the humanist nobleman: *otium cum dignitate*. But he certainly is no more than that. He is no absolute model. For that, after all, he is too cautious and too mediocre, and it is quite possible (so far Castro may be right) that there is a shade of irony in the manner in which Cervantes describes his style of life, his manner of hunting, and his views on his son's literary inclinations.

Cervantes's attitude is such that his world becomes play in which every participating figure is justified by the simple fact of living in a given place. Only Don Quijote in his madness is not justified, is wrong. He is also wrong, absolutely speaking, as against the temperate and peaceable Don Diego, whom Cervantes—"with inspired perversity," as Castro puts it—makes the witness of the adventure with the lion. It would be forcing things if one sought to see here a glorification of adventurous heroism as against calculating, petty, and mediocre caution. If there is possibly an undertone of irony in the portrait of Don Diego, Don Quijote is not possibly but unqualifiedly conceived not with an undertone of ridicule but as ridiculous through and through.

The chapter is introduced by a description of the absurd pride he takes in his victory over Carrasco (disguised as a knight) and a conversation on this theme with Sancho. The passage bears rereading for the sake of the realization it affords that there is hardly another instance in the entire book where Don Quijote is ridiculed—also in ethical terms—as he is here. The description of himself with which he introduces himself to Don Diego is foolish and turgid. It is in this state of mind that he takes on the adventure with the lion. And the lion does nothing but turn its back on Don Quijote! This is pure parody. And the additional details are fit for parody too: Don Quijote's request that the guard should give him a written testimonial to his heroism; the way he receives Sancho; his decision to change his name (henceforth he will be the Knight of the Lion), and many others.

Don Quijote alone is wrong as long as he is mad. He alone is wrong in a well-ordered world in which everybody else has his right place. He himself comes to see this in the end when, dying, he finds his way back into the order of the world. But is it true that the world is well-ordered? The question is not raised. Certain it is that in the light of Don Quijote's madness and confronted with it, the world appears well-ordered and even as merry play. There may be a great deal of wretchedness, injustice, and disorder in it. We meet harlots, criminals as galley slaves, seduced girls, hanged bandits, and much more of the same sort. But all that does not perturb us. Don Quijote's appearance, which corrects nothing and helps no one, changes good and bad fortune into play.

The theme of the mad country gentleman who undertakes to revive knight-errantry gave Cervantes an opportunity to present the world as play in that spirit of multiple, perspective, non-judging, and even non-questioning neutrality which is a brave form of wisdom. It could very simply be expressed in the words of Don Quijote which have already been quoted: "allá se lo haya cada uno con su pecado, Dios hay en el cielo que no se descuida de castigar al malo, ni de premiar al bueno." Or else in the words which he addresses to Sancho in part 2, chapter 8, at the end of the conversation about monks and knights: "muchos son los caminos por donde lleve Dios a los suyos al cielo [many are the paths by which God brings his children to heaven]." This is as much as to say that in the last analysis it is a devout wisdom. It is not unrelated to the neutral attitude which Gustave Flaubert strove so hard to attain, and yet it is very different from it: Flaubert wanted to transform reality through style; transform it so that it would appear as God sees it, so that the divine order—insofar as it concerns the fragment of reality treated in a particular work—would perforce be incarnated in the author's style. For Cervantes, a good novel serves no other purpose than to afford refined recreation, "honesto entretenimiento." No one has expressed this more convincingly in recent times than W. J. Entwistle in his book on Cervantes where he speaks of recreation and connects it very beautifully with re-creation. It would never have occurred to Cervantes that the style of a novel—be it the best of novels—could reveal the order of the universe. On the other hand, for him too the phenomena of reality had come to be difficult to survey and no longer possible to arrange in an unambiguous and traditional manner. Elsewhere in Europe men had long since begun to question and to doubt, and even to begin building anew with their own materials. But that was in keeping neither with the spirit of his country nor with his own temperament, nor finally with his conception of the office of a writer. He found the order of reality in play. It is no longer the play of Everyman, which provides fixed norms for the judgment of good and evil. That was still so in *La Celestina*. Now things are no longer so simple. Cervantes undertakes to pass judgment only in matters concerning his profession as a writer. So far as the secular world is concerned, we are all sinners; God will see to it that evil is punished and good rewarded. Here on earth the order of the unsurveyable is to be found in play. However arduous it may be to survey and judge phenomena, before the mad knight of La Mancha they turn into a dance of gay and diverting confusion.

This, it seems to me, is the function of Don Quijote's madness. When the theme—the mad hidalgo who sets forth to realize the ideal of the "caballero andante [knight-errant]"—began to kindle Cervantes's imagination, he also perceived a vision of how, confronted with such madness, contemporary reality might be portrayed. And the vision pleased him, both by reason of its multifariousness and by reason of the neutral gaiety which the knight's madness spreads over everything which comes in contact with it. That it is a heroic and idealized form of madness, that it leaves room for wisdom and humanity, was no doubt equally pleasing to him. But to conceive of Don Quijote's madness in symbolic and tragic terms seems to me forced. That can be read into the text; it is not there of itself. So universal and multilayered, so noncritical and nonproblematic a gaiety in the portrayal of everyday reality has not been attempted again in European letters. I cannot imagine where and when it might have been attempted.

JOSÉ ORTEGA Y GASSET

Master Pedro's Puppet Show

As the thread of the adventure [in *Don Quixote*] develops we experience an increasing emotional tension, as if by accompanying the former in its course we felt ourselves violently pulled away from the line followed by inert reality. At each step this reality pulls, threatening to make the event conform with the natural course of events, and it is necessary for a new impulse from the adventurous power to free it and push it towards greater impossibilities. We are carried along in the adventure as if within a missile, and in the dynamic struggle between it, as it advances on an escaping tangent, and the center of the earth which tries to restrain it, we side with the missile. This partiality of ours increases with each incident and adds to a kind of hallucination, in which we take the adventure for an instant as actual reality.

Cervantes has represented in a marvelous way this psychological reaction of the reader of fables in the experience undergone by the spirit of Don Quixote in the presence of Master Pedro's puppet show. The horse of Don Gaiferos in his headlong gallop leaves a vacuum behind him, into which a current of hallucinating air rushes, sweeping along with it everything that is not firmly fixed on the ground. There the soul of Don Quixote, light as thistledown, snatched up in the illusory vortex, goes whirling like a dry leaf; and in its pursuit everything ingenuous and sorrowing still left in the world will go forevermore.

The frame of the puppet show which Master Pedro goes around presenting is the dividing line between two continents of the mind. Within, the

---

From *Meditations on Quixote*. © 1961 by W. W. Norton & Co.

puppet show encloses a fantastic world, articulated by the genius of the impossible. It is the world of adventure, of imagination, of myth. Without there is a room in which several unsophisticated men are gathered, men like those we see every day, concerned with the daily struggle to live. In their midst is a fool, a knight from the neighborhood, who, one morning, abandoned his town impelled by a small anatomical anomaly of the brain. Nothing prevents us from entering this room: we could breathe in its atmosphere and touch those present on the shoulder, since they are made of the same stuff and condition as ourselves. However, this room is, in its turn, included in a book, that is to say, in another puppet show larger than the first. If we should enter the room, we would have stepped inside an ideal object, we would be moving in the hollow interior of an esthetic body. (Velázquez in *The Maids of Honor* offers us an analogous case: he is painting a picture of the king and queen and at the same time he has placed his studio in the picture. In *The Spinners* he has united forever the legendary action represented by a tapestry to the humble room in which it was manufactured.) Along a conduit of simple-mindedness and dementia emanations come and go from one continent to the other, from the puppet show to the room, from the room to the puppet show. One would say that the important thing is precisely the osmosis and endosmosis between the two.

JORGE LUIS BORGES

Pierre Menard,
Author of Don Quixote

The *visible* works left by this novelist are easily and briefly enumerated. It is therefore impossible to forgive the omissions and additions perpetrated by Madame Henri Bachelier in a fallacious catalogue that a certain newspaper, whose Protestant tendencies are no secret, was inconsiderate enough to inflict on its wretched readers—even though they are few and Calvinist, if not Masonic and circumcised. Menard's true friends regarded this catalogue with alarm, and even with a certain sadness. It is as if yesterday we were gathered together before the final marble and the fateful cypresses, and already Error is trying to tarnish his Memory. . . . Decidedly, a brief rectification is inevitable.

I am certain that it would be very easy to challenge my meager authority. I hope, nevertheless, that I will not be prevented from mentioning two important testimonials. The Baroness de Bacourt (at whose unforgettable "vendredis" I had the honor of becoming acquainted with the late lamented poet) has seen fit to approve these lines. The Countess de Bagnoregio, one of the most refined minds in the Principality of Monaco (and now of Pittsburgh, Pennsylvania, since her recent marriage to the international philanthropist Simon Kautsch who, alas, has been so slandered by the victims of his disinterested handiwork) has sacrificed to "truth and death" (those are her words) that majestic reserve which distinguishes her, and in an open letter published in the magazine *Luxe* also grants me her consent. These authorizations, I believe, are not insufficient.

From *Ficciones.* © 1962 by Grove Press.

I have said that Menard's *visible* lifework is easily enumerated. Having carefully examined his private archives, I have been able to verify that it consists of the following:

a) A symbolist sonnet which appeared twice (with variations) in the magazine *La Conque* (the March and October issues of 1899).

b) A monograph on the possibility of constructing a poetic vocabulary of concepts that would not be synonyms or periphrases of those which make up ordinary language, "but ideal objects created by means of common agreement and destined essentially to fill poetic needs" (Nîmes, 1901).

c) A monograph on "certain connections or affinities" among the ideas of Descartes, Leibnitz and John Wilkins (Nîmes, 1903).

d) A monograph on the *Characteristica Universalis* of Leibnitz (Nîmes, 1904).

e) A technical article on the possibility of enriching the game of chess by means of eliminating one of the rooks' pawns. Menard proposes, recommends, disputes, and ends by rejecting this innovation.

f) A monograph on the *Ars Magna Generalis* of Ramón Lull (Nîmes, 1906).

g) A translation with prologue and notes of the *Libro de la invención y arte del juego del axedrez* by Ruy López de Segura (Paris, 1907).

h) The rough draft of a monograph on the symbolic logic of George Boole.

i) An examination of the metric laws essential to French prose, illustrated with examples from Saint-Simon (*Revue des langues romanes*, Montpellier, October, 1909).

j) An answer to Luc Durtain (who had denied the existence of such laws) illustrated with examples from Luc Durtain (*Revue des langues romanes*, Montpellier, December, 1909).

k) A manuscript translation of the *Aguja de navegar cultos* of Quevedo, entitled *La boussole des précieux*.

l) A preface to the catalogue of the exposition of lithographs by Carolus Hourcade (Nîmes, 1914).

m) His work, *Les problèmes d'un problème* (Paris, 1917), which takes up in chronological order the various solutions of the famous problem of Achilles and the tortoise. Two editions of this book have appeared so far; the second has as an epigraph Leibnitz's advice "Ne craignez point, monsieur, la tortue," and contains revisions of the chapters dedicated to Russell and Descartes.

n) An obstinate analysis of the "syntactic habits" of Toulet (*N.R.F.*,

March, 1921). I remember that Menard used to declare that censuring and praising were sentimental operations which had nothing to do with criticism.

o) A transposition into Alexandrines of *Le Cimetière marin* of Paul Valéry (*N.R.F.,* January, 1928).

p) An invective against Paul Valéry in the *Journal for the Suppression of Reality* of Jacques Reboul. (This invective, it should be stated parenthetically, is the exact reverse of his true opinion of Valéry. The latter understood it as such, and the old friendship between the two was never endangered.)

q) A "definition" of the Countess of Bagnoregio in the "victorious volume"—the phrase is that of another collaborator, Gabriele d'Annunzio—which this lady publishes yearly to rectify the inevitable falsifications of journalism and to present "to the world and to Italy" an authentic effigy of her person, which is so exposed (by reason of her beauty and her activities) to erroneous or hasty interpretations.

r) A cycle of admirable sonnets for the Baroness de Bacourt (1934).

s) A manuscript list of verses which owe their effectiveness to punctuation.*

Up to this point (with no other omission than that of some vague, circumstantial sonnets for the hospitable, or greedy, album of Madame Henri Bachelier) we have the *visible* part of Menard's works in chronological order. Now I will pass over to that other part, which is subterranean, interminably heroic, and unequalled, and which is also—oh, the possibilities inherent in the man!—inconclusive. This work, possibly the most significant of our time, consists of the ninth and thirty-eighth chapters of part 1 of *Don Quixote* and a fragment of chapter 22. I realize that such an affirmation seems absurd; but the justification of this "absurdity" is the primary object of this note.**

Two texts of unequal value inspired the undertaking. One was that philological fragment of Novalis—No. 2005 of the Dresden edition—which outlines the theme of *total* identification with a specific author. The other was one of those parasitic books which places Christ on a boulevard, Hamlet on the Cannebière and Don Quixote on Wall Street. Like any man of good taste, Menard detested these useless carnivals, only suitable—he used to say—for evoking plebeian delight in anachronism, or (what is worse) charm-

---

*Madame Henri Bachelier also lists a literal translation of a literal translation done by Quevedo of the *Introduction à la vie dévote* of Saint Francis of Sales. In Pierre Menard's library there are no traces of such a work. She must have misunderstood a remark of his which he had intended as a joke.

**I also had another, secondary intent—that of sketching a portrait of Pierre Menard. But how would I dare to compete with the golden pages the Baroness de Bacourt tells me she is preparing, or with the delicate and precise pencil of Carolus Hourcade?

ing us with the primary idea that all epochs are the same, or that they are different. He considered more interesting, even though it had been carried out in a contradictory and superficial way, Daudet's famous plan: to unite in *one* figure, Tartarin, the Ingenious Gentleman and his squire. . . . Any insinuation that Menard dedicated his life to the writing of a contemporary *Don Quixote* is a calumny of his illustrious memory.

He did not want to compose another *Don Quixote*—which would be easy—but *the Don Quixote*. It is unnecessary to add that his aim was never to produce a mechanical transcription of the original; he did not propose to copy it. His admirable ambition was to produce pages which would coincide—word for word and line for line—with those of Miguel de Cervantes.

"My intent is merely astonishing," he wrote me from Bayonne on December 30th, 1934. "The ultimate goal of a theological or metaphysical demonstration—the external world, God, chance, universal forms—are no less anterior or common than this novel which I am now developing. The only difference is that philosophers publish in pleasant volumes the intermediary stages of their work and that I have decided to lose them." And, in fact, not one page of a rough draft remain to bear witness to this work of years.

The initial method he conceived was relatively simple: to know Spanish well, to re-embrace the Catholic faith, to fight against Moors and Turks, to forget European history between 1602 and 1918, and to *be* Miguel de Cervantes. Pierre Menard studied this procedure (I know that he arrived at a rather faithful handling of seventeenth-century Spanish) but rejected it as too easy. Rather because it was impossible, the reader will say! I agree, but the undertaking was impossible from the start, and of all the possible means of carrying it out, this one was the least interesting. To be, in the twentieth century, a popular novelist of the seventeenth seemed to him a diminution. To be, in some way, Cervantes and to arrive at *Don Quixote* seemed to him less arduous—and consequently less interesting—than to continue being Pierre Menard and to arrive at *Don Quixote* through the experiences of Pierre Menard. (This conviction, let it be said in passing, forced him to exclude the autobiographical prologue of the second part of *Don Quixote*. To include this prologue would have meant creating another personage—Cervantes—but it would also have meant presenting *Don Quixote* as the work of this personage and not of Menard. He naturally denied himself such an easy solution.) "My undertaking is not essentially difficult," I read in another part of the same letter. "I would only have to be immortal in order to carry it out." Shall I confess that I often imagine that he finished it and that I am reading *Don Quixote*—the entire work—as if Menard had conceived it? Several nights ago, while leafing through chapter 26—which he had never attempted—I recognized our friend's style and, as it were, his voice in this exceptional phrase: *the nymphs of the rivers, mournful and humid Echo.* This effective combination of two adjectives, one moral and the other physical, reminded me of a line from Shakespeare which we discussed one afternoon:

> Where a malignant and turbaned Turk . . .

Why precisely *Don Quixote,* our reader will ask. Such a preference would not have been inexplicable in a Spaniard; but it undoubtedly was in a symbolist from Nîmes, essentially devoted to Poe, who engendered Baudelaire, who engendered Mallarmé, who engendered Valéry, who engendered Edmond Teste. The letter quoted above clarifies this point. "*Don Quixote,*" Menard explains, "interests me profoundly, but it does not seem to me to have been—how shall I say it—inevitable. I cannot imagine the universe without the interjection of Edgar Allan Poe

> Ah, bear in mind this garden was enchanted!

or without the *Bateau ivre* or the *Ancient Mariner,* but I know that I am capable of imagining it without *Don Quixote.* (I speak, naturally, of my personal capacity, not of the historical repercussions of these works.) *Don Quixote* is an accidental book, *Don Quixote* is unnecessary. I can premeditate writing it, I can write it, without incurring a tautology. When I was twelve or thirteen years old I read it, perhaps in its entirety. Since then I have reread several chapters attentively, but not the ones I am going to undertake. I have likewise studied the *entremeses,* the comedies, the *Galatea,* the *Exemplary Novels,* and the undoubtedly laborious efforts of *Pérsiles y Sigismunda* and the *Viaje al Parnaso.* . . . My general memory of *Don Quixote,* simplified by forgetfulness and indifference, is much the same as the imprecise, anterior image of a book not yet written. Once this image (which no one can deny me in good faith) has been postulated, my problems are undeniably considerably more difficult than those which Cervantes faced. My affable precursor did not refuse the collaboration of fate; he went along composing his immortal work a little *à la diable,* swept along by inertias of language and invention. I have contracted by mysterious duty of reconstructing literally his spontaneous work. My solitary game is governed by two polar laws. The first permits me to attempt variants of a formal and psychological nature; the second obliges me to sacrifice them to the 'original' text and irrefutably to rationalize this annihilation. . . . To these artificial obstacles one must add another congenital one. To compose *Don Quixote* at the beginning of the

seventeenth century was a reasonable, necessary and perhaps inevitable undertaking; at the beginning of the twentieth century it is almost impossible.
It is not in vain that three hundred years have passed, charged with the most
complex happenings—among them, to mention only one, that same *Don
Quixote*."

In spite of these three obstacles, the fragmentary *Don Quixote* of Menard is more subtle than that of Cervantes. The latter indulges in a rather
coarse opposition between tales of knighthood and the meager, provincial
reality of his country; Menard chooses as "reality" the land of Carmen
during the century of Lepanto and Lope. What Hispanophile would not have
advised Maurice Barrès or Dr. Rodríguez Larreta to make such a choice!
Menard, as if it were the most natural thing in the world, eludes them. In
his work there are neither bands of gypsies, conquistadors, mystics, Philip
the Seconds, nor autos-da-fé. He disregards or proscribes local color. This
disdain indicates a new approach to the historical novel. This disdain con-
demns *Salammbô* without appeal.

It is no less astonishing to consider isolated chapters. Let us examine,
for instance, chapter 38 of part 1 "which treats of the curious discourse that
Don Quixote delivered on the subject of arms and letters." As is known,
Don Quixote (like Quevedo in a later, analogous passage of *La hora de todos*)
passes judgment against letters and in favor of arms. Cervantes was an old
soldier, which explains such a judgment. But that the *Don Quixote* of Pierre
Menard—a contemporary of *La trahison des clercs* and Bertrand Russell—
should relapse into these nebulous sophistries! Madame Bachelier has seen
in them an admirable and typical subordination of the author to the psychology of the hero; others (by no means perspicaciously) a *transcription* of
Don Quixote; the Baroness de Bacourt, the influence of Nietzsche. To this
third interpretation (which seems to me irrefutable) I do not know if I would
dare to add a fourth, which coincides very well with the divine modesty of
Pierre Menard: his resigned or ironic habit of propounding ideas which were
the strict reverse of those he preferred. (One will remember his diatribe
against Paul Valéry in the ephemeral journal of the superrealist Jacques Reboul.) The text of Cervantes and that of Menard are verbally identical, but
the second is almost infinitely richer. (More ambiguous, his detractors will
say; but ambiguity is a richness.) It is a revelation to compare the *Don
Quixote* of Menard with that of Cervantes. The latter, for instance, wrote
(*Don Quixote,* part 1, chap. 9):

la verdad, cuya madre es la historia, émula del tiempo, depósito

de las acciones, testigo de lo pasado, ejemplo y aviso de lo pre-
sente, advertencia de lo por venir.

[truth, whose mother is history, who is the rival of time, depos-
itory of deeds, witness of the past, example and lesson to the
present, and warning to the future.]

Written in the seventeenth century, written by the "ingenious layman"
Cervantes, this enumeration is a mere rhetorical eulogy of history. Menard,
on the other hand, writes:

la verdad, cuya madre es la historia, émula del tiempo, depósito
de las acciones, testigo de lo pasado, ejemplo y aviso de lo pre-
sente, advertencia de lo por venir.

[truth, whose mother is history, who is the rival of time, depos-
itory of deeds, witness of the past, example and lesson to the
present, and warning to the future.]

History, *mother* of truth; the idea is astounding. Menard, a contemporary of William James, does not define history as an investigation of reality,
but as its origin. Historical truth, for him, is not what took place; it is what
we think took place. The final clauses—*example and lesson to the present,
and warning to the future*—are shamelessly pragmatic.

Equally vivid is the contrast in styles. The archaic style of Menard—in
the last analysis, a foreigner—suffers from a certain affectation. Not so that
of his precursor, who handles easily the ordinary Spanish of his time.

There is no intellectual exercise which is not ultimately useless. A philosophical doctrine is in the beginning a seemingly true description of the
universe; as the years pass it becomes a mere chapter—if not a paragraph
or a noun—in the history of philosophy. In literature, this ultimate decay is
even more notorious. "*Don Quixote*," Menard once told me, "was above all
an agreeable book; now it is an occasion for patriotic toasts, grammatical
arrogance and obscene deluxe editions. Glory is an incomprehension, and
perhaps the worst."

These nihilist arguments contain nothing new; what is unusual is the
decision Pierre Menard derived from them. He resolved to outstrip that
vanity which awaits all the woes of mankind; he undertook a task that was
complex in the extreme and futile from the outset. He dedicated his conscience and nightly studies to the repetition of a pre-existing book in a
foreign tongue. The number of rough drafts kept on increasing; he tena-

ciously made corrections and tore up thousands of manuscript pages.* He did not permit them to be examined, and he took great care that they would not survive him. It is in vain that I have tried to reconstruct them.

I have thought that it is legitimate to consider the "final" *Don Quixote* as a kind of palimpsest, in which should appear traces—tenuous but not undecipherable—of the "previous" handwriting of our friend. Unfortunately, only a second Pierre Menard, inverting the work of the former, could exhume and rescuscitate these Troys. . . .

"To think, analyze and invent," he also wrote me, "are not anomalous acts, but the normal respiration of the intelligence. To glorify the occasional fulfillment of this function, to treasure ancient thoughts of others, to remember with incredulous amazement that the *doctor universalis* thought, is to confess our languor or barbarism. Every man should be capable of all ideas, and I believe that in the future he will be."

Menard (perhaps without wishing to) has enriched, by means of a new technique, the hesitant and rudimentary art of reading: the technique is one of deliberate anachronism and erroneous attributions. This technique, with its infinite applications, urges us to run through the *Odyssey* as if it were written after the *Aeneid,* and to read *Le jardin du Centaure* by Madame Henri Bachelier as if it were by Madame Henri Bachelier. This technique would fill the dullest books with adventure. Would not the attributing of *The Imitation of Christ* to Louis Ferdinand Céline or James Joyce be a sufficient renovation of its tenuous spiritual counsels?

---

*I remember his square-ruled notebooks, the black streaks where he had crossed out words, his peculiar typographical symbols and his insect-like handwriting. In the late afternoon he liked to go for walks on the outskirts of Nîmes; he would take a notebook with him and make a gay bonfire.

MICHEL FOUCAULT

Representing: Don Quixote

With all their twists and turns, Don Quixote's adventures form the bound-
ary: they mark the end of the old interplay between resemblance and signs
and contain the beginnings of new relations. Don Quixote is not a man given
to extravagance, but rather a diligent pilgrim breaking his journey before all
the marks of similitude. He is the hero of the Same. He never manages to
escape from the familiar plain stretching out on all sides of the Analogue,
any more than he does from his own small province. He travels endlessly
over that plain, without ever crossing the clearly defined frontiers of difference, or reaching the heart of identity. Moreover, he is himself like a sign, a
long, thin graphism, a letter that has just escaped from the open pages of a
book. His whole being is nothing but language, text, printed pages, stories
that have already been written down. He is made up of interwoven words;
he is writing itself, wandering through the world among the resemblances of
things. Yet not entirely so: for in his reality as an impoverished hidalgo he
can become a knight only by listening from afar to the age-old epic that
gives its form to Law. The book is not so much his existence as his duty.
He is constantly obliged to consult it in order to know what to do or say,
and what signs he should give himself and others in order to show that he
really is of the same nature as the text from which he springs. The chivalric
romances have provided once and for all a written prescription for his adventures. And every episode, every decision, every exploit will be yet another

From *The Order of Things: An Archaeology of the Human Sciences.* © 1970 by
Random House, Inc. Pantheon Books, 1970.

sign that Don Quixote is a true likeness of all the signs that he has traced
from his book. But the fact that he wishes to be like them means that he
must put them to the test, that the (legible) signs no longer resemble (visible)
people. All those written texts, all those extravagant romances are, quite
literally, unparalleled: no one in the world ever did resemble them; their
timeless language remains suspended, unfulfilled by any similitude; they
could all be burned in their entirety and the form of the world would not
be changed. If he is to resemble the texts of which he is the witness, the
representation, the real analogue, Don Quixote must also furnish proof and
provide the indubitable sign that they are telling the truth, that they really
are the language of the world. It is incumbent upon him to fulfil the promise
of the books. It is his task to recreate the epic, though by a reverse process:
the epic recounted (or claimed to recount) real exploits, offering them to our
memory; Don Quixote, on the other hand, must endow with reality the signs-
without-content of the narrative. His adventures will be a deciphering of the
world: a diligent search over the entire surface of the earth for the forms
that will prove that what the books say is true. Each exploit must be a proof:
it consists, not in a real triumph—which is why victory is not really important—but in an attempt to transform reality into a sign. Into a sign that the
signs of language really are in conformity with things themselves. Don Quixote reads the world in order to prove his books. And the only proofs he
gives himself are the glittering reflections of resemblances.

His whole journey is a quest for similitudes: the slightest analogies are
pressed into service as dormant signs that must be reawakened and made to
speak once more. Flocks, serving girls, and inns become once more the
language of books to the imperceptible degree to which they resemble castles,
ladies, and armies—a perpetually untenable resemblance which transforms
the sought-for proof into derision and leaves the words of the books forever
hollow. But non-similitude itself has its model, and one that it imitates in
the most servile way: it is to be found in the transformations performed by
magicians. So all the indices of non-resemblance, all the signs that prove that
the written texts are not telling the truth, resemble the action of sorcery,
which introduces difference into the indubitable existence of similitude by
means of deceit. And since this magic has been foreseen and described in
the books, the illusory difference that it introduces can never be anything
but an enchanted similitude, and, therefore, yet another sign that the signs
in the books really do resemble the truth.

Don Quixote is a negative of the Renaissance world; writing has ceased
to be the prose of the world; resemblances and signs have dissolved their
former alliance; similitudes have become deceptive and verge upon the vi-

sionary or madness; things still remain stubbornly within their ironic identity: they are no longer anything but what they are; words wander off on their own, without content, without resemblance to fill their emptiness; they are no longer the marks of things; they lie sleeping between the pages of books and covered in dust. Magic, which permitted the decipherment of the world by revealing the secret resemblances beneath its signs, is no longer of any use except as an explanation, in terms of madness, of why analogies are always proved false. The erudition that once read nature and books alike as parts of a single text has been relegated to the same category as its own chimeras: lodged in the yellowed pages of books, the signs of language no longer have any value apart from the slender fiction which they represent. The written word and things no longer resemble one another. And between them, Don Quixote wanders off on his own.

Yet language has not become entirely impotent. It now possesses new powers, and powers peculiar to it alone. In the second part of the novel, Don Quixote meets characters who have read the first part of his story and recognize him, the real man, as the hero of the book. Cervantes's text turns back upon itself, thrusts itself back into its own destiny, and becomes the object of its own narrative. The first part of the hero's adventures plays in the second part the role originally assumed by the chivalric romances. Don Quixote must remain faithful to the book that he has now become in reality; he must protect it from errors, from counterfeits, from apocryphal sequels; he must fill in the details that have been left out; he must preserve its truth. But Don Quixote himself has not read this book, and does not have to read it, since he is the book in flesh and blood. Having first read so many books that he became a sign, a sign wandering through a world that did not recognize him, he has now, despite himself and without his knowledge, become a book that contains his truth, that records exactly all that he has done and said and seen and thought, and that at last makes him recognizable, so closely does he resemble all those signs whose ineffaceable imprint he has left behind him. Between the first and second parts of the novel, in the narrow gap between those two volumes, and by their power alone, Don Quixote has achieved his reality—a reality he owes to language alone, and which resides entirely inside the words. Don Quixote's truth is not in the relation of the words to the world but in that slender and constant relation woven between themselves by verbal signs. The hollow fiction of epic exploits has become the representative power of language. Words have swallowed up their own nature as signs.

Don Quixote is the first modern work of literature, because in it we see the cruel reason of identities and differences make endless sport of signs and similitudes; because in it language breaks off its old kinship with things and enters into that lonely sovereignty from which it will reappear, in its separated state, only as literature; because it marks the point where resemblance enters an age which is, from the point of view of resemblance, one of madness and imagination. Once similitude and signs are sundered from each other, two experiences can be established and two characters appear face to face. The madman, understood not as one who is sick but as an established and maintained deviant, as an indispensable cultural function, has become, in Western experience, the man of primitive resemblances. This character, as he is depicted in the novels or plays of the Baroque age, and as he was gradually institutionalized right up to the advent of nineteenth-century psychiatry, is the man who is *alienated* in *analogy*. He is the disordered player of the Same and the Other. He takes things for what they are not, and people one for another; he cuts his friends and recognizes complete strangers; he thinks he is unmasking when, in fact, he is putting on a mask. He inverts all values and all proportions, because he is constantly under the impression that he is deciphering signs: for him, the crown makes the king. In the cultural perception of the madman that prevailed up to the end of the eighteenth century, he is Different only in so far as he is unaware of Difference; he sees nothing but resemblances and signs of resemblance everywhere; for him all signs resemble one another, and all resemblances have the value of signs. At the other end of the cultural area, but brought close by symmetry, the poet is he who, beneath the named, constantly expected differences, rediscovers the buried kinships between things, their scattered resemblances. Beneath the established signs, and in spite of them, he hears another, deeper, discourse, which recalls the time when words glittered in the universal resemblance of things; in the language of the poet, the Sovereignty of the Same, so difficult to express, eclipses, the distinction existing between signs.

This accounts, no doubt, for the confrontation of poetry and madness in modern Western culture. But it is no longer the old Platonic theme of inspired madness. It is the mark of a new experience of language and things. At the fringes of a knowledge that separates beings, signs, and similitudes, and as though to limit its power, the madman fulfils the function of *homosemanticism*: he groups all signs together and leads them with a resemblance that never ceases to proliferate. The poet fulfils the opposite function: his is the *allegorical* role; beneath the language of signs and beneath the interplay of their precisely delineated distinctions, he strains his ears to catch that "other language," the language, without words or discourse, of resemblance. The poet brings similitude to the signs that speak it, whereas the madman loads all signs with a resemblance that ultimately erases them. They share, then, on the outer edge of our culture and at the point nearest to its essential divisions, that "frontier" situation—a marginal position and a profoundly archaic silhouette—where their words unceasingly renew the power of their strangeness and the strength of their contestation. Between them there has opened up a field of knowledge in which, because of an essential rupture in the Western world, what has become important is no longer resemblances but identities and differences.

MANUEL DURÁN

Cervantes's Swan Song: Persiles and Sigismunda

I. CERVANTES'S FAVORITE NOVEL

It seems probable that *Persiles and Sigismunda*, Cervantes's last novel, was his favorite work. It is certain that he never invested as much care and love in the composition of any of his other works. In his opinion, or at least he so states towards the end of his life, this novel was the most perfect of all. In his dedication to the Count of Lemos, which appears in the second part of *Don Quixote*, referring to *Persiles*, which he thought at that time he would finish within four months, he states: "I myself now take my leave by offering Your Excellency *The Trials of Persiles and Sigismunda*, . . . It ought to be the worst or the best that has been written in our language—I am referring, of course, to books designed for entertainment. As a matter of fact, I repent having said 'the worst,' for according to the opinion of my friends it should be extremely good" [tr. Samuel Putnam].

Persiles was published in Madrid in 1617, one year after Cervantes's death. Its last pages seem to have been finished hurriedly. Its author, who had built such illusions about this novel, must have felt anguished about the idea of dying without putting the finishing touches on it, and worked with feverish intensity during the last months of his life. The fourth book of *Persiles* consists of only fourteen chapters, compared with the twenty-three, twenty-two and twenty-one of the other books or sections. Moreover, these last chapters are much shorter than the rest. This fact and some examples

From *Cervantes*. © 1974 by Twayne Publishers, a division of G. K. Hall & Co., Boston.

of carelessness of style in a work otherwise so scrupulously written lead us to believe that perhaps Cervantes was unable to revise these pages.

This novel was published by Cervantes's widow in Madrid in 1617, as we have stated, and in the same year by several other publishers in Valencia, Barcelona, Pamplona, and Brussels. Probably Cervantes had begun writing it at the same time as the second part of *Don Quixote*. He finished it a few days before dying. In his dedication to the Count of Lemos he states poignantly, "There is an old song, once famous, which begins, 'Having placed my foot in the stirrup.' I wish its words did not fit so closely my own predicament, since I can now use almost these very words:

> Puesto ya el pie en el estrivo
> Con las ansias de la muerte,
> Gran señor, esta te escrivo.

> [Having placed my foot in the stirrup,
> A prey to the agony of death,
> Great Lord, this I write to you.]

Yesterday they gave me extreme unction, and today I write you these lines; time is short, my agony grows, hopes diminish. And in spite of all this, I keep alive because of my desire to go on living."

With this novel, therefore, Cervantes takes leave of life and of glory, and the farewell of its preface reminds us of the death of Don Quixote.

The complete title of the novel is *The Trials of Persiles and Sigismunda, A Northern Adventure*. The words "Northern Adventure" better describe the first two books of the novel, which are set in the foggy Nordic shores. It is a Northern Europe described with all the fantasy of the Baroque period. *Persiles* could be described as a romance and a novel of adventures, a "thriller for lovers." Its situations are based on the usual pair of lovers upon whom Fate visits the most unexpected trials and dangers, but who must finally win; the book ends with the happy union of the lovers. Cervantes makes these situations, which the Byzantine novels had already explored, fit a more modern era, conferring upon his couple all possible poetic and Christian virtues, and substituting for the bright Mediterranean world the shadowy Northern one.

The plot is not too hard to follow. Persiles, the prince of Thule, and Sigismunda, the daughter of the king of Friesland, pretending to be brother and sister under the false names of Periandro and Auristela, journey through the vast seas and lands of Europe, starting from the faraway frozen Northern shores near the pole, going south by sea and land, crossing Portugal, France, and Italy until they reach Rome. They must obtain from the Pope a blessing for their love, a love which emerges chaste and pure from the most terrible trials and adventures. The complicated plan of the novel, which is based on a main narrative line that is frequently interrupted, permits the author to suggest the constant intervention of a blind fate under whose mysterious and capricious influence the characters look for happiness only to be frustrated time and time again.

The first two sections of this novel are developed by Cervantes along the lines of a wild succession of adventures: shipwrecks, kidnappings, separations, dreams, premonitions. It is a dream world, similar often to the dream world of Shakespeare's *The Tempest,* a world of unreality, ghosts, constant doubts about the reality of everyday life, a world in which, like Calderón's Segismundo in *Life is a Dream,* we are never quite sure whether we are awake or dreaming. Periandro, for example, narrates a splendid vision full of color and delight in which he saw emerald meadows, fruits of every kind, precious stones, in a setting of mild skies, a splendid procession of chariots and allegorical figures, and he states: "I broke the dream and the beautiful vision disappeared," and when asked, "Then you were dreaming?" "Yes," he replies, "since everything good that happens to me turns out to be a dream."

Persiles turns out to be a huge book of adventures, a poetic novel of chivalry, which rights the failure of the hero in *Don Quixote.* It is of unequal interest with respect to its plot and its development, yet nevertheless is written in a style which is perhaps the richest in nuances, most elegant and terse Cervantes ever employed.

II. A POETIC SYNTHESIS

Everything Cervantes knew about poetry, rhythm, harmony in language can be found in the pages of *Persiles*: some of his sentences truly contain "the sound of music." The novel is, as the Italian critic Arturo Farinelli puts it, "Cervantes's last romantic dream." It unites the two aesthetic criteria applied by Cervantes to his own works: idealization and realism. The idealization is here much more visible, it dominates the whole novel, yet from time to time we can also find sentences, sayings, observations, which remind us of *The Glass Scholar* and other *Exemplary Novels.* This is especially true of the second half of *Persiles,* books 3 and 4, where we leave behind the mysterious Northern shores and come down to the bright world of Mediterranean sunlight. Cervantes knows his surroundings much better: he had invented every detail in his descriptions of Northern Europe; he can now rely on his experience and his memory, and perspicacious observations reappear at this moment. As soon as he brings his characters to the squares and towns of the contemporary world, he regains his true nature as a humorist and a keen observer of human nature, human foibles, local color.

Cervantes's novel is also a geographic synthesis, a recapitulation of everything the author knew, directly or indirectly, about Europe, its lands, its mountains, rivers, seas, inhabitants, and customs. To be sure, we are not dealing with a scientific treatise: on the contrary, Cervantes takes great liberties with geography as we understand it today. We must take into account the fact that the books on this subject available to Cervantes were, on the whole, closer in style and accuracy to Marco Polo's famous description of his trip to the Orient than to our modern maps and the descriptions of the *National Geographic* magazine.

Accuracy in geographic details was certainly not among the virtues of the great writers of this period. Two examples shall suffice. In *The Tempest*, Shakespeare assumes that Milan is either a seaport or is situated very close to the sea. Thus, when Prospero narrates his sad story to Miranda, he states:

> The King of Naples, being an enemy
> To me inveterate, hearkens my brother's suit;
>
> A treacherous army levied, one midnight
> Fated to the purpose, did Antonio open
> The gates of Milan; and, i' the dead of darkness,
> The ministers for the purpose hurried thence
> Me and thy crying self
> In few, they hurried us aboard a bark,
> Bore us some leagues to sea.
>
> (act 1, scene 2)

Calderón de la Barca, in his masterpiece *La vida es sueño* (*Life is a Dream*) describes how his hero, Segismundo, having been brought to the King's palace, becomes infatuated with his cousin Estrella, who is already betrothed to another man, and tries to kiss her hand against her will; a servant interferes, and Segismundo, furious, throws him off the balcony. The servant had been warned by Segismundo, who had told him, in very few words, that he would defenestrate him if need be, but had rejected Segismundo's menace:

> Con los hombres como yo
> no puede hacerse eso.

[With men like me
you cannot do such a thing.]

Segismundo then proceeds to throw him down from the high balcony:

Cayó del balcon al mar:
¡Vive Dios, que pudo ser!

[He fell down from the balcony into the sea:
By my faith, I could do it!]

(act 2, scene 6)

Yet Calderón could have known (should have known) that the capital of Poland, the city where the King's palace rose, was at that time Kraków, certainly not a seaport. And yet he assumed the King's castle was surrounded by the sea or at least built on the seashore.

Cervantes did not lack for sources of information, however unreliable. We should remember his era was not inclined towards scientific precision. Facts and fantasy often mixed in the travel books he may have read. Perhaps some of the sources that inspired him, if not with respect to concrete details, but rather as a cultural background that explains his cavalier attitude towards geography, were the descriptions of the New World so widely read during his lifetime. Columbus, Hernán Cortés, Bernal Díaz del Castillo, so many other explorers and conquerors, had given the Spaniards an image of the new lands beyond the sea that was at the same time realistic and fantastic. America was different, huge, fabulous. The magnificent exotic cities such as Tenochtitlan were a source of wonder. They seemed to belong in the pages of a novel, a fiction such as *Amadís de Gaula* or the other novels of chivalry. The real world turned out to be more fantastic than the imagination of most writers: it was a mirage come true. Aristotle in his *Poetics* had claimed that art should imitate Nature. Yet in these strange descriptions of the New World one could almost believe that—as Oscar Wilde would claim much later—Nature was imitating art. How could one tell the fantasy apart from the commonplace and factual? Should one even try?

There were numerous books on geography and travel available to Cervantes, and he must have been familiar with some of them: they were easily available in the Spanish libraries and bookstores of his time. Books such as the works of Archbishop Olao Magno of Uppsala, a well-known geographer of the sixteenth century; the *Jardín de flores curiosas* (*Garden of Curious Flowers*) by Antonio de Torquemada; the *De las cosas maravillosas del mundo* (*All About the World's Wonders*) by Francisco Thamara; Pero Mexía's

Silva de Varia lección (*Gatherings from Many Sources*), and, of course, classical works such as Marco Polo's description of his travels, the famous works of Pliny, Strabo, and Ptolemy. Many of their tales rivaled in exotic strangeness the marvelous accounts given by Spanish travellers and explorers who came back from the New World or the Pacific Ocean, the "Mar del Sur" or Southern Seas, and often described strange animals, cities of gold, vast cities built in the middle of a lake or on top of a mountain, temples and citadels not unlike the fabled Egyptian pyramids.

And yet it would be wrong to underline excessively Cervantes's disregard of geography; in a way, the opposite is true. Or, rather, the essential facts are true, the details are imagined. All his locations, except one, can be found on the maps of his time, even such seemingly fantastic places as the Island of Fire and the Island of the Hermits. Cervantes does know geography. What happens occasionally is that he is more interested in what we may call "symbolic geography." Let us not forget that the travels of his two lovers take them from the Nordic mists to the clear light of the South. The trip ends in Rome, an exceptional city, the spiritual center of the world. It begins in a strange place, a country not found on any of the maps current in the sixteenth century, in the mythical island of Thule. If we pay attention to this unique lapse, we realize that Cervantes was trying to establish two poles, at the beginning and the end of his book, one remote, mysterious, and on the whole imperfect, negative, the other positive, sacred, luminous. The true allegorical dimensions of Cervantes's novel begin so to appear. As Alban K. Forcione states [in *Cervantes's Christian Romance*], in one notable case the importance of symbolic space causes Cervantes to sacrifice geographical precision and verisimilitude. Rome, as "cabeza del mundo [Head or Center of the world]," "Eternal City," and a real city, was well-suited to be the goal of Cervantes's heroes. However, those maps of the time that had the greatest pretensions to scientific accuracy offered no city or country with such symbolic power for the origins of the quest. Hence Cervantes turns to classical geography, locating Periandro's kingdom on Thule. He underscores its traditional associations as a hallowed kingdom and "the end of the earth." The name for this strange land, assumed to be the last land to the West, "the end of the world," can be found in Vergil, in his *Georgics* (book 1), and Cervantes is well aware of it, since he quotes the pertinent passage from Vergil in chapter 12 of book 4 of *Persiles*. It is curious to observe, at the same time, that Cervantes seems aware of the odd choice he has made as to the point of geographic departure of his characters' adventures, and characteristically he retraces his steps and underplays the symbolism to be found in Thule. Shortly after the allusion to Vergil, a character says: "Tule, que agora vulgarmente se llama Islanda . . . [Thule, which nowadays people call Iceland . . .]" (book 4, chap. 12). Yet the impression remains: Cervantes is making use here of allegorical space. Could it be that *Persiles* was intended to be much more than a romance, than an endless series of melodramatic adventures, much more than a "Renaissance soap opera"? In order to make perfectly sure that this is the case, it is wise to examine Cervantes's sources: only thus can we ascertain what he imitates and what he innovates, and thus find out what his purpose was.

III. THE SOURCES OF *PERSILES*

The main source for *Persiles* has been identified by most critics as Heliodorus' *Aethiopica,* a Hellenistic romance of the third century A.D. The main reason for this identification is obvious: Cervantes himself points out his indebtedness to Heliodorus when, in his preface to the *Exemplary Novels,* he claims that his work in progress (the *Persiles,* at that time, was still without a title) would try to compete with Heliodorus' novel. It was indeed then a famous novel. Tasso had been influenced by it when in *Gerusalemme Liberata* he created his most interesting feminine character, Clorinda. Its fame would not soon vanish: it was still a "best seller" in France during the seventeenth century. Racine devoured its pages on the sly, as his stern teachers considered the book to be too mundane and frivolous for a good Jansenist mind. It had been translated from the original Greek into French by Jacques Amyot in 1547; the first translation into Spanish, anonymous, was based upon Amyot's version and was published in Antwerp in 1554. The second Spanish version was obtained by comparing a Latin translation and the Greek text. The translator, Fernando de Mena, had it published at Alcalá de Henares in 1587. It is possible that Cervantes owned both Spanish translations, as the *Aethiopica,* otherwise known by its subtitle, *Theagenes and Chariclea,* was one of the favorite books of the Renaissance. The typical characteristics of this novel, as well as of *Apollonius of Tyre* and other romances of the Hellenistic period, are the separation of two lovers, hair-breadth escapes from a series of appalling perils and adversities, a final reunion, and a happy ending.

The *Aethiopica* is a long novel, the longest of all the Hellenistic romances, and perhaps the one to offer its essential traits in the most typical form. Its ten books offer the reader a plot both simple and complex. Let us try to summarize it, since the book is not easy to find for the average reader: its ancient glory has vanished, it is no longer in print in most countries, and on the whole it has not been popular with modern Classical scholars. Chariclea, a beautiful maiden about whose ancestors nothing is known, lives in Delphi, the ancient oracular shrine and precinct of Apollo. She is a priestess at the temple. Theagenes, a Thessalian prince, falls in love with her, suddenly and dramatically, during a party given at the temple, and she reciprocates his love. Protected and accompanied by Calasiris, an Egyptian priest living in Delphi, Theagenes and Chariclea flee together to Egypt, but not before swearing eternal love and chastity until the moment they should marry. The novel is made up of the numerous adventures that befall the lovers before their marriage. There are storms at sea, attacks by pirates and bandits, wars, ambushes, betrayals, mistaken identities, sudden recognitions, live characters confused with dead ones, dead ones that speak, witchcraft, and obstacles of every imaginable kind continually slow up both the action and the happy ending. Finally the lovers arrive in Ethiopia as war prisoners slated to be sacrificed in a barbarous ritual. But in that very moment it is learned that the girl is the daughter of the King of Ethiopia, Idaspe, and Persina, the Queen. And so the last obstacles are overcome and the marriage finally takes place. As in other Greek novels which have been handed down to us, the *Aethiopica* is dominated by the theme of love as a virtuous and proper feeling, crowned by matrimony; it abounds in mannered sentimentality and makes a clear distinction between good and bad characters, with the good ones always winning out at the end, and shows excessive delight in harrowing adventures and in marvelous happenings. Its psychology is rudimentary and conventional, and the characters, seen from the outside, are reduced to caricature-like marionettes. But spectacular descriptions and a kaleidoscope of adventures help to camouflage an inner vacuity. A vague religiosity, expressed by the cult of Apollo-Helios, is an important ingredient but does not quite succeed in giving unity to the novel.

Finally, the modern reader can easily see through the melodrama, the rhetorical tricks, the conventions: nevertheless, there is something appealing about the basic situation of two young lovers in trouble. The resilience of this novel can be appreciated if we point out that Tasso, Cervantes, countless second-rate novelists in the seventeenth and eighteenth centuries enjoyed it, and moreover, as most lovers of Italian literature may realize—although this fact has been almost completely ignored by serious critics—we can still find echoes of the *Aethiopica*'s plot in the best and most popular Italian novel of the nineteenth century, Alessandro Manzoni's *I Promessi Sposi* [*The Betrothed*], which means that the influence of Heliodorus was to reach, directly or indirectly, into the Romantic era. Few novels can boast about such an enduring presence.

Cervantes wanted to accomplish two goals. The first and foremost aim was, perhaps, to please his readers, to compose a novel which would be successful. This goal was easily attained: *Persiles* enjoyed an immediate success comparable to that of *Don Quixote*. The years that followed its posthumous publication in 1617 witnessed ten editions in Spanish, translations into French, Italian, and English, and imitations in drama and prose fiction. This success was not of short duration: in the eighteenth century, new editions, translations and imitations continued to appear. At the beginning of the nineteenth century, a serious scholar, the Swiss Jean-Charles Simonde de Sismondi, could claim, in his *De la littérature du midi de l'Europe,* published in 1813, that many readers considered it to be Cervantes's masterpiece. Obviously, the best way to produce a modern best seller, Cervantes concluded, was to imitate an old best seller. Cervantes turned to a model that was universally praised for its sound structure, its moving situations, its use of suspense.

Yet winning the applause of the crowds was not enough for Cervantes. He wanted to please the most demanding critics. They were all, or almost all, imbued with the ideas about literature that Aristotle had propounded in his *Poetics.* One of the rules suggested for the epic poems, the highest form of literature, was to begin in the middle of a significant episode, in order to involve the reader in the action. It is curious to observe that Heliodorus makes use of this technique, and that Cervantes follows suit, thereby bringing his romance one step closer to what we might call an "epic narrative," a prose epic. In the case of Heliodorus, his French translator, Jacques Amyot, had already remarked, in the preface to his version, upon this strange technique: "is strangely organized, for he begins in the middle of his tale, as Heroic Poets often do. Which at first creates a great surprise among his readers, and awakens in them a passionate desire to hear the beginning of the story; and yet he compels them to go on reading through the ingenious linking of his plot, so that one is not quite certain about what happens at the beginning of the first book until one reads the end of the fifth book. And when the reader reaches this point, he is still more anxious to find out about the end than he was when he started his reading of the novel. In this fashion his critical judgment remains always in suspense, until he reaches the conclusion, which satisfies him fully, as are satisfied those who finally enjoy the fact that they have at last reached a goal long desired."

These remarks by the French translator of Heliodorus raise an interesting problem. Both *Aethiopica* and *Persiles* are links in a chain which stretches from Classical literature to the present, and which establishes the novel as an accepted literary genre. Modern readers do not realize how difficult it was for the novel to be born and be accepted: It was the "ugly duckling," the disinherited genre. Aristotle does not even mention it in his *Poetics,* a basic book which sets the tone for literary critics from the fourth century B.C. up to the Romantic era. Was it perhaps a careless omission on his part? It does not seem possible. The Greeks did not assign a Muse to the art of the novel. They had a Muse presiding over the creation of historians, one for choreographers, one for astronomers, no muse for aspiring novelists. Critics acquainted with Chinese literature report the same strange phenomenon: the novel is in Chinese letters, until very recent times, a despised genre, one utterly lacking in prestige, to be left to rank amateurs and pornographers.

It is possible that novelists such as Heliodorus, trying to establish their craft in spite of the lack of official academic recognition, may have borrowed some of the techniques prescribed by Aristotle and his followers for epic poets and dramatists, such as the *in-medias-res* beginning and the need for unity of the work and verisimilitude in its plot.

Heliodorus, about whom very little is known, must have felt in his creative years the pull of two opposite forces. On the one hand, he wanted to please his readers; on the other, he did not want to antagonize the masters of rhetoric and Aristotelian critics who exerted a strong influence upon the most cultivated and influential public of that era. Similarly, perhaps yet with greater urgency, Cervantes felt the need to placate both groups. This tension was not uncommon during the Renaissance. Both Lope de Vega and Shakespeare were keenly aware of these two goals.

IV. ARISTOTLE'S INFLUENCE

It seems evident that both Heliodorus and Aristotle were essential in the birth of *Persiles*: both were its sources, if we understand the word "sources" in a wide sense, not only the materials that an author can use in his work but also the techniques that can give shape to his materials. Cervantes was highly sensitive to the critical currents of his age. His *Don Quixote* is, as some of the modern critics as Edward C. Riley are aware, both a novel and a tract of literary criticism. How could Cervantes fail to take into account, while writing *Persiles,* the very principles of criticism that he had propounded in *Don Quixote*?

The answer is simple: he did take them into account. *Persiles,* no less than *Don Quixote,* although in a less obvious fashion, is a critique and a purification of the "wrong" type of novel, the romances of chivalry. As Alban Forcione states, "If it could ever be said that a work of literature is almost exclusively a product of literature and literary theory, it could be said of Cervantes's final work *Los Trabajos de Persiles y Sigismunda.* Everywhere the eclectic character of the work is visible: in its undisguised appropriation of scenes and passages from Vergil's *Aeneid* and Heliodorus' *Ethiopian History,* in its inclusion of an Italian novella and many brief reminiscences from biblical tradition, medieval romance, and other works of classical antiquity, and in its presentation of various recurrent topics of imaginative literature which are as old as literature itself. Moreover, the specific literary theories which inspired the fusion of so many widely disparate elements into a coherent whole are everywhere apparent in its texture. They are revealed in occasional digressions about aesthetic problems and in brief remarks of the self-conscious narrator drawing attention to the criteria governing his selective processes in the inclusion of a specific element. But more basically they become deeply imbedded in the action of the work itself informing an extended dramatic situation and its development in the second book."

The discovery and diffusion of Aristotle's *Poetics,* on the one hand, and the aesthetic critique of the romances of chivalry, on the other, had created for Cervantes the need to establish new rules for his fiction. Foreign critics were unsparing in their judgment of contemporary Spanish fiction. Cervantes was probably aware of the harsh words used by the Italian critic Giovanni Battista Pigna, who in his treatise *I romanzi,* published in 1554, states that "nearly all the Spanish romances are full of worthless follies, being founded, as they are, solely on miraculous occurrences and with their supernatural spirits of one sort or another always bringing about things far removed from the natural world and from true pleasure, which is generally produced by legitimate marvels. . . . [The Spanish romances] have the custom of presenting journeys by horse without taking into account the sea which lies between the rider and destination, and they present journeys by ship although there is land there to oppose such passage; they make the short roads long and the long ones short, and they include places which are not in the world; moreover, they lose themselves continually in love affairs and empty reasonings. There are nearly always in the battles described by the Spanish romances the most impossible things accepted as the most true."

Around the middle of the sixteenth century, literary critics started to make systematic use of Aristotle's *Poetics* for their attacks on the romances of chivalry. Their objections to this literary genre were manifold: lack of verisimilitude, lack of artistic unity, lack of sound moral teachings. In Spain the attack of intelligent critics such as Luis Vives was based mainly upon moral grounds, but also on traditional arguments derived from Plato: these books were a waste of time, a distraction from serious scientific work. Literature of this kind, Plato had claimed, is fictitious, it consists of lies. Vives denies that there can be any pleasure for the reader "in things that they (the

authors of romances of chivalry) feign so foolishly and openly," as, for instance, when they describe a battle in which one knight kills thirty opponents
and two giants, and recovers with miraculous swiftness from the wounds he
sustained in battle. Vives concludes, "Is it not madness to be carried away
by such idiocies and to be impressed by them?"

As Alban Forcione ably states, "it is only against this background of
literary theorizing that we can properly understand Cervantes's undeniably
high literary aspirations in the conception of the *Persiles,* his desire to rival
Heliodorus, his theorizing concerning the purification of the romance of
chivalry and the creation of an epic in prose, the important thematic role
that contemporary literary theory—particularly those problems surrounding
the polemics over Ariosto and Tasso—has in both the *Quixote* and the
Persiles, the creation of the *Persiles,* and finally the literary humor which
functions so successfully in the context of the *Quixote* but gives the *Persiles*
a puzzling ambivalence." Cervantes had dealt with literary theory in *Don
Quixote,* especially in the chapters where the knight's literary taste is discussed by the Curate, at the beginning of the novel (part 1, chap. 6), in
which the scrutiny of the knight's library takes place) and in chapters 49
and 50 of the same part where Don Quixote and the Canon of Toledo argue
at length about the truth and literary merit of the romances of chivalry.

The Canon of Toledo had undoubtedly read with care Aristotle's *Poetics.* Judged by Aristotle's formula that an epic poem should have for its
subject "a single action, whole and complete, with a beginning, a middle,
and an end," the romances of chivalry, which in the sixteenth century were
often classified as epic poems, turned out to be at best many actions of one
man, at worst many actions of many; their composition was faulty, even
chaotic. One of the Canon's criticisms of these novels centers on their structural disorder. The Canon, who, as we have said, had read Aristotle, seems
to have been equally acquainted with Horace's aesthetic ideas, as expounded
in the *Epistle to the Pisos,* or, as it is more generally known, *Ars Poetica.*
Horace begs the poets to avoid creating a composition that recalls to the
reader's mind the chaotic appearance of a monster. Aristotle wants the work
of literature to resemble a unified, living organism which must be entirely
visible to the glance of the beholder. The Canon makes use of an analogy
which was used by many theorists of the century who criticized the multiplicity of plot and protagonist in the romances of chivalry: "I have never
seen a book of chivalry with a whole body for a plot, with all its limbs
complete, so that the middle corresponds to the beginning, and the end to
the beginning and middle, for they are generally made up of so many limbs
that they seem intended rather to form a chimera or a monster then a well-

proportioned figure." He proceeds to invoke the principle of verisimilitude, another important line of attack of the critics of that period when dealing with fantastic fiction: "What beauty can there be, or what harmony between the parts and the whole, or between the whole and its parts, in a book or story in which a sixteen-year-old lad deals a giant as tall as a tower one blow with his sword . . . ?" Chapter 47 of *Don Quixote* (part 1) is also relevant to this aesthetic debate: in it the Canon declares that "in works of fiction there should be a mating between the plot and the readers' intelligence. They should be so written that the impossible is made to appear possible, things hard to believe being smoothed over and the mind held in suspense in such a manner as to create surprise and astonishment while at the same time they divert and entertain so that admiration and pleasure go hand in hand. But these are things which he cannot accomplish who flees verisimilitude and the imitation of nature, qualities that go to constitute perfection in the art of writing."

And yet Cervantes is not wholly convinced by the arguments of the Aristotelian critics. His mental reservations come to the surface time and time again. He must have thought them, on the whole, pedantic. Moreover, they were not acquainted with the problems of a professional writer of fiction. The words "and the mind held in suspense," in the above quotation, are revealing. Only through suspense (which presupposes an identification, partial or complete, between reader and hero) can the reader enjoy a long novel. His reservations about the harsh judgment meted out to the romances of chivalry may have prompted him to state (ironically, he places these words in the mouth of the Canon, who had been so merciless in his criticism): "for all the harsh things that he had said of such books, the Canon added, he had found one good thing about them, and that was the chance they afforded for a good mind to display its true worth, for they offered a broad and spacious field over which the author's pen might run without impediment, describing shipwrecks, tempests, battles, and encounters . . . he could picture here a lovely lady, modest, discreet, and reserved, and there a Christian knight, gentle and brave, setting a lawless, barbarous braggart over against a prince, courtly, valorous and benign, letting us see at once the loyalty and devotion of the vassals and the generosity of their lords." Chapter 47 concludes on a positive note: these books, the Canon claims, "indeed, by their very nature, provide the author with an unlimited field in which to try his hand at the epic, lyric, tragic, and comic genres and depict in turn all the moods that are represented by these most sweet and pleasing branches of poetry and oratory; for the epic may be written in prose as well as in verse."

Here we have, in a nutshell, the plan that Cervantes was to follow in his *Persiles*. He would write a romance that would please the crowds but at the same time be as similar as possible to a prose epic. It would be a novel that, according to the Canon's words, "keeping the mind in suspense, may so astonish, hold, excite, and entertain, that wonder and pleasure go hand in hand." He would avoid, as far as possible, the presentation of realities that did not exist in the natural world, e.g., giants as big as towers, imaginary geographical settings, such as the lands of Prester John of the Indies, and countries that Ptolemy never knew nor Marco Polo visited.

As Alban Forcione sees it, "it is clear that the Canon of Toledo's plan for the ideal book of chivalry was Cervantes's general formula for the *Persiles*, and it is tempting to believe that the hundred pages which the Canon claims to have written and abandoned are Cervantes's first sketch of his final work. Just how far the composition of the *Persiles* can be related to the suggestive literary dialogue is conjectural. Nevertheless, Cervantes's desire to follow the classical rules—unity, verisimilitude, decorum, the legitimized marvelous, rhetorical display, moral edification, and instructive erudition—is everywhere evident in the *Persiles,* both in subject matter and structure and in the various comments of the self-conscious narrator concerning criteria governing his creative and selective process" [*Cervantes, Aristotle and the "Persiles"*].

What Cervantes knew instinctively, and his contemporary Aristotelian critics forgot, was that a long narrative in prose had to be built around certain poles of tension, around emotional cores. Tension could not be sustained indefinitely: pauses were also essential. The romances of chivalry were organized along such lines. But in these romances tension was provided by the frantic moments of activity of the hero or heroes, the struggles, the scenes of battle, which, in turn, meant that for this tension to be relieved many implausible factors had to be introduced. Tension was created by pitting a hero against impossible odds: it was brought down to a lower level by having the hero overcome every obstacle, which in turn compelled the writer to resort to magic and the supernatural. These romances are, in modern terms, much closer to the adventures of Superman than to the modern thrillers of espionage built around our contemporary hero, James Bond. Cervantes would follow Heliodorus, a sounder model than the authors of the romances of chivalry; tension would be created in his *Persiles,* suspense and empathy achieved, through psychological devices, especially through the constant dangers menacing the happiness of the young couple and the painful separations forced on them by their enemies, by accidents, storms, and sheer bad luck. Where the writers of romances of chivalry tried mainly to create admiration in their readers by describing the extravagant and superhuman adventures of one or several heroes, Cervantes wants to elicit from his readers feelings of compassion, sympathy, concern.

And yet Cervantes's novel differs from Heliodorus' *Aethiopica* in many respects. This fact had already been noticed in 1854 by the English translator of the *Persiles,* who signs her Preface with the initials "L. D. S." and has been identified as Louisa Dorothea Stanley: she points out that "though the *plan* of *Persiles and Sigismunda* is taken from Heliodorus, I do not think they have *any* resemblance in style, and there is far more vivacity and humour in the narrative and characters (in Cervantes's novel), and more nature too, in spite of the high flown romance that surrounds them." She goes on to warn the reader: "I fear the modern reader will find the numerous episodes tedious; and story after story, which every additional personage we meet, thinks it necessary to relate, will perhaps try his patience; yet there is great beauty in many of these, at least in the original language." Her statement is plausible. The Spanish text does sound more harmonious, does have a more supple rhythm than its English versions. Modern readers do find many of the pages somewhat tedious. This is perhaps due to two factors. The first is easily explained: Cervantes's main literary device, or perhaps main stylistic device, is suspense. But our readers are used to a faster pace and a stronger dose of suspense. Cervantes's suspense is subtle and slow in developing, as the main narrative, the one that can create suspense inasmuch as the fate of the two young lovers depends on what happens in this main tale, is constantly interrupted by new characters and new tales related to these characters. Cervantes's contemporaries had apparently an inexhaustible supply of patience and were perhaps inclined towards masochism.

The second factor which prevents us from enjoying *Persiles* to the full is that Cervantes is operating, throughout the novel, at several levels. The superficial level, the one that the reader understands right away, is made up of the adventures of the two star-crossed lovers. The deeper meaning has been pointed out by modern critics: Thus Alban Forcione states that the *Persiles* is a quest romance in which the heroes must abandon an imperfect society, journey through strange worlds full of menacing forces, and suffer numerous trials and struggles before reaching their destination. Here their sufferings are rewarded with superior wisdom, and they can return to elevate their society to the state of perfection which they themselves embody. This process of purification, of groping from darkness and shadow towards light, of attaining wisdom through suffering and through faithful, chaste love, is not unlike the process prescribed by Plato in his *Republic,* in which men are described inside a cave, surrounded by shadows; the light shines outside the cave, but only philosophers will be able to venture outside the cave, after which they should return to the cave in order to enlighten their fellowmen and bring to them the fruits of wisdom.

At another level the quest of the young lovers reenacts the basic myth of Christianity: Man in his fallen state must wander in the sublunary world of disorder, suffering in the world of human history, and be reborn through expiation and Christ's mercy. Here again we move from darkness towards light, from a realm menaced by war, an oppressive king, and the threat of sterility to the city of Rome, which traditionally brings to our mind the Kingdom of the Blessed.

Possibly the taste of most modern readers does not favor extended allegory in a novel. In any case, few readers of Cervantes's novel are aware, nowadays, of the mythical and allegorical dimensions of the book. It can be doubted that many readers of Cervantes's own time were aware of it, in spite of the fact that allegory was far from dead during the Renaissance.

In this respect, the *Persiles* is entirely different from its model, *Aethiopica*; Cervantes's pride, his ambition as a writer, prevented him from following too closely a model and forced him to endow his novel with a complicated symbolical scaffolding that some readers would be capable of understanding and appreciating. He places a few clues here and there, strategically, all along his work, clues which indicate to the alert reader that Cervantes is not content with producing a mere romance. For instance, in the very first pages we find the theme of bondage, the theme of darkness, the quest for freedom. The in-medias-res beginning adds to the tension and suspense. Chapter 1 bears the following title: "Periander is drawn up out of the Dungeon: he goes out to Sea on a Raft: A Tempest comes on, and he is saved by a Ship." What follows is a scene worthy of a Gothic novel, a scene, moreover, that would bring to mind to Cervantes's readers the scenes of Calderón's *La vida es sueño* if it had been published or staged at that time (as is well known, Calderón's play follows Cervantes's novel, not vice versa).

Darkness and danger are everywhere in these first lines: "Near the mouth of a deep and narrow dungeon, which was more like a tomb than a prison to its wretched inmates, stood Corsicurbo, the barbarian. He shouted with a terrible voice, but, although the fearful clamour was heard far and near, none could hear his words distinctly, except the miserable Clelia, an unhappy captive, buried in this abyss. 'Clelia,' he said, 'see that the boy who was committed to your custody two days ago, be bound fast to the cord I am about to let down; see that his hands are tied behind him, and make him ready to be drawn up here: also look well if among the women of the last prize there are any beautiful enough to deserve being brought amongst us, and to enjoy the light of the clear sky that is above us.' So saying, he let down a strong hempen cord, and for some brief space he and four other barbarians pulled it, until, with his hands tied strongly behind him, they drew up a boy, seemingly about nineteen or twenty years of age, drest in linen like a mariner, but beautiful, exceedingly."

A novel, unlike an opera, does not usually start with an overture. Yet the first chapter of the *Persiles* has the same function as an opera overture: it introduces the main themes, the theme of ascension from darkness to light and the theme of geographical flight towards freedom. Vertical movement and horizontal travel are related, the symbolic ascent and the painful horizontal movement towards freedom, light, wisdom.

Periandro, the young man in the first chapter, is, of course, Persiles, the lover of Sigismunda; their travels, both real and symbolic, become the unifying thread in this long and complex novel. Travels, tribulations, dangers: the pages of Cervantes's novel remind us of *Pilgrim's Progress* and of the serial film, *The Perils of Pauline*. Symbols and pathos abound: we long for comic relief. We discover the importance of the motif of "los trabajos" ["the works"] in the Spanish title of the novel, which becomes a principle of unity. The Spanish dictionaries of the Renaissance, specifically the dictionary compiled by Covarrubias, offer two meanings of the word *trabajos*. It means "work" or "task," and also "ordeal" or "trial." This second meaning is especially relevant. The novel narrates an ordeal, a trial, in which two young people will be able to prove their lasting love and also their patience, perseverance, and faith in God in adversity.

Light and darkness alternate along the pages of Cervantes's novel. The events unfold according to a pattern that avoids the impossible, miraculous effects dear to the writers of romances of chivalry and justly criticized by the Aristotelian critics. Cervantes tries to respect verisimilitude. But he wants to organize the many strands that are woven into his complex tapestry in as clear a pattern as possible. No scene repeats exactly a previous scene, yet we have often an impression of *déjà-vu*. This is perhaps due to the fact that all his characters are searchers: they want to find peace and wisdom, they want to emerge from the shadows into the light, they are moreover, in their search, looking for a central point in which they will find peace and wisdom. Many contemporary anthropologists and specialists of comparative religions would conclude that Cervantes's characters are not, in this respect, unique, bizarre, atypical. On the contrary, these characters retrace their steps, undergo similar adventures, repeat their efforts, simply because they are looking for the same goal: the center of the world.

Yet their search takes them through a labyrinth. It is a path with blind alleys, strange encounters. Oriental cultures have evolved a unique graphic design in which a labyrinth, often a circle surrounded by a square and divided into connecting sections, stands for the universe: men can accept it as a map, one to be followed in their wanderings, in search of the goal, the center, where circle, square, and labyrinth will finally disappear when the wanderer attains his goal, union with the cosmos. The composition of the *Persiles* resembles in many ways this Oriental design, this *mandala,* and this labyrinth. In it we find also blind alleys, connecting roads, strange encounters.

The connecting stories, the unfolding tales, the recurrent patterns of Cervantes's novel compel us to conjecture that Heliodorus and Aristotle were not his only guides, his basic sources. Oriental literature abounds in complex works where the unfolding of the plot brings us to numerous crossroads, to blind alleys, to "the tale-within-the-tale." The most outstanding example of such labyrinthine composition is, of course, *The Thousand and One Nights,* the complicated juxtaposition and interpolation of stories that have delighted countless generations of Oriental and Western readers. It is not necessary to prove—an impossible task—that Cervantes was acquainted with this Arabic-Persian-Oriental compilation. We might point out that he was one of the very few European writers of his century to have lived for a while in a Moslem environment, yet this would not be a conclusive proof. Let us state simply that the *Persiles,* just like *The Thousand and One Nights,* reminds us of a labyrinth.

And yet it differs from the Oriental collection of tales in one significant respect: the beginning and the end of the labyrinth are clearly marked in Cervantes's novel, in a way that gives it true symbolic meaning. To be sure, both the complex book built around the story of Scheherazade and the complicated story woven by Heliodorus around his two young lovers have clear beginnings and ends. Yet they lack symbolic content. Heliodorus, it is said, was Bishop of Tricca, in Thessaly, and wrote in a time when the rise of Christianity should have made both him and his readers sensitive to religious meanings. It is Cervantes, a lay writer, who is closer to real religious writing: his fable compels us often to gaze upwards, to the heavenly places from which Fate, or Providence, pulls the strings; and it is organized in a seesaw movement between the sad moments of "purgatory," i.e., the times when the lovers are imprisoned or isolated from each other, and the ecstatic visions of bliss. The vision of Rome from the top of a hill is one of these moments: the young lovers proceed to renew their vows and rekindle their hope; their heavenly vision does not exclude earthly love; as Persiles says to his beloved Sigismunda, "Already is the air of Rome playing on our cheeks, and the hopes that have supported us are beating in our hearts; already it seems to me that I am in possession of the beloved object so long desired. Look well, O Lady, whether your feelings still remain unchanged; scrutinize well your heart, and see if it is still firm and true to its first intentions, or will be after you have fulfilled your vow, which I doubt not that it will, for your royal blood cannot deceive nor give false promises. Let me then hear you say, O lovely Sigismunda, that the Periander you see before you, is the Persiles that you saw in the palace of my royal father; the same Persiles who pledged his word to you to be your husband there, and who would gladly fulfill that promise in the Deserts of Lybia, should our adverse fortune take us there. . . . Why should we not be the fabricators of our own fortune? They say every man makes his own from beginning to end. I will not answer for what I may do after our happy fate has united us; the inconvenience of our present divided state will soon be over, when we are one; there are fields enough where we can maintain ourselves, cottages wherein we may find shelter and clothes to cover us; for as to the happiness two souls made one can feel, it is as you say unequalled by any other, and we could not enjoy *this* beneath the gilded roofs of a palace." Love creates its own sacred places. Man—and woman—take at last a firm hold on their destiny. We know at this moment that the novel is going to have a happy ending.

V. THE FINAL MESSAGE

A Spanish critic, Augustín González de Amezúa, has pointed out the aspects of Heliodorus' novel that made it so attractive to Cervantes and to the Spaniards of the Golden Age: "Heliodorus' novel marks the acceptance and glorification of two human values triumphant above others in Spain's Golden Age. On the one hand, a love for adventure, for the unknown, the marvelous; on the other, a latent idealism, an aspiration towards an idyllic world, with the worship of the noblest virtues and feelings of man: faithfulness in love, purity, a spirit of abnegation and sacrifice, faithfulness to one's own ideas, all of which make the protagonists of Heliodorus' *Aethiopica* into admirable prototypes of human virtue. All these values, I repeat, were dearly beloved by the Spaniards of that period, whether simple novelists or men of erudition, and in finding them sublimated in a novel which contained as well a fine composition and rare literary beauty, they saw in Heliodorus a great novelist, one admired and emulated by all."

Yet Cervantes's novel was far better than its model. It meant, for him as well as for his readers, an escape to a world of marvelous adventures, a world of dangers and of freedom, of destiny and of love. There is a link between Cervantes's last novel and the romances of chivalry that he had criticized in *Don Quixote*: both in the romances and in the *Persiles* the heroic effort of the main characters is victorious at the end. The *Persiles* is more realistic than *Aethiopica,* and of course much more in tune with history, geography, and common sense, than the romances of chivalry. It is also a work of art: its style is extremely pleasant to the Spanish eye and the Spanish ear (many passages, read aloud in the original, have musical overtones: harmony, rhythm, well-rounded sentences, amplifications and variations on a main theme; it is possible to speak of "leit-motifs," just as in Wagner's music, through which Cervantes presents throughout his book the theme of purgatory, i.e., the separation and anguish of the two unhappy lovers, and paradise, i.e., the hope of reunion and fulfillment).

It is no wonder, then, that this novel attained an immediate success comparable to that of *Don Quixote.* Cervantes seems to have had a premonition of this success: the fact that he was working on a novel that was sure to become a "best seller" may have sustained his strength and given him a new lease on life. He had to finish his manuscript at all costs.

Ten editions were published in the years immediately following its posthumous publication in 1617, as well as translations into French, Italian, and English, and imitations in prose fiction and in drama. New imitations and editions appeared in the eighteenth century. At the beginning of the nineteenth century, the Swiss scholar Sismondi could still claim that many readers considered it to be Cervantes's masterpiece.

Many modern critics, as well as many modern readers, have been less kind to Cervantes's last novel. Thus Mack Singleton, for instance, claims (against the opinion of practically every other Hispanist who has dealt with the subject) that the *Persiles* was for Cervantes merely a "pot boiler," a clumsy adventure story written by Cervantes in his youth and wisely kept well hidden by its author until money was short and death was fast approaching.

Yet contemporary criticism is becoming increasingly interested in Cervantes's last novel. It is seen by some as a neglected masterpiece. As one of these critics states, "it is only in the last twenty-five years that criticism has begun to take the *Persiles* seriously, to see it in its historical circumstances rather than in the context of contemporary literary preferences, and to consider it as an independent work of art. The exploration of the great impact of Neoclassical literary theory on Cervantes, as well as the study of Renaissance discussions and evaluations of Heliodorus's *Aethiopica,* has thrown much light on Cervantes's intentions and aspirations in his final work. We may still agree with Menéndez y Pelayo that Cervantes's decision to imitate the Greek romance was a lamentable piece of folly, but we may at least admit that Renaissance critical opinion considered the work to be an artfully constructed epic in prose and a model for all who dared to scale the heights of Parnassus."

More than its episodic panorama and its proliferating action, what interests the modern critics in this novel is its structure, its pattern: a coherent cycle of catastrophe and restoration linked symbolically to the Christian vision of man's fall and redemption. Cervantes wanted to create an epic in prose. What he did in fact write was an allegorical romance in which recurrent motifs and myths manage to unify the action by endowing it with a ritualistic quality.

Every light projects a shadow. Every positive aspect in this novel can be seen as the opposite of a mistake or a defect—at least to the modern reader. The characters of *Persiles* move ecstatically, like stars in orbit. This is a source of strength in one sense, but also a weakness. For these characters were created perfect: they do not evolve. Their creator placed them on a Platonic pedestal at the very beginning of the tale, and there they remain, surrounded by a magic halo, eternal, changeless. The reader misses the complex and exciting process that makes Don Quixote occasionally sensitive to the common sense of Sancho Panza, that makes Sancho respond to the lofty goals of his master and thus become slowly "quixote-like" or "quixotized." Our own experience, and the writings of modern psychologists, have made us aware of the changing nature of man, of man's recurrent crises of identity, of human interaction. It is not that man's obsessions (if love can be called an obsession) can no longer be the subject of modern novels. It is rather that we are as much aware of man's changeable nature as we are of man's faithfulness or his obsessive nature. This modern awareness makes the *Persiles,* with its perfect, changeless lovers, difficult to accept. We long for the "flesh and blood" characters that Cervantes creates in his best novellas and also in *Don Quixote.* The young lovers in the *Persiles* are models of human behavior: can we identify with such lofty paradigms? Cervantes's last novel is also atypical in one respect: there is very little humor in its adventures. The familiar landmarks, which we may accept as symbolic, are there: the city and the open road. The city is a place of rest and fulfillment, the open road stands for the trials and perils that await those that would reach the city.

Jung has written that "wandering is a symbol of longing, of the restless urge which never finds its object, of nostalgia for the lost mother" and also "The city is a maternal symbol, a woman who harbours the inhabitants in herself like children." As the characters in his novel were about to reach their goal, Cervantes was preparing to make his own serene departure from the world of unfulfilled desire that he had known all through his life, hoping to find repose at the bottom of Being. In his prologue to the *Persiles* (and it is a well-known fact that a prologue to a novel is always written after the novel has been completed), Cervantes makes his final adieu to his friends and readers. He envisions himself as following the path that took his lovers into serene happiness. He takes leave of the world, symbolized in the picturesque figure of a student who overtakes him on the road, pays homage to him as the "delight of the Muses," and leaves him at the gate of Toledo to follow his own way. Cervantes embraces the student: it is an embrace of reconciliation between the man and the adversities that had troubled him for so long. He does not go away with an embittered heart. On the contrary, he keeps hoping that he will some day, somehow, be able to work again, to influence once more his readers: "Here we reached the bridge of Toledo, over which my road lay, and he separated from me to go by that of Segovia. As to what will be said of my adventure, Fame will take care of that, my friends will have pleasure telling it, and I greater pleasure in hearing it. He again embraced me, I returned the compliment. He spurred on his ass, and left me as sorrily disposed as he was sorrily mounted. He had however furnished me with abundant materials for pleasant writing, but all times are not alike. Perhaps a time may come when, taking up this broken thread again, I may add what is now wanting and what I am aware is needed. Adieu to gaiety, adieu to wit, adieu, my pleasant friends, for I am dying, yet hoping to see you all again happy in another world." These are probably the last words he wrote, just as the *Persiles* is his swan song.

ROBERTO GONZÁLEZ-ECHEVARRÍA

The Life and Adventures of Cipión:
Cervantes and the Picaresque

Few fields have been more thoroughly scrutinized of late than the picaresque. Clearly because of their interest in the novel as a theoretical issue,
critics have returned repeatedly to *Lazarillo, Guzmán* and *Buscón*, searching
for the origins of a novelistic genealogy. Studies by such established critics
as Carlos Blanco Aguinaga, Stephen Gilman, Claudio Guillén, Javier Herrero, Fernando Lázaro Carreter, Alexander A. Parker, Francisco Rico, Gonzalo Sobejano and Bruce Wardropper provide a plethora of interpretations
of the individual texts, as well as insights into the origins and development
of the picaresque [see Bibliography for references]. All of this work has not
been without controversy, and at times the field has been left like the one in
the Góngora ballad, in which the horses "buscaban/entre la sangre lo verde
[searched for green amidst the blood]." The richness of this critical tradition
could very well have discouraged a young critic like Harry Sieber; fortunately,
it did not. [In *Language and Society in* La Vida de Lazarillo de Tormes]
Sieber has managed to cull from these studies much of what is worthwhile
and also to make quite a strong reading of his own of *La vida de Lazarillo
de Tormes*. This is a substantial accomplishment, given that no picaresque
novel has been more minutely analyzed than the first. Sieber has raised the
level of criticism of *Lazarillo* and by extension of the picaresque, and though
he has done it partly because the level was already high, he has taken his
leave from previous work on this specific novel and on the topic in general.

From *Diacritics* 10, no. 3 (September 1980). © 1980 by The Johns Hopkins University Press.

It is clear, however, that *Language and Society in Lazarillo de Tormes* is heir to the long and distinguished Anglo-American tradition of Hispanic studies, a tradition whose main virtue has been to practice close readings of texts. The tradition goes back to Edward M. Wilson, Parker, Wardropper, Gilman and more recently Elias Rivers and many other distinguished contributors to Golden Age studies. The guiding principle for these critics has been belief in organic form or structure, conceived as the product of an artistic intention that a sedulous reader can recover. Work on the *comedia* or on poetry has focused on the interconnectedness of metaphors within a given play, and on the relation of metaphoric systems to other levels of signification, mainly the plot in the case of the theater. Similar efforts have been made with the picaresque, though here the readings have often led to moral allegories. But because the question of form presents such peculiar problems in the picaresque, the awareness of more complex theoretical issues than organic or artistic form has been keener among its critics. Albert A. Sicroff's detailed study of the language of *Lazarillo* ["Sobre el estilo del *Lazarillo de Tormes*"]—a worthy predecessor to Sieber's work—and Rico's point of view analysis of the same novel [*La novela picaresca y el punto de vista* (Barcelona, 1970)] are good examples of this. Guillén [in his *Literature as System*] and Lázaro Carreter [*Lazarillo de Tormes en la novela picaresca*] made important contributions by underlining the relationship between the picaresque and various forms of autobiographical writing. Parker's book [*Literature and the Delinquent: The Picaresque Novel in Spain and Europe*], on the other hand, was the first sustained effort to link the picaresque to society, though Américo Castro, Gilman and Sicroff had already provided tangential but important insights of their own in this area. At the heart of Parker's controversial book there is an anachronism. His notion of delinquency appears to be tinged with a sociological view of crime that is more pertinent to the nineteenth-century novel than to the picaresque, which promotes a notion of criminality rooted in theology. Lázaro Carreter's and Guillén's arguments are more convincing, though it seems to me that to apply the notion of genre to the picaresque is futile. The picaresque is not one of the norms that tradition bequeaths as a genre in the Renaissance, and though one of its characteristics is that it assumes an autobiographical form, one would be hard put to define autobiography as a genre. Autobiography usually needs the cloak of a specific rhetorical vehicle (confession, for instance) and only becomes an independent form of narrative after the nineteenth century, as is well known.

Sieber decided from the start to scuttle questions of genre. He thereby avoided having to deal either with the thematic issues raised by Parker or the formalistic arguments advanced by Guillén. Working from within more recent critical thought, Sieber saw that the key both to the problem of form and to the relation of the picaresque to society was language. Though he offers enough methodological and historical justifications for his choice, a few more can be added. The sixteenth century was obsessed with questions of language, and especially so in Spain and its recently discovered American empire. This obsession not only took the form of learned disquistions by the likes of Luis Vives or Fray Luis de León, but was a constant practical problem that surfaces in many guises in the works of Bartolomé de las Casas and others involved in the conversion of Indians to Christianity. The sixteenth century also witnessed an explosion of writing, not only in literature, philosophy and theology, but in the massive output of the bureaucracy organized to govern the wide and unwieldy Spanish empire. It was also in the sixteenth century that Spanish underwent its most radical linguistic transformation. *Lazarillo* was written at a time when the socio-linguistic changes taking place in the empire were quick and profound. There can be little doubt that the novel reflects the nearly convulsive nature of those changes in the social and the linguistic realms.

The chief virtue of *Language and Society* is that it reads *Lazarillo* as a linguistic performance whose aim is constituting the presence of the fictional author: "It [*Lazarillo*] is the story of this process, of these successive acts of mobilizing language, that constitutes both the subject of my essay and the hidden discourse of Lázaro's *Vida*. The nature of this 'life' is not a reflection or a representation of an individualized sixteenth-century experience. Rather it is the 'life' of the individualizing acts of language through which such an experience takes form. I will argue that Lázaro's 'trabajos y fatigas [trials and difficulties]' refers to an experience that involves a struggle with language too difficult not to be shared." This insight into the elaboration of the text and its fiction leads Sieber to conclusions, the importance of which he exploits with varying degrees of success: Lázaro "converts" to a writer and his relations with his various masters, including the "Vuestra Merced [your worship]" to whom the discourse is addressed, are chiefly linguistic, though they are simultaneously a part of his psychosexual development. Lázaro's sexual autobiography is the story of his initiation into the complexities of the linguistic code, and with it, the language of society at all levels. The combined analyses of these various levels of performance will constitute the enduring value of Sieber's book.

If Lázaro's awakening to the intricacies of language is the true story of *Lazarillo*, the relations with the various masters are the individual lessons. Sieber reads these instances with admirable subtlety and exemplary attention to detail, to the point that sometimes the readings stand out quite apart from the main narrative of *Language and Society*. The readings are carried out mainly at two levels. One could be called contextual and is above all a commentary aimed at elucidation through scholarly spade-work. Sieber's minute reading of the very short and suggestive fifth *tratado* unveils repressed homosexual connotations in such convincing manner that his commentary should become the standard one. The same is true of his dazzling break of the dress code in the fourth *tratado*. The second level could be called symbolic, in that it assigns a stable, though initially hidden meaning to parts of the text. Thus: "The bull's horns function as a visible sign of Lázaro's cuckoldry at the end of the novel and they point also to the 'gran ruido [great noise],' the rumors of the 'malas lenguas [gossip mongers]' of his neighbors, which threaten his comfortable life as Toledo's public voice." In these interpretations Sieber betrays his debt to Anglo-American Hispanism, and though his readings here are also convincing, they hark back to notions of organic form, artistic unity and symbolic meaning that are not as radical as the critical ideology underlying other parts of his book. At this level Sieber re-enacts vis-à-vis his critical fathers an operation that he reads very well in the episode in *Lazarillo*, where the protagonist's half-brother flees from his black father, blind to his own color. The symbolic is produced in that scene out of fear. The reflective fear in *Language and Society* might be to transgress the laws of the criticism that precedes it. This sort of process occurs only because of the intensity of the critical operation being performed and the risks that Sieber is taking and should not be seen as a negative aspect of the book. On the contrary, I believe that Sieber's book gains considerable value by the very troublesome way in which it *performs* what it discovers in the picaresque. For instance, the very same process of blindness resulting from an obsessive attachment to the *verbum visibile* that afflicts Lazarillo also afflicts Sieber. This is apparent in the repetition of *Lazarillo*'s structure in *Language and Society*. *Language and Society* contains seven chapters and a prologue, each a commentary on the same portions of *Lazarillo*, a rather transparent strategy whose sense the reader must ponder. It is too far fetched to think that it places Sieber's text in relation to Lazarillo's in the same position as Lazarillo's in relation to *Vuestra Merced*? But Lazarillo's relation to *Vuestra Merced* is not as submissive as it seems, as Sieber himself points out, and in repeating *Lazarillo*'s text Sieber is submitting perhaps too readily to its own forms of blindness. For instance, though *La vida de Lazarillo de Tormes* begins with a prologue that casts everything that follows as a performance from a given point in time, Sieber sometimes "forgets" the rhetorical diachrony of the *tratados* and sees a real teleology leading up to the insights of the prologue. But clearly all is written in *Lazarillo* as a way of persuading *Vuestra Merced* of something from the point of view (and time) of Lázaro's adult mastery of the codes of language and society. To forget the fictionality of this teleology is to fall prey to the blindness of the "verbum visibile," the temporal unfolding of the text as we read. Sieber is not always deluded in this fashion; most of the time he is quite aware of the rhetoricization of the *vida*.

The very intensity of Sieber's reading endows his text with a theoretical power that it may lack at a conceptual level (where, for instance, it is difficult to find a continuity to the "Lacanian" reading of the first *tratado*). Sieber struggles to maintain a balance between his exegetical work and an overall thesis on *Lazarillo*, haunted both by scholarship and by the need to interpret. His close readings are so admirably detailed, so well supported with contextual reference, that they become independent of the whole argument of the book. Instead of converging, close reading and overall interpretation go in separate directions, the more the latter intensifies. It is as if the visible details manage to repress the overall interpretation, as if scholarship shielded Sieber from the ideological grasp of his critical fathers. It is rather more in this respect that *Language and Society* acquires a compellingly picaresque character than through its repetition of the *tratados*. The visible detail delays and makes increasingly difficult interpretation (the ultimate task of historico-thematic Anglo-American criticism), just as Lázaro finds it difficult to find coherence in society's various codes: the linguistic, the sexual, the religious. Only through his willed blindness to his wife's morals can Lázaro make his life coalesce with society, just as a certain blindness to detail can lead to interpretation of the text, in the sense of making it subservient to a given theme.

So ultimately the greatest value in Sieber's book is the way in which it plays out the major preoccupation in the picaresque: the emergence of writing and its relation to authority. Sieber's analyses have essentially theoretical scope in that they seek to uncover that relation through the hypostases of the paternal figure who embodies the law and the emerging pícaro-writer. The emergence of the picaresque is thus a sort of psychodrama staged in the text itself, through which authority is subverted and preserved at the same time. Lázaro learns enough from the blind man to blind him, but his authority at the end is based on his own willed blindness to his wife's infidelity. The very complex inscription of these issues in the text of *Lazarillo* has never been read with more subtlety than in *Language and Society*.

The problematics that Sieber mobilizes in his book had been dealt with by Cervantes at the turn of the sixteenth century in a way that tells a good deal about the origins of the novel. I would argue that to read that problematic in Cervantes's work is a more concrete (even institutional) way of understanding the relation between literature and society than Sieber's, but that is not at odds with his readings at all. Cervantes was forced by circumstances to deal with the picaresque. It is known that, though published later, Quevedo's *Buscón* was written in the very first years of the new century, in the wake of *Guzmán* (1599). An apocryphal second part to Alemán's novel came out three years after the original—in 1602—and Alemán had to hurry to press with his own second part. In 1605 López de Ubeda published his *Pícara Justina,* a feminine picaresque, while just a few years later, in Paris, H. de Luna published a *Segunda parte de la vida de Lazarillo de Tormes* (1620). The years around the turn of the century mark a peak in the production of picaresque novels. Though Cervantes never wrote a picaresque following Alemán's model, he did leave a complex critique of how this new literature was changing the rules of the game. This speculation is contained in "The Deceitful Marriage" and "The Dogs' Colloquy," intertwined tales that can be taken to constitute a sort of "metapicaresque."

It was no formalist whim nor thematic compulsion that made a unity of "The Deceitful Marriage" and "The Dogs' Colloquy" and much less an afterthought of Cervantes. The relationship between the two tales is determined by their "reading" of the picaresque. Even the framing-story alludes to a basic picaresque conceit: a roguish adventurer tells his story to someone in authority. Lazarillo tells the story of his life to a *Vuestra Merced,* a Your Lordship, who may very well be a judge. This implicit device of the picaresque is blown up in Cervantes's two linked stories, where we are told in detail how this narrative scene is set. Rather than begin his tales with the conventional formula of the picaresque, mentioning the protagonist's birth and parents, Cervantes indicates what, within the implicit fiction must literally be the first incident: the meeting of the teller and his listener and their agreement to have the story told. Here Ensign Campuzano, who is being released from the Hospital de la Resurrección in Valladolid, meets by chance with Licentiate Peralta, a lawyer friend of his, and they both repair to the latter's quarters.

Claudio Guillén, in his influential piece of the picaresque, uses as his point of departure Don Quijote's adventure with the galley slaves in which Cervantes pokes fun at the convention of autobiography that supports the picaresque novel ["Genre and Countergenre"]. Ginés de Pasamonte, one of the prisoners, says that he has not finished writing his life because he is not through living it, having only written his own picaresque novel up to the point when he was last arrested. The allusion to the *Guzmán de Alfarache,*

in which the pícaro undergoes the conversion that leads him to write the
novel when a galley slave could not be clearer, as is the suggestion that
autobiography can have no clear resolution and therefore no plot. But it
hardly seems to be casual that Ginés de Pasamonte is a prisoner, as is Guzmán, nor that Lazarillo appears to be telling his life to a judge. The pícaro
is often in trouble with the law. In his autobiography he speaks not to God,
as did Augustine, but to a temporal authority. Cervantes has reenacted this
scene in the framing story, and though the situation is much more relaxed,
Ensign Campuzano is also telling his life to a representative of the law. The
pícaro, as Parker emphasized, is a delinquent, therefore the story of his life
takes the form of a legal deposition. The picaresque developed the form of
life as a unit of narrative by mimicking one of the formulas of forensic
rhetoric much in use at the time: the "relación [report]." Lazarillo's life is
told not simply in a letter, as Lázaro Carreter has argued, but in the kind of
letter which functions as a legal deposition or makes a petition to a higher
authority based on services rendered. Harry Sieber's penetrating analysis of
Lazarillo's relationship with Your Lordship corroborates this. The fact that
Lázaro refers constantly to the situation in which he finds himself with the
Archpriest as a "caso [case]" underscores, it seems to me, that the text of
the novel passes for a relación. Although caso was a fairly common word in
the Golden Age, as it is even now in the same context, it may be well to
remember here what Covarrubias says about it: "It is equivalent to an event
that has occurred; thus lawyers call caso the issue or proposition on which
the legal determination is based; *and in legal actions the first thing on which
they must agree is the case or the fact, which is all one and the same*" [my
italics].

Further historical evidence can be adduced. The vastness of the Spanish
empire in the sixteenth century and the myriad adventures in which so many
of its citizens were involved made of the relación a very common sort of
document. A modern writer has evoked in these terms the world of petti-
foggery and bureaucratic strife typical of the Spanish colonies in the sixteenth
century: "Each time the New Spanish fleet set sail for home, the ships'
masters were entrusted with commissions, letters, lies, and slanders to be
taken back to Spain and delivered to anyone who could best use them to
harm someone else. . . . While the Governor was trying to discredit the
King's officers in an eight page letter, the Bishop would be denouncing the
Governor for living in concubinage. . . . And so a chain was formed, always
ready to break at the weakest or most unexpected point. One man was
denounced for having bought aphrodisiac herbs from a Negro witch doctor
who was whipped at Cartagena de Indias; the Town Crier was accused of

the abominable sin . . ." [Alejo Carpentier, "The Highroad of Saint James," in his *War of Time*]. All of these adventures and misadventures, by people who were marginal to society, found their way to legal or quasi-legal documents in which lives large and small were told in search of acquittal or social advancement. The relación became the vehicle for such narratives. In it, the protagonist identified himself by telling his life and then told the relevant incidents in which he had been involved. Conventional literary history veils the fact that many of the "crónicas de la conquista [chronicles of the conquest]" were relaciones. There is hardly a text more like *Lazarillo* or *Guzmán* than Bernal Díaz del Castillo's *Historia verdadera de la conquista de la Nueva España* [*The True History of the Conquest of New Spain*], Hernán Cortés's *Cartas de relación* [*Letters of Relation*] or Ramón Pané's *Relación acerca de las antigüedades de los Indios* [*Report Concerning the Ancient Times of the Indians*]. The recourse to the relación was so pervasive and popular that by 1636, in the Viceroyalty of Nueva Granada, the lascivious and witty Juan Rodríguez Freyle wrote his well-known *El Carnero* [*The Sheep*] using the device wholesale. The *Carnero* was a history of the Viceroyalty drawn from the archives of the Real Audiencia, or so claims its compiler, covering the tenure of several viceroys, plus "some cases [casos] that occurred in this kingdom, that appear in the history to be exemplary, and not to be imitated owing to the harm they would do to conscience." These casos, as all readers of Rodríguez Freyle know, had to do very often with cuckoldry in a manner not too dissimilar from that of *Lazarillo*'s. The lives of insignificant soldiers, the domestic foibles of petty bureaucrats, the adventures of obscure friars were told as relaciones, not in the classical rhetorical molds known only to the humanists. Reams of legal paper crossed the Atlantic in both directions in the sixteenth century, and streams of documents crossed Spain's arid plains toward Europe. Not a few of those documents were relaciones, much like the one Lázaro writes for Your Lordship.

What better form to express the life of a pícaro than a legal formula, when he was forever on the verge of being entangled in the law? Cervantes, who had himself been a soldier and felt on his shoulders the weight of the law, picked up this element of the picaresque and shows its importance in the story framing "The Deceitful Marriage" and "The Dogs' Colloquy." It is indeed significant that one of the characters is a picaresque soldier who has recently returned from Flanders, and the other a lawyer who "hears" his case. When Lazarillo says that his case has not been heard before, he is also using a legalism. Covarrubias, again: "To hear [Oyr]: the acceptance by the authorities of demands, reasons, or proofs from the litigating parties before a resolution is made." By assuming the form of a relación, the picaresque is implicitly claiming that by doing so it is truer to life, that it is a document showing a real life enmeshed in the society of the times. The question of truth, as the correspondence between what is written and what actually happens, is not one to have troubled literature much before the Renaissance. In the picaresque, and so Cervantes recognizes, the question is violently introduced and the appeal to a form of legal rhetoric is evidence of it. Now literature must deal not only with abstractions such as moral truth, but also answer to the pressures of social reality. In the framing story Cervantes posits this dilemma clearly. In addition, the picaresque text then appears as the result of guilt, exoneration or achievement before a paternal figure who embodies power and authority.

Not only by its ambience, but more significantly by the relationship among its characters, the framing story sets the whole text encompassing "The Deceitful Marriage" and "The Dogs' Colloquy" in a critical posture before the picaresque. It is already significant that the relationship has been altered: the tale is told to a curious reader, not to the slightly inquisitorial one of *Lazarillo*. The Licentiate is not performing his function as a lawyer. Like the reader of *Don Quijote,* he is an "idle reader." The change in the picaresque formula is significant.

In "The Deceitful Marriage" and "The Dogs' Colloquy" Cervantes reveals how the picaresque has an inner connectedness provided by the way in which the turning points in the picaresque life allude to the origin and organization of writing through a metaphoric field of allusion drawn from sexuality. By uncovering this metaphoric stratum on the picaresque text, Cervantes lays bare the contradiction at the core of this new form of writing: its pretense to truth and authority sustained by taking the form of a legal document, and at the same time the elusiveness of its dense system of inner relations. By pointing to the relationship between sexuality and writing, Cervantes is suggesting too that the turning points in a pícaro's life are also tropes that tell the story of the writer and his text's coming into being.

A pícaro writes of his birth and family, of his masters, his marriage and the conversion that leads him to write his autobiography. In all cases the early events lack distinctiveness. They do not constitute a clear beginning either for a life or for a story. Lázaro is born of a González and a Pérez, the two most common surnames in Spanish. Guzmán has, according to his mother's rather explicit feminine calculations, two fathers. Given the morality of Pablos' mother, his legitimacy could also be doubted. The masters, who become surrogate fathers, come and go. Picaresque life is made of maddening repetitions that the pícaro-writer seeks to control by writing the text of his life, by giving it fictive substantiality in a *relación*: a substantiality that would domesticate the repetitions, turning them into meaningful, unique instances, organized as a teleology that leads up to the moment he writes. By means of marriage and conversion, the pícaro seeks to legitimize his beginnings and the starting point of his story. But of course, both turning points become as difficult to control as the wild dissemination they attempt to cover. Lázaro's marriage to the Archpriest's mistress only augurs that the next pícaro will be born of a union that can hardly guarantee the identity of his father. Pablos repeats his father's error when he joins up at the end with La Grajales, a prostitute whose progeny could not be untarnished. Marriage, for a pícaro, turns out to be the repetition of an initial moment in picaresque life, when the protagonist is born out of a confusing sexual situation: the proliferating González's and Pérez's, the multiplicity of fathers, the public mothers. If marriage is going to be the pícaro's social contract, that contract winds up being as unreliable a text as the pícaro himself and the life that he later writes.

The same elusiveness is present in conversion, which is the other crucial turning point in a picaresque life. In *Lazarillo* the prologue is the best example of the notorious ambiguities of autobiographical writing. The account of a conversion can only breed a new account and the typical infinite regression is set in motion. López de Ubeda has taken to its ultimate consequences the relationship between beginning to write a picaresque life, sexuality and conversion in the interminable chapters in which Justina struggles with a hair that has stuck to the tip of her pen, and in the process tells a great deal about the difficulties of beginning to write a picaresque life—particularly when hers leads to marriage with none other than Guzmán de Alfarache. Writing leads to a textual marriage, within the disseminatory power of literature, not to an outside union by means of which authority will be restored.

By focusing on the moment of marriage, Cervantes is calling attention to a crucial turning point in the picaresque: the end that "determines" its beginning. Besides, as is well known, marriage is an important convention in the literature of the times, particularly in the *comedia*. Marriage in the theater always signals a happy ending, a restoration of order in society, insurance that reproduction will follow rules that contain it. In Cervantes's works marriage often appears as a dubious endeavor, which rarely ensures order and tranquility, though there are cases such as "Gitanilla" and "The Power of Blood" where it provides a happy closure. But in "The Deceitful Marriage" Cervantes is focusing on marriage as the end/beginning of a picaresque life, blowing it up, as it were, to study both the pícaro and the origin of his new vocation of writing. When Estefanía disappears with his counterfeit gems, Campuzano thinks that he has had the last laugh. But he soon lands in the hospital and discovers that it was Estefanía who laughed last. The tale has a very tightly structured plot that leads from deceit to counterdeceit to delayed action deceit: it is a kind of inverted romance. There is no small measure of irony in that a marriage that began beyond all the mystifications of love should turn out to be a crescendo of falsehoods. The pure chance of their first encounter engenders an interlocking sequence of events that winds up with the dissolution of the marriage, a counter-ending in terms of the *comedia,* but also a step beyond the ending within the realm of the picaresque.

And what is beyond the ending of the picaresque? The issue of the picaresque marriage is the elusive, ambiguous and inconclusive picaresque text. The pícaro "fathers" a picaresque novel. Campuzano's true progeny is the story that he has just told and also the text that the Licentiate Peralta is about to read. Just as the pícaro is born of this uncontrollable kind of sexual dissemination, so the picaresque text is born of this textual multiplication. The relación, no matter how many notary publics sign it, can only be a pretext, never a binding document.

Ginés the Pasamonte's quip about not having finished his picaresque novel because he had not finished living it is Cervantes's way of pointing to a convention of all autobiographical writing: the memorialist must undergo a conversion, must become another to be able to have enough distance from his former self. In *Lazarillo* this occurs when he decides to take sides with the good people ["acogerme a los buenos"], submit to the "laws" of society by marrying. In *Guzmán,* the protagonist undergoes a religious conversion at the end, as we have already seen. In "The Deceitful Marriage" conversion is spoofed by its taking the form of a social disease. The fact that the hospital is the Hospital de la Resurrección should not be lost. Conversion as death and resurrection is a common enough metaphor. There is a mild, Cervantine irony running through the Ensign's illness and his becoming a writer, an irony that turns into more raucous humor in the next tale, in which the pícaros have become dogs.

If "The Deceitful Marriage" and "The Dogs' Colloquy" were framed by the story of the two friends meeting outside of the Hospital de le Resurrección, the story of Berganza's life is framed by at least two stories. The first has to do with the night in which the dogs speak; the second, somewhat nebulous, tells why they can speak and whether they will continue to have the ability to speak. Just as there are multiple stories, so there are various justifications for the dogs' ability to speak: first, that they are really humans, changed to dogs by virtue of their mothers' commerce with the devil; second, that it is the Ensign's feverish imagination that produced their speech as in a dream; third, as the Licentiate suggests, that the Ensign has written a sort of fable or apologue in the manner of the classics, in which animals speak. To this already vast array, it could be added that the Ensign may be giving a veiled, transformed version of his own picaresque life. As Ruth El Saffar argues, it is clear that the Ensign is a writer. But these possibilities, like the multiple stories, are not mutually exclusive. Multiplication and amplification abound in Berganza's tale.

Berganza tells his life according to the picaresque formula: he begins by mentioning his parents, tells of his childhood, his early masters and winds up, of course, at the moment when he and Cipión acquire speech suddenly. The most significant aspects of the picaresque formula in Berganza's life are both his origin and conversion, which are multiplied and expanded. Right in the center of his story, Berganza speaks of his meeting with La Camacha, a witch who tells him how he and Cipión were the product of another witch's, La Montiela, relations with the devil. Who were Berganza's parents? The slaughterhouse dogs or La Montiela and the devil? The undifferentiated and wild multiplication of Pérez's and González's in *Lazarillo,* the two fathers in *Guzmán* appears here in the figure of Montiela and her bizarre sexuality. There is an uncontrolled side to reproduction here that is akin to that of writing, a demonic origin that conspires against the possibility of finding a true, unpolluted beginning, a non-duplicitous source of reproduction. This appeal to Montiela is also a way of indicating the true genealogy of the picaresque, which winds back to the garrulous *Celestina.* (The dialogue form of the second novella is an homage to *Celestina*'s own dialogic form.) Celestina, whose main occupation was restoring virginities, was a true figure of the writer; one who passes patchwork for the original. If the pícaro's origins were confused because of the lack of chastity of his mother, Cervantes is going back here to their true mother—Celestina, that *pharmakos* in which both alchemy and writing are blended for the first time in Spanish literature. This is the sense of the very uncharacteristically salacious nature of these Cervantes stories.

Montiela not only explodes the pícaro's tale of origin, she also ruins the determining power of conversion within the picaresque fiction. She decreed, enigmatically when the puppies were born that:

> They will return to their true form
> when they see the mighty speedily brought down
> and the humble exalted
> by that hand which has power to perform it.

In other words, the dogs will be able to undergo a radical transformation at judgment day, not before. Conversion, so the text suggests, is yet another ruse of the picaresque author. The fact that the dogs have gained ability to speak indicates that their change has been rather partial. Cervantes has foreclosed any chiliastic reading of the picaresque by making the temporal mechanism of conversion hinge on a literal figuration. (I am using figuration here in the sense Auerbach gave the term *figura,* that is to say, the relation between a past and a present event that renders the latter meaningful—the most common figures being those linking the Old and New testaments ["Figura," in *Scenes from the Drama of European Literature*]. The future of the picaresque is not the demystified hero, nor the author of romances; the future of the picaresque text is yet another text. By postponing the perfect text to a nether future, Cervantes makes all fictions of concord, all dreams of order and intelligibility as much a part of fiction as conversion, marriage and the other conventions of picaresque life. The future text is the life and adventures of Cipión. That unwritten text is Cervantes's move beyond the picaresque.

At the end of "The Dogs' Colloquy," Berganza tells of four madmen whose conversation he overheard at the Hospital. The four are, a poet who has written an unfinished epic poem, a mathematician who claims to be close to locating the fixed point, an alchemist who is near the discovery of the philosopher's stone and an "arbitrista" [a schemer] who has the answer to Spain's economic problems. It is clear that all four are searching for a kind of absolute knowledge and perfection that would only be possible if Montiela's fiction of concord became a reality. In the meantime they are confined in the Hospital as madmen: all four live in an absolute future at odds with the present. The most suggestive of the four is the poet, who gives the following reasons for his lamentations:

> "And haven't I good reason to complain?" he went on. "Having kept to the rules that Horace lays down in his *Ars of Poetry* that one shouldn't publish a work until ten years after it is finished, I have one which took me twenty years to write, not to mention twelve more I had it by me, a work with a vast subject, an admirable and novel plot, dignified lines and entertaining episodes, marvellously balanced, with the beginning matching the middle and the end: so that poem is lofty, tuneful, heroic, pleasing and substantial; yet I can't find a noble patron to whom I can address it. I mean a nobleman who is intelligent, liberal and magnanimous. What a wretched age and depraved century we live in!"
>
> "What is the work about?" asked the alchemist. The poet re-

plied, "It's about what Archbishop Turpin didn't get 'round to writing about King Arthur of England, with a further supplement to the 'Story of the Quest of the Holy Grail.' It's all in heroic verse, partly in octaves and partly in free verse; but all in dactyls and nouns at that, without a single verb."

Who is this poet if not a Cervantine figure, a modern author worried about the fate of his work within the market of the day, yet hoping to revive a heroic age? What is the book that he has written if not a sort of pre-Quijotic adventure, retelling the adventures of knights? And isn't Cervantes giving a figure of himself as author of the *Quijote* when the poet assumes the position of Archbishop Turpin, the apocryphal editor of chivalric tales (rather than the author)? The mixture of epic with humor, parody, questions about authorship and representation define *Don Quijote,* and these are the elements that prevail in the work-in-progress of this Borgesian poet who is also planning to omit all verbs from his discourse. Isn't this the same mixture that one would expect to find in the life of Cipión? After all, though merely a dog, Cipión bears a heroic, epic name, one that in the context of the Spanish peninsula had historical resonances as well and that, as *Numancia* shows, was important in Cervantes's conception of heroism. In short, his life may very well be much like that of Don Quijote himself. The future work that Cervantes's intertwined tales announce is not the *Persiles,* but the *Quijote.* The life and adventures of Cipión become the life and adventures of Don Quijote.

The picaresque is made up of the past life of the pícaro and his present activity as writer. The picaresque is the novel of the writer: the portrait of the artist as a young man. The *Quijote,* on the other hand, is not burdened by the past like the pícaro. The hero of that novel begins his adventures precisely and significantly when he is beyond the reach of family and the more immediate constraints of making a living. Don Quijote's adventures begin as a result not of life but of literature, not of writing, but of reading. Don Quijote is the novel of the reader. If "The Deceitful Marriage" was recounted, re-enacted by Campuzano to his friend, "The Dogs' Colloquy" is read by Campuzano as the reader reads the text. Naturally, the past still weighs on Don Quijote, as does the present. He aims to bring about that moment when the humble overpower the lofty, but settles for less, constantly forced by the contingencies of the present. It is this, I believe, that would have prevailed in the life of Cipión, so much a tale of the reader that it is left up to us to imagine.

Cervantes's analysis of the picaresque focuses on two features of the new literature: the emergence of the modern writer and the relationship between the literary text and the other codes through which authority is transmitted in society. The first of these was of paramount importance to Cervantes and his contemporaries (Alemán, Lope) who were among the first professional writers in Spain. Cervantes's social status and aspirations were not wholly different from those of the pícaro. Like Pablos, Cervantes pined for the opportunity to cross the Atlantic in search of social advancement in the New World. Like the pícaro Cervantes accepted the values of society and pretended as best he could to live by them. The new novel, as it emerged then, was appropriately a marginal form of writing without substantial antecedents in the classical tradition. It was a combination of rhetorical molds, a simulacrum of other texts with social acceptance. The picaresque lacked an official model; therefore it mimicked real, official documents to render effective its "performance" of the functions of society's texts. Because it has no prescribed form, the novel often must pretend to be a non-literary document. It can appear as a relación, the report of a scientific expedition, as history, a correspondence, a police report, a chronicle, a memoir, and so on. One fruitful way to study the history of the novel and its relation to society would be to take notice of what it pretends to be throughout the centuries. Is not Cervantes suggesting that the novel mimicks whatever kind of text a given society invests with power at a certain point in history?

Sieber argues convincingly that *Lazarillo* is a sexual autobiography in which the emergence of the symbolic issues from the relationship between the language of authority and that of the callow pícaro, the modern writer. This is an insight that, supported as it is by so much valuable documentation, can truly begin to show how subversive the new literature really was in Golden Age Spain. But Cervantes had already also shown that to remain within the dialectic of authority is not the fate of the new writing begun in *Celestina*. Otis Green rightly pointed out that "the ideology of Cervantes is not rigorous, except for his firmly held belief in an ultimate overarching harmony wherein the positives and the negatives agree" ["Lope and Cervantes: *Peripeteia* and Resolution"]. More than agreeing, however, in a text whose "origin" is ultimately a Celestinesque pharmacological mixture, they commingle; feminine picaresque like Pícara Justina obviously heirs to the old bawd, performed an equally corrosive function on the genealogy of voices that constitute the picaresque. The deconstruction of picaresque formulas is Cervantes's most radical view of the new narrative and its presence in *Don Quijote* is a crucial element in that text.

Cervantes's insight into the nature of the emerging novel contains an important lesson for literary critics and historians. We speak of the birth and growth of the modern novel, of the French and English novels being heirs to the picaresque, of Cervantes having fathered the modern novel. We say all this, allowing ourselves to be carried away by the force of our own metaphors. Cervantes, by mocking this very metaphorical system, has shown that the novel itself has no such genealogical purity, that it is enmeshed in a vast textual field that is renewed in history. *The Life and Opinions of Tristram Shandy, Finnegans Wake* and *Three Trapped Tigers* are also part of the field of force created in the explosion of Celestina's lab.

MARY GAYLORD RANDEL

The Language of Limits and the Limits of Language: The Crisis of Poetry in La Galatea

Todo su gusto y pasatiempo era cantar al son de su rabel los succesos prósperos o adversos de sus amores, llevado de la natural condición suya.

[All his pleasure and pastime was singing of his loves' prosperous or adverse events to the sounds of his rebec, carried away by his natural condition.]

One might say of the "*libros de pastores* [pastoral novels]" what the narrator says of "el enamorado Lauso [enamored Lauso]" in book 5 of *La Galatea* (2, 123). [All references to *La Galatea* cite the edition of Juan Bautista Avalle-Arce, Clasicos Castellanos, by volume and page number. Translations are by H. Oelsner and A. B. Welford, the Fitzmaurice-Kelly edition.] They find their whole and sole pleasure in songs of love. If the shepherd symbolizes love by the very nature of his calling, the world of literary pastoral is one in which not love but *talk about love* dominates, in which shepherds are not obliged actually to tend sheep but rather to engage in constant reflection on that "occupation." The pastoral world, in short, is a world of representation and of self-representation, as Cervantes makes clear in the "fingida Arcadia [imitation Arcadia]" episode of *Don Quixote* [part 2, chapter 58; because of the large number of editions in use, I have chosen to refer to passages from *Don Quixote* in the text of the article, by part and chapter number, preceded by the initials *DQ*, to distinguish from passages of *La Galatea*. All emphasis in quoted passages has been added.]

From *MLN* 97, no. 2 (March 1982). © 1982 by The Johns Hopkins University Press.

From its beginnings, the literature of shepherds has presented what Elias
Rivers calls the "pastoral paradox of natural art." While it promotes an ideal
of Golden Age innocence, it insists on its own position as art. Pastorals have
tended to be highly conscious of their own traditions; their world is a world
of inherited words. Classical versions of pastoral, furthermore, were written
entirely in verse, many of them consisting largely of poetic competitions. By
virtue of their fidelity to tradition, the contestants of these matches vie implicitly not only with their immediate rivals, but with the tradition which
their songs carry on. The "natural" language of shepherds does not simply
accept imitation of poetic models. It makes that imitation a central principle
of its art. Pastoral, then, advertising itself as poetry, can readily become
poetry about poetry. Quite predictably, we often find pastoral works ad-
dressing the nature, the claims and the status of the poetic enterprise.

   La Galatea provides a particularly rich illustration of this tendency. In
his prologue, Cervantes, invoking "la inclinación que a la poesia siempre he
tenido [the inclination I have always had toward poetry]" (1, 6), complains
about the disfavor which poetry (and especially the eclogue) suffers in his
day. He makes his first major literary effort an implicit defense of poetry:

> no puede negarse que los estudios desta facultad—en el pasado
> tiempo, con razón, tan estimada—traen consigo más que media-
> nos provechos, como son enriquecer el poeta considerando su
> propia lengua, y enseñorearse del artificio de la elocuencia que
> en ella cabe, para empresas más altas y de mayor importancia.

> [one cannot deny that the studies of this faculty—in the past,
> rightly, so highly esteemed—bring with them more than average
> advantages: such as enriching the poet in his own language, and
> allowing him to appropriate the artifice of eloquence comprised
> in it, which may be employed in enterprises both loftier and of
> greater importance.]

                                                                   (1, 6)

Cervantes's enthusiasm associates him with a host of sixteenth-century de-
fenders of the vernacular and its poetic aspirations. *La Galatea*'s obvious
concern with poetry does not, however, end here. Tirsi and Damón, "dos
nombrados y famosos pastores [two elect and famous shepherds]," who
represent the celebrated poets, Francisco de Figueroa, "el Divino [the Di-
vine]" and Pedro Laínez, join the shepherds on the banks of the Tagus in
book 2. These poets guide the company toward the wedding of book 3, the
debate of book 4 and finally to the commemorative rites at the tomb of

another poet, Meliso (Diego Hurtado de Mendoza), in book 6. Along the road to the tomb, Tirsi and Damón participate—both as poets and as judges—in numerous poetic contests. At graveside in the Valley of the Cypresses, the shepherds witness the marvellous nocturnal appearance of Calíope, the muse of poetry, who offers a lavish verse tribute to one hundred of Cervantes's poet contemporaries. By their sheer bulk, Calíope's imposing hyperboles oblige us to focus on the place of verse in what we have come to call the pastoral novel.

Two prevalent notions interfere with our disposition to read *La Galatea* as primarily a defense of poetry. Cervantes himself promoted both of these conceptions, which have become persistent axioms of Cervantes criticism. One is the idea of the "failure" of *La Galatea,* suggested in the prologue ("en esta parte [la voluntad de agradar] la obra no responde a su deseo [in this part (the wish to please) the work does not respond to its desire]" [1, 9]) and in the famous judgment voiced in the *escrutinio* [scrutiny] of *Don Quixote* ("propone algo, y no concluye nada [it proposes something and concludes nothing]" [*DQ* 1, 6]). The other is the portrait of Cervantes as "failed poet." Again in the *escrutinio,* the priest describes *La Galatea's* author as "más versado en desdichas que en versos [more versed in misfortune than in verses]." The prologue of the *Ocho comedias y ochos entremeses* [*Eight Comedies and Eight Interludes*] reports the book dealer's blunt verdict: "de la prosa se podría esperar mucho, pero del verso nada [One can expect great things of prose, but of poetry, nothing]." Despite equally frequent tributes to poetry scattered throughout his works, we have most often elected to accept at face value—that is, as signs valid apart from contexts—Cervantes's self-deprecating remarks about his poetic talents. These negative self-appraisals have tended to bolster "disappointed" modern reactions to *La Galatea* and to provide readers with an excuse for skipping over its verses in search of Cervantes, the apprentice novelist.

La Galatea, while it purports to defend poetry, is not exclusively a verse pastoral or eclogue, but a pastoral romance, the Renaissance hybrid of prose and verse modeled on Sannazaro's *Arcadia.* Recently Joaquín Casalduero cautioned against viewing this hybrid form as a simple pretext to "reunir unas cuantas poesías [to join a few poems together]." He challenges readers to uncover the "íntima necesidad [intimate need]" that causes verse to give way to prose and prose to verse, in alternating rhythm. The question is highly suggestive. It pinpoints, in fact, another pastoral paradox, the formal paradox of the pastoral romance, which uses prose to privilege verse, at the same time that it acknowledges the insufficiency of the verse. Pastoral romance is thus always meta-poetry. That is, by virtue of the decision to supplement verse with prose, it always makes an implicit commentary on the original vehicle. In what follows we propose to show how *La Galatea* explicitly makes the power of poetry its central concern, and how the text exploits the alternation of prose and verse to dramatize a struggle with the very limits of language.

Cervantes, says Casalduero, attacks the pastoral composition at its center. From the temple of Love in Montemayor's *La Diana,* we move in *La Galatea* to the sacrament of marriage, for Casalduero a sign of Cervantes's Christian social and moral consciousness, new to the genre. Two weddings, mirror images of each other, share the center of *La Galatea*: the public wedding of Daranio and Silveria toward the end of book 3 and the secret vows of Rosaura and Grisaldo at the beginning of book 4. These events raise many questions which are left unresolved. The "justice" of both matches remains in doubt. The weddings, toward which the shepherds journey and from which they move on in a symbolic, unwitting, pilgrimage toward Death, serve as foreshadowing of Galatea's own destiny. If the weddings occupy the off-centered center, the work does not give a prominent place to the consideration of marriage in itself. The dramatic encounter of Rosaura and Grisaldo briefly claims the narrative foreground with its intensity, but the wedding of Daranio and Silveria seems strangely remote. It functions as silent backdrop to a series of poetic events, particularly the Eclogue.

In effect a "pastoral within a pastoral," the Eclogue situates the traditional poetic competition within a pastoral romance. Its stilted form, its commitment to abstract expression and its static quality stand in marked contrast to the tangle of love-lives that surrounds it. Even before it begins, Cervantes seems to invite us to reject it as a form of discourse inadequate to the task of evoking the intricacies of sentimental life. He introduces his four shepherd-poets, famed for their "disputas y competencias [disputes and rivalries]," with elusive irony:

> muchas veces se habían juntado a encarecer cada cual la causa de su tormento, procurando cada uno mostrar como mejor podía que su dolor a cualquier otro se aventajaba, tiniendo por suma gloria ser en la pena mejorado; y tenían todos tal ingenio, o por mejor decir, tal dolor padecían, que como quiera que le significasen, mostraban ser el mayor que imaginar se podía.

> [often times they had gotten together, and each one exaggerated the cause of his torment, trying to show as best he could that his pain was greater than all the others, for they believed improvement by suffering was the greatest glory; and all of them were so

ingenious, or rather suffered such great pain, that whatever they
might make known, they showed it to be the greatest imaginable.]

(1, 198)

Orompo, Marsilio, Crisio, Orfenio, representing respectively the pain of
Death, Disdain, Absence and Jealousy, renew an old question: Which of them
is the most wretched and most deserving of pity? Cervantes turns the standard oxymoron of "sweet pain" into the paradoxical emblem of poetic competition. Whoever can prove himself most miserable— by eloquence or by
the "truth" of his grief—will be most glorious.

Yet there is more at stake here than Montemayor's axiom that "los que
sufren más son los mejores [those who suffer the most are the best]." This
passage and the Eclogue which follows oblige us to suspend that consideration. How, they ask us, are we to go about answering the question? Does
one judge the merits and miseries of a soul on the basis of rhetorical skill or
on the basis of actual suffering? Orompo describes himself as

> Un pastor que se atreve
> con *razones fundadas*
> *en la pura verdad de su tormento,*
> mostrar que el sentimiento
> de su dolor crecido
> al tuyo se aventaja,
> por más que tú le estimes,
> levantes y sublimes.
>
> [A shepherd who avers,
> Reasoning from his woes,
> Founding his words upon the truth therein,
> That it must needs be seen
> His sorrow doth surpass
> The sorrow thou dost feel,
> The higher thou mayest raise it,
> Exalt it, and appraise it.]

(1, 209–10)

The Eclogue, we now perceive, is *a poetic competition about poetic competition.* Cervantes here makes the central issue of pastoral art not sentiment
but the way that sentiment can be expressed. Orompo's words call into
question the power of language to communicate truth about the self.

Orompo echoes Salicio's famous refrain from Garcilaso's first Eclogue
(itself an echo of an earlier poem). He addresses, however, not his *tears* but

his *words*: "Salid de lo hondo del pecho cuitado, / *palabras sangrientas* con muerte mezcladas; / y si los sospiros os tienen atadas, / abrid y romped el siniestro costado [Come from the depths of my grief-stricken breast, / Oh words of blood, with death commingled come, / Break open the left side that keeps you dumb]" (1, 205). And even if his words break out of his heart's prison, will they succeed as self-representation and communication?

> Porque aunque salgáis, palabras, temblando,
> ¿con cuáles podréis decir lo que siento,
> *si es incapaz mi fiero tormento*
> *de irse cual es al vivo pintando?*
> Mas ya que me falta el cómo y el cuándo
> de *significar mi pena* y mi mengua,
> aquello que falta y no puede la lengua,
> suplan mis ojos, contino llorando.
>
> [Although ye issue trembling at my cry
> With what words can ye utter what I feel,
> If my fierce torment is incapable
> Of being as 'tis painted vividly?
> Alas, for neither means nor time have I
> To express the pain and sinking at my heart
> But what my tongue doth lack to tell its smart,
> My eyes by constant weeping may supply.]
>
>   (1, 206)

Orfinio, victim of "*celos* [jealousy]," rejects eloquence as a valid standard for judging sentiment: "que no está en la elegancia / y modo de decir el fundamento / y principal sustancia / del verdadero cuento, / que en la pura verdad tiene su asiento [A truthful history / In the pure truth doth find its resting-place. / For it can never be, / That elegance and grace / Of speech can form its substance and its base]" (1, 215–16). This passage is most often read as confirmation of Cervantes's campaign against affectation. Language must make the "pure truth," as Orfinio says, its sustaining base. Yet his words voice an anxiety: "truth" may give words a foundation; but only words, trembling in their incapacity, can provide evidence of that truth.

The indictment of refined speech—whether through distrust of its excess expressive capacity or through the agonizing realization of its insufficiency— is nothing less than an indictment of pastoral as a whole. In this most poetic of genres, shepherd-lovers rehearse and exalt their intimate feelings in verse. They operate on the tacit premise that subtlety of feeling can best be communicated by the subtle refinement of language called "poetry." Cervantes plays with that assumption by permitting several characters to champion less polished speech as proof of sincerity. But the private anxiety of the individual sufferer-competitor that he will be found unworthy of sympathy is secondary to the questions which the competition poses about the relationship of language to its object, to the "truth." Is the idea of language as mimesis a viable one in the area of feeling? In short, can the self ever aspire to "irse cual es al vivo pintando?"

The traded verses of the Eclogue seem largely oblivious to this problem. Each shepherd argues the pressing nature of his own particular claim. Only Orompo perceives the devastating logic of their competition, an interminable duel of hyperboles, a "Nunca pusieran fin [Never-ending series]": "Y como *el uno lo que el otro pasa / no siente,* su dolor solo exagera, / y piensa que al rigor del otro pasa [As each the woes through which his fellows pass / Feels not, he praiseth but the grief he knows, / Thinking it doth his fellows pangs surpass]" (1, 222). The performance of the four ends in a kind of truce: the shepherds offer final summations of their cases without conceding. An outsider, Damón, must decide the question. The Eclogue must end, because each shepherd ultimately *listens only to himself.* As attempted communication of intimacy, the Eclogue has failed.

Nonetheless Damón, without hesitation, "dejando a todos satisfechos de *la verdad* que con tanta llaneza les había mostrado [leaving everyone satisfied with the truth he had shown them so simply]" (1, 232), names Orfinio's torment, Jealousy, winner of the contest. Damón's discourse introduces a pair of favorite Cervantine themes: *celos* and the figure of the "*curioso impertinente* [man who was too curious]" (from the interpolated tale of that name in *Don Quixote* and the story of Timbrio and Silerio in *La Galatea* itself). These themes have such a recognizable profile in Cervantes's work generally that readers have not felt the need to articulate their particular function within *La Galatea.* In a work which poses to itself the problem of the power and limits of its own discourse, the figure of the "*celoso-curioso* [jealous-curious man]" clearly paints the limit of distress. As *curioso,* burning for absolute certainty, and as *celoso,* beyond all of language's power of persuasion and consolation, condemned to invent *ex nihilo* his own seductive fictions, he inhabits a *purgatory of language,* which cannot reach that which it claims for its foundation and its object.

> No hay antídoto que le preserve, consejo que le valga, amigo que
> le ayude, ni disculpa que le cuadre; todo esto cabe en el enamo-
> rado celoso, y más: que cualquiera sombra le espanta, cualquiera

niñeria le turba, y cualquiera sospecha, falsa o verdadera, le des-
hace . . . Y no habiendo para la enfermedad de los celos otra
medicina que las disculpas, y no queriendo el celoso admitirlas,
siguese que esta enfermedad es sin remedio, y que a todas las
demás debe anteponerse.

[for there is no antidote to preserve it, counsel to avail it, friend
to aid it, nor excuse to fit it; all this is contained in the jealous
lover, and more—every shadow terrifies him, every trifle disturbs
him, and every suspicion, false or true, undoes him . . . And since
there is no other medicine than excuses for the disease of jealousy,
and since the jealous man suffering from it does not wish to admit
them, it follows that this disease is without remedy, and should
be placed before all others.]

                                                           (1, 230)

The true lover, Damón adds, shares the jealous lover's purgatory, if not his
frenzy. Neither can have certainty beyond fear in love: "Teme y tema el buen
enamorado . . . y este temor ha de ser tan secreto *que no le salga a la lengua
para decirle, ni aun a los ojos para significarle* [The good lover fears, and let
him fear . . . and this fear must be so secret, that it does not come to his
tongue to utter it, nor yet to his eyes to express it]" (1, 231). The discreet
lover's language must serve him as a mask.

From the Eclogue and subsequent commentary, we draw two remarkable
conclusions. First, language cannot tell the truth; it fails absolutely as a
mimetic mirror in the domain of feeling. Second, language *should not* tell
the truth; its mask necessarily, rightfully, conceals. Finally, the paradoxical
result: despite language's lamentable inadequacy, the greatest misery comes
of finding one's self beyond its civilizing power. The Eclogue's concern with
discourse and what it struggles to tell suggests a key to the unity of the
episodes which proliferate around it. Fragments of discourse leave as much
mystery as information in their wake. The relentless pace of narrative interruption—introducing other figures with more stories to tell—creates a chain
of partial understandings and misunderstandings. Daranio and Silveria,
unique among the wordy shepherds in their speechlessness, are only more
mysterious in degree than the other characters in *La Galatea*. Their absolute
silence is only slightly more perplexing than the faltering aid which discourse
lends to the exploration of intimacy. Again and again, the text's lurching
movements, sudden breaks and incompletions—its interruptive aesthetic—
remind us that we cannot know with certainty, that "el uno lo que el otro
pasa no siente."

La Galatea's shepherds and shepherdesses break into song when they overflow with emotion, when they contemplate a beloved person or a private grief. "No se calle mi tormentio [Let my torment not be silenced]," says Timbrio; "salga con la voz el alma, / *para mayor sentimiento* [let my soul come forth with my voice, / for the greatest surge of feeling]" (2, 108). As the language of the soul, verse aims to intensify, even to exaggerate feeling. Timbrio offers his verses here as the handmaidens of hyperbole. Verse is presumed better equipped than prose to maintain a high emotional temperature and to reproduce emotion in the listener. Charged with saying the most that language can say, verse nonetheless presents itself as a problematical vehicle of communication.

Of course, it is always the challenge of poetry to say what it means by not saying what it means. "Poetry," writes Jonathan Culler, "lies at the center of the literary experience because it is the form that most clearly asserts the specificity of literature, its difference from ordinary discourse by an empirical individual about the world. The specific features of poetry have the function of differentiating it from speech and altering the circuit of communication within which it is inscribed." Within the mimetic world created by the book, the shepherd's decision to "speak in song" necessarily changes the nature and aims of his communication. Verse in *La Galatea* always attaches to a specific "I," identified by name at the head of the composition. If speaking in verse means choosing to speak *from* the deepest seat of emotion, however, it also means deciding not to speak directly, exclusively, *to* anyone. Even though the song may be addressed rhetorically to a certain figure, it reaches for a wider audience. While claiming to be in some sense more intimate, poems become at the same time more impersonal. In the pastoral romance, verse tends to function as a kind of *indirect direct discourse*: it always presents the paradox of alluding to and simultaneously avoiding its fictional context.

A shepherd (like Elicio at the opening of book 1) may sing to no one but his own "Amoroso pensamiento [amorous fancy]" (1, 18), hinting at his circumstances, but aware of no audience. Such songs are, of course, in what Cesáreo Bandera calls a "mundo de mirones [world of bystanders]," fated to be overheard by listeners who eventually reveal their presence and pursue the significance of what they have chanced to hear. Or a shepherd or shepherdess may be asked to sing in order to demonstrate the sweetness of his or her voice. The poem is always presumed to address a circumstance or a person which may or may not be recognized by its listeners. If the addressee happens to be present, the verses may press a specific complaint by innuendo, without ever revealing an identity. If the addressee is absent, the verses may say more than they would dare to say in his or her actual presence. Verses may even be delivered from a presumed speaker to a presumed addressee, while the poem's impersonal discourse hides the actual identity of either from the character-listeners. The most complex instance involves the two friends, Timbrio and Silerio. Silerio tells of his own sentiments to Nísida *as though they were*—and in fact they *are*—Timbrio's (1, 150–51). Later he sings of his love *for* Nísida *to* Timbrio *as though it were for* Blanca (1, 159–60). In these situations, the language of verse is *double-talk*. It does and simultaneously does not want to be understood. It claims, through the privilege it enjoys over prose, a special significance for its message, but it cloaks that significance in a *mask of language*.

This bizarre kind of communication which hopes to succeed and simultaneously works to blunt its own purpose has a familiar name in the courtly ethos: discretion. As an ethic, discretion dictates reserve. The lover must remain silent lest he endanger his beloved's reputation. But even in private, in the protected intimacy of her presence, he must not—like the *curioso impertinente*—say all. He must repress his inmost fears and offer his lady the image of his trust. He must mask her to others and himself to her. As an aesthetic principle, then, discretion imposes the *language of the mask*, another name for the inner distancing action of language, its irrevocable separateness from the thoughts whose image it presents. The shepherd paints an image of self—a "*semejante a sí mismo* [self-likeness]," in Alarcón's phrase—which is and is not his own.

By convention and by desire, *La Galatea*'s shepherds speak a verse language both abstract and heavily metaphorical. Abstractions naturally work to obscure intratextual references. The dependence on metaphor, however, creates a different kind of difficulty. The theorists of Cervantes's day wrestled with the connection between metaphor and clarity of style. Fernando de Herrera, while recommending clarity, acknowledges that "*palabras propias* [proper words]," which call things by their own names, do not always have the force of "*palabras ajenas* [foreign words]" or metaphors. Metaphors are desirable, provided they are used judiciously. Keep the comparison just, says Herrera, and the expression will retain both clarity and energy. Cervantes, however, makes the notion of transparent metaphor problematical. When Orompo laments in the Eclogue that he cannot find the means to express his pain and loss, the subsequent exchange of verses makes it clear that metaphor is at the heart of the problem. Each of the four poets in turn takes up a well-worn metaphor (the *locus amoenus,* the fruits of love and the *albergue* or haven of repose) and tries to make the metaphor *stand for* his own grief. He attempts, in other words, to make it *more proper,* to *appro-*

priate it, but in the end none succeeds in taking permanent possession of any of these images. The proliferation of metaphors traces only the search for that oxymoronic impossibility, the *proper metaphor.*

The obstacles which metaphoric speech erects to communication become acutely obvious in book 4, when Lenio and Tirsi debate the nature of Love. Their traded poems belong to the medieval tradition of *"preguntas* [questions]," where the answer imitates the form of the question. After hearing Lenio's poem, Tirsi offers one "que parece que en competencia de la tuya se hizo [that seems to have been written in competition with yours]" (2, 68). Each lays claim to a traditional body of metaphors (*"fuego, hielo, lazo, red, yugo, ejército, ciego* [fire, ice, bond, snare, yoke, army, blind]," etc.) to bolster his own view of Love. With subtle irony, Cervantes permits Lenio to boast that "la voz levanto / al verdadero canto / que en vituperio del amor se forma, / con tal verdad, / con tal manera y forma, / que a todo el mundo su maldad descubre / y claramente informa / del cierto daño que el amor encubre [When I employ my tongue / To utter the true song / Which in reproach of Love himself I form, / So rich in truth, in manner, and in form, / That unto all Love's malice it reveals, / And clearly doth inform / The world of the sure hurt that Love conceals]" (2, 55). The next moment Lenio's adversary Tirsi congratulates himself for the "verdades que . . . he declarado [truths that . . . I have declared]" (2, 68). Cervantes makes Tirsi in some degree conscious of the dependence of his "truth" on metaphor. When Tirsi attacks his adversary's version of the figure of Cupid, he alleges, "Porque píntanle niño, ciego, desnudo, con las alas y saetas, *no quiere significar* otra cosa, sino que el amante ha de ser niño [Because they depict him as a child, blind and naked, with wings and arrows, he does not desire to signify anything else, but that the lover has to be a boy]" (2, 67). The dependence on metaphor makes poetry always a *"querer significar* [desire to signify]," a desire to invest things with meaning. Since poetic language cannot say directly what it means without saying less than it means, it must expose itself to the perils of metaphor. In the contest between Lenio and Tirsi, the *shepherds'* desire for meaning stands squarely on Tirsi's side. That is to say, Tirsi's listeners want Love's language to signify purity, faith, innocence, beauty and trust—not suffering and despair. Despite the fact that *La Galatea's* narratives alternately support and contradict that vision, by showing that Love is both glory and inferno, even critics fall into the trap of equating desire with truth.

Lenio's and Tirsi's philosophical and poetic exchange occupies a position similar to that of book 3's Eclogue. As an explicit, traditional *"cuestión de amor* [question of love]," it is really a question within a question. The status of the prose debate and supporting verses is metaphorical: they stand for, before or in front of, the narrative fabric, and thus inevitably apart from it. The extreme views they oppose are never reconciled, either with each other or with the narrative. Despite the tacit promise that there is some "truth" about Love to which language can provide access, the debate and the text as a whole cultivate contradictions as obstacles to reduction. With both verse eclogue and debate held at arm's length from narrative, books 3 and 4 suggest a model for describing the structure of the work as a whole. In *La Galatea* narrative itself stands conspicuously apart from its subject. Galatea's book does not tell *her* story: she functions as the silent center. "*Desdén*" is merely the name of her opacity. The "*Primera parte* [first part]" makes her image its premise, its hyperbolic limit, which the text points to but does not approach. The text, in this sense, is never at one with itself. Galatea's and Elicio's destinies are available to us—even to them—only as foreshadowing. In the genre which supposedly allows its characters to concern themselves with being rather than contingency, wholeness shines precisely by its absence. The text's internal distances—between philosopher and philosopher, poet and poet, between debate and verse and narrative and event—confirm the inevitable exteriority of all discourse to the vision of truth or of self that it pursues.

The games people play in *La Galatea* revolve around the ambiguous signifying power of language. Following the Eclogue and Damón's discourse on jealousy, the old man Arsindo puts a question to the poet-visitors. Two shepherds, Francenio and Lauso, have written verse glosses of a couplet which had been composed during a game of "propósitos." A sort of poetic game of "telephone," "los propósitos" involves a chain of whispered communications. The first speaker whispers a verse into the ear of his neighbor, who completes the couplet and passes the whole on around the circle. On the occasion in question the first speaker and his neighbor happened to be lovers. To his "Huyendo va la esperanza [Hope doth fly and will not stay]," she returned "Tenella con el deseo [With desire to check its flight]" (1, 233). The *agudeza* [sharpness] of the reply won general approval. The poets applauded it by composing glosses of their own, and between these glosses the visiting poets are now asked to decide. Damón and Tirsi decline to make the choice, on the grounds that "la guirnalda se debe dar a la pastora que dio la ocasión a tan curiosa y loable contienda [the garland should be given to the shepherdess who was the cause of so curious and praiseworthy a contest]" (1, 235). The sequence as a whole alludes to an intimate communication, the couplet which that secret exchange produces, and the verses which the imitative chain of admiration-rivalry produces. The initial energy of the couplet derives from a mysterious sentimental transaction that lies before and beyond language. In the amplifications of their discourse the glossers, desiring to exploit the rich implications of the original, concentrated verses, instead dilute its energy. Their verses in fact prove most interesting to the other shepherds as veiled allusions to their own sentimental adventures. In terms of the original moment, however, more verses have produced not more truth but less.

In a symmetrical position in book 6 we find another game: *enigmas* or riddles. This eminently literary game of verse riddles is really nothing other than a metaphor matching. Each speaker presents a catalog of metaphors; the listener who can name the unspoken referent of the series wins the chance to continue the game with a catalog of his own. The play reaches its climax with Elicio's riddle:

> Es muy escura y es clara;
> tiene mil contrariedades;
> encúbrenos las verdades
> y al cabo nos las declara.
>
> Nace a veces de donaire,
> otras, de altas fantasías,
> y suele engendrar porfías
> aunque trate cosas de aire
>
> Cuál es necia, cuál curiosa,
> cuál fácil, cuál intricada,
> pero sea o no sea nada,
> decidme *qué es cosa y cosa.*

> ['Tis obscure, and yet 'tis clear,
> Thousand opposites containing,
> Truth to us at last explaining,
> Which it hides from far and near;
>
> Born at times from beauty rare
> Or from lofty fantasies,
> Unto strife it giveth rise,
> Though it deals with things of air
>
> Sometimes foolish sometimes witty;
> Easy, or with tangles fraught,

> Whether naught it be or not,
> Say, what is this thing so pretty?]
>   (2, 245)

"Qué es cosa y cosa," the popular form of the riddle's question, asks roughly, "can you guess what this is?" Timbrio supplies the answer: "Con lo mesmo que yo pensé que tu demanda, Elicio, se escurecía, con eso mesmo me parece que se declara, pues el último verso dice que te digan qué es cosa y cosa, y así yo te respondo a lo que me dices, y digo que tu pregunta es el 'qué es cosa y cosa' [With the very thing by which I thought your query was obscured, Elicio, it appears to me to be solved, for the last line says, that they are to say what is this thing so pretty. And so I answer you in what you ask me, and say that your question means that which we mean by a pretty thing]" (2, 246). The "answer" turns out to be none other than the question itself: "encúbrenos las verdades / y al cabo nos las declara." The "truth" of the reply only reiterates its own question: what does this mean?

These formal entertainments mirror two games which *La Galatea*'s characters play in real earnest: hide-and-seek and what Geoffrey Stagg calls the "matter of masks." The riddle contest is interrupted by a "real" game of hide-and-seek that involves Gelasia, Galercio, Lenio and ultimately Maurisa, Arsindo, Theolinda, Artidoro and Leonarda. In fact, *La Galatea*'s narrative structure follows the shepherds and shepherdesses through a woodsy labyrinth, pursuing and fleeing, finding and losing one another, by design and by chance. In Cervantes's hands, the hackneyed pastoral topic of unsynchronized love recovers its energy, emerging not only as a sentimental problem but as an aesthetic question as well. The lack of synchrony becomes a basic principle, a "natural law" of the book's universe. The central experience of *La Galatea,* in physical, sentimental and linguistic terms, is that of being perpetually *out of phase,* of pulling backward or forward to a condition whose full enjoyment seems ever to elude the grasp.

"Rostros rebozados [Hidden faces]" merges hide-and-seek and the mask in another unacknowledged game in which identity is withheld for strategic reasons, as when Nísida, Blanca and Timbrio approach Silerio's hermitage (2, 98ff.). Geoffrey Stagg reminds us that the desire for positive identification of characters propelled the sixteenth-century reader beyond the confines of the book. That reader mirrors the characters themselves, who strain throughout *La Galatea* to uncover and fix identities. With the riddles, the metaphor-matching duels, and the opacity of the lovers' lyrical double-talk, the name of the game is really the *game of the name.* "Name" stands here for the power of language to establish presence and identity. In *La Galatea,* the name always turns out to be another game, the answer poses a new question. The riddles offer the shepherds a kind of ritual satisfaction. They *play at* achieving the desired moment of naming, a satisfaction which is denied to many of them in the world of the book outside of the game. The play verses of the riddles suggest that the shepherds' earnest verses obey similar aims. Their metaphorical enterprise is self-consuming. Metaphors strain for names, for the full presence which will render them needless.

In another important respect, *La Galatea*'s verses are self-consuming. Poetry operates in the limit region of sentiment, where it always risks extinguishing itself. Elicio's songs in praise of Galatea regularly give way to paroxysms and fainting spells. When Galatea learns of her father's plans to marry her to a "Lusitanian shepherd," her songs of grief dissolve: "lo que no puede mi lengua, / mis ojos te lo señalen [what my tongue cannot say / my eyes tell you]" (2, 134). The intense sentiments which it is verse's mission to cultivate threaten to obliterate the vehicle of their expression. One of *La Galatea*'s most dramatic moments, the reunion of Timbrio and Silerio in book 5, comes as a breaking off of poetry. Timbrio, his face concealed, sings a sonnet which he had composed "en el tiempo del hervor de mis amores [in my loves' fervorous time]," and which (like his passion) is familiar to Silerio. He does not, however, succeed in finishing, "porque el oir Silerio su voz y el conocerle todo fue uno, y sin ser parte a otra cosa, se levantó de do sentado estaba y se fue a abrazar del cuello de Timbrio, con muestras de tan estraño contento y sobresalto, que *sin hablar palabra*, se transpuso y estuvo un rato sin acuerdo [for Silerio's hearing of his voice and recognition of him took place together, and unable to do aught else, he arose from where he was seated, and went to embrace Timbrio's neck with tokens of such strange content and surprise, that without speaking a word he became faint and was for a while without consciousness]" (2, 103). As the verses succeed, they become perfectly superfluous. To the extent that the story of Timbrio and Silerio presents an unusually successful communication of intense emotion, it serves also to illustrate the dangers of success. So eloquently does Timbrio communicate his affection for Nísida that Silerio actually experiences that emotion, thereby becoming his best friend's rival. "*El uno lo que el otro pasa no siente*": the exteriority of language to both speaker and listener in fact affords a necessary protection. Lovers who invoke their inmost feelings do not consciously aim at kindling identical sentiments in others. When the lover of the popular song says, "If you knew Suzy like I know Suzy," he does not really want to share that experience, only to validate his exclamation ("Oh, oh, oh what a gal!").

Poetry's hyperbolizing mission—the communication of extremes of beauty and sentiment—is placed in jeopardy by both success and failure. It should not surprise us, then, to hear the Muse of Poetry herself, the Calíope of the *Canto,* owning up to serious difficulties as she faces the challenges of sustaining her verse hyperboles through the celebration of a full hundred *ingenios.* The music of "la más sonora voz que imaginarse puede [the most sonorous voice imaginable]" (2, 190) holds her listeners enrapt. Not only her extraordinary voice (she is the very fountain of eloquence) but her subject, the veneration of that eloquence and its practitioners, makes her song into a kind of poetry to the second power. What first appears to be a cheerful but tedious catalog of superlatives turns out, on closer inspection, to be the Muse's meditation on the limits of the art she patronizes. Calíope spends many of the more than one hundred octaves lamenting *her own* inadequacy. For human eloquence, the task she faces would be hopeless ("hacerlo humana lengua es disparate [for the human tongue to do it is foolish]," [2, 217]), but in the heady regions of hyperbole even the Muse finds herself at a loss for words: "Que no podrá *la ruda lengua mía,* / por más caminos que aquí tiente y pruebe, / hallar alguno así cual le deseo / para loar lo que en tí siento y veo [For my rough tongue will never able be, / Whate'er the ways it here may try and prove, / To find a way of praising as I would / All that I feel and see in thee of good]" (2, 218). At the outer limit of eloquence, she discovers silence: "Con las palabras más calificadas, / con cuanto ingenio el cielo en mi reparte, / os *admiro y alabo aqui callando,* / y llego do llegar no puedo hablando [With words significant of noble deed, / With all the skill that Heaven doth impart, / I marvel, praise in silence, thus I reach / A height I cannot hope to gain by speech]" (2, 219). None other than the custodian of the poetic word here confesses her ultimate impotence. As she finishes singing, the Muse is immediately engulfed in the miraculous flames from which she appeared. The flames ("poco a poco consumiéndose [consumed little by little]") soon disappear altogether; Calíope's enterprise has quite literally consumed itself. The shepherds must accreditate ("*acreditar*") the truth of her praise. Telesio, sage and elder shepherd, must second and supplement the Muse's poetic tribute with a prose discourse on the merits of Spanish poetry.

In the hybrid form of pastoral romance, the limit of poetry always takes the form of a *return to prose.* His *song* concluded or interrupted, the shepherd can usually be persuaded to tell his *story* as validation of his verses. Timbrio invites his friends to judge the success of his long narration: "Ved si, por la [vida] que he pasado y la que agora paso, me puedo llamar el más lastimado y venturoso hombre de los que hoy viven [See if, by my past and present life, I may not call myself the most pitiful and fortunate man alive today]" (2, 121–22). A story's capacity to amaze *authorizes* its narrator's poetic ejaculations; poems in turn validate narrative hyperboles. Don Quixote makes Poetry first lady of the sciences: "ella se ha de servir de todas, y todas se han de autorizar con ella [she must be served by all of them, and all must be authorized by her]" (*DQ*, 2, 16). Poetry will use all the other sciences; they will take their authority from her. Verse and prose in *La Galatea* coexist in this sort of relation of mutual dependence, each requiring the reinforcement of the other. Nor does this amount to a comfortable symbiosis of prose and verse, the one flowing harmoniously into the other. The dynamic of narrative, propelled by the desire of both character-narrators and curious character-readers to make it complete ("por no dejar imperfecto mi comenzado cuento [to not leave incomplete the story I have begun]," in Teolinda's words [1, 80]), seeks scenes of recognition and presence, scenes which should belong to verse in its capacity as custodian of exalted sentiment. Yet at the moment of its greatest power, poetry discovers its limit. Either it breaks off, obliterated by its own success, into the speechless silence of delight or pain, or it leaves its significance cloaked in a veil of language, sending the curious hearer back once again to disentangle the threads of narrative.

"La poesía," says Don Quixote, defender of poetry as well as of damsels, "es como una doncella tierna y de poca edad, y en todo estremo hermosa, . . . pero esta tal doncella no quiere ser manoseada, ni traída por las calles, ni publicada por las esquinas de las plazas ni por los rincones de los palacios [Poetry is like a tender, young and extremely beautiful maiden, . . . But this maiden does not care to be handled, or dragged through the streets, nor to be shown at the corners of the marketplace, or in the antechambers of palaces]" (*DQ* 2, 16). Her intimacy and fragility must be safeguarded; she must not be paraded daily through the public plazas of discourse. Like the damsel, poetry will arouse desires she cannot satisfy. Hers is the language of the limit, and poetry is the limit of language. In trying her strength, we test the capacity of eloquence to fulfill its most delicate charge, the communication of human experience and feeling.

Not only in the Eclogue and the *Canto*, but throughout the six books, the shepherds constantly invoke language's inadequacy for expressing sentiment: "¿Qué palabras serán bastantes? [What words would suffice?]" (1, 101), "no es para decirse el bien que siento [it is not enough to say how good I feel]" (2, 27), "no podre enearecer el dolor [I will not be able to express my pain sufficiently]" (2, 116), "digan ellas lo que sintieron, si se atreven [let them say what they feel, if they dare]" (2, 117), to quote only a few instances. The "inexpressibility topos," a standard disclaimer often used to voice the false modesty of the super-articulate, in *La Galatea* calls attention to the limit regions in which hyperbole operates. The work's insistent concern with the power of language gives coherence to a whole range of familiar pastoral topics: persuasion, consolation, unwitting failures of communication, deceit and disdain. Even the interpolated tales (of Lisandro, Teolinda, Timbrio and Silerio, and others), which have been seen to represent the world of history or of action within the book, are also stories about communication. In these tales, lovers often speak to one another first in the masked language of verse. Their stories subsequently demonstrate the potential for misreading of verbal and visual signs even within the intimacy of mutual desires. The motif of doubles (look-alikes and think-alikes, rivals and friends) dramatizes the gap which separates appearance and expression from feeling. Silerio's hermitage offers him temporary refuge from the chaos of human communication: "desengañado de las cosas deste falso mundo en que vivimos, he acordado de volver el pensamiento a mejor norte, y gastar lo poco que de vivir me queda en servicio *del que estima los deseos y las obras en el punto que merecen* [disillusioned by the things of this false world in which we live, I have decided to turn my thoughts to a better pole-star, and spend the little that is left of my life in the service *of He who esteems desires and works as they deserve to be esteemed.*] (1, 187). Only God knows the truth of desires. The crisis of poetry in *La Galatea* only describes at the limit the crisis of all language.

As *La Galatea*'s central preoccupation, the ultimate impotence of words inscribes itself clearly in the work's "ending." Galatea learns shortly before the book ends that her father plans to marry her to a "Lusitanian shepherd," obliging her to leave the banks of the Tagus. Under this threat, she at last acquiesces to Elicio's offer of assistance. Suddenly much like the Erastro who once proposed to teach Lenio a lesson in love with his fists (1, 86), Elicio plans three strategies. First he will try persuasion with Galatea's father, then threats to discourage his rival. Failing all else, he will resort to force (2, 263). As his fellow shepherds fall in behind him, vowing to "cumplir la palabra," we suspect with them that words will ultimately fail to keep order in the fictional world. The book's final moment, that of *keeping the word,* is also the moment of *breaking the word.* Words can only carry thought and feeling to the limit, where desire reaches beyond discourse.

Cervantes's references to poetry and the pastoral should, by their very range, suggest to us the author's capacity for ironic distance from himself. His wry smile suggests that he is not at one with himself about a poetic enterprise as immensely appealing as it is fraught with peril. In the context of *La Galatea*'s testing of the limits of language and poetry, Cervantes's protestations about the distance between his texts and his desires assume a new value. The *themes* of *La Galatea*'s shortcomings and its author's meager poetic talents acquire their full resonance from the text's concern with the failure of language itself and the super-language of verse to produce a "pure truth" of thought and desire. Cervantes's defense of poetry, then, also indicts; his version of pastoral is also a subversion. The text's ambivalence about poetry helps us to see why its verses are so rarely read. In a sense, we have already accepted what the text discovers. We already distrust pastoral's claim that refined language can best render intense feeling or describe an essential self. We regard the mask of language with suspicion, but we find its veil more powerful than the unveiling. By attending to narrative, we perhaps acknowledge that a literary vehicle which exploits the dynamic of desire and curiosity exerts a greater pull than "still-life" in verse. Like all poetry, *La Galatea* makes promises which it cannot keep ("propone algo, y no concluye nada"). Cervantes ultimately subverts the pastoral not by asking it to be something other than pastoral, but by asking pastoral to deliver on its own promises.

JUAN BAUTISTA AVALLE-ARCE

Novelas ejemplares: *Reality, Realism, Literary Tradition*

In the year 1613 Miguel de Cervantes Saavedra brought out in Madrid a collection of twelve short stories, which he entitled collectively *Exemplary Novels*. After a slow and dubious start in the literary world, Cervantes was then at the height of his fame. His years in the Spanish army were far behind him in time, and so were his years of captivity in Algiers. His first published novel had come out more than a quarter of a century earlier. That book, *La Galatea*, a highly experimental pastoral novel, had met with an all too modest success, although Cervantes clung to the pastoral theme to his, literally, dying days. He had written an unspecified number of plays, which he chose not to publish until a few years after the *Exemplary Novels*. But the competition with Lope de Vega, the Monster of Nature, had proved too strenuous, and Cervantes had given up writing for the theater. In 1605 he had published the most successful novel in literary history: the first part of *Don Quixote*. Its success had been immediate and immense, and Cervantes had left the reading public dangling with the written promise of a second part, whose very sketchy outline appeared at the end of *Don Quixote* of 1605.

It is interesting to reconsider the fact that Cervantes deliberately chose not to follow up the success of *Don Quixote*. He decided not to publish the promised continuation, to postpone it, and this decision had the gravest consequences. The continuation was destined to come out all right—not

From *Mimesis: From Mirror to Method, Augustine to Descartes,* edited by John D. Lyons and Stephen G. Nichols, Jr. © 1982 by the Trustees of Dartmouth College. Dartmouth College/University Press of New England, 1982.

135

written by Cervantes but by an imitator who called himself Alonso Fernández de Avellaneda, whose real identity will remain unknown forever, short of a literary miracle. But Avellaneda's continuation would not appear until the year after the publication of the *Exemplary Novels*. It was a strange and fateful decision for Cervantes to postpone the obvious and imminent success of the second part of *Don Quixote* in favor of publishing these short stories. His decision underscores the special place that the *Exemplary Novels* had in the literary estimation of their author.

He had been at work on them since before the publication of *Don Quixote* in 1605. We know this because "Riconete y Cortadillo ["Rinconete and Cortadillo"] the third of the *Exemplary Novels,* is mentioned in chapter 47 of the *Don Quixote* of 1605. Furthermore, we have a different manuscript version of "Rinconete y Cortadillo" from the one Cervantes chose to publish in 1613. And we have a very different version of "El celoso extremeño ["The Jealous Hidalgo"] as well, thanks to the literary curiosity of a priest from Sevilla named Francisco Porras de la Cámara, who, no later than 1605, collected a manuscript the two above-mentioned short stories. I cite some of these facts to bring into perspective the artful and deliberate care with which Cervantes treated his collection of short stories. He was at work on two of them before 1605, and when he published these same two stories in 1613 the revisions were more than considerable.

In the preface to the *Exemplary Novels* Cervantes goes out of his way to call the reader's attention to the literary revolution he is about to start. As he writes in the preface (I should point out that I use throughout this paper Harriet de Onís's translation): "I am the first to essay novels in the Castilian tongue, for the many which go about in print in Spanish are all translated from foreign languages, while these are my own, neither imitated nor stolen. My genius begat them, and my pen gave them birth." This, far from being a show of literary arrogance, is nothing but the naked truth, as the slightest consideration of the Italianate short stories of Juan de Timoneda makes very evident. I mention Timoneda's name because he was the most successful of Cervantes's predecessors in this genre. In other words, Cervantes set out in the *Exemplary Novels* to invent a new literary genre in Spanish. He was fully aware of the novelty of the experiment, and he wanted his reader to be equally aware.

Let me briefly consider the first and the last of the *Exemplary Novels* to emphasize my point. The first one is "La gitanilla" ["The Gypsy Maid"], and it should be obvious that Cervantes set a very special store by it, since he chose to give it the place of honor in the collection. Why? It should be clear that the first story in a collection must successfully ensnare the reader and not let him wander. Which qualities contributed to making "La gita-nilla" a successful reader-trap? I think that the most successful single quality is the literary typology contained in that short story. Gypsies had arrived in Spain by the early fifteenth century, and they had been officially outlawed by the state as early as the reign of the Catholic kings. Officially condemned as vagrant and thieves, gypsies had no room in literary history, save for a few bit parts in the earliest Spanish theater. Cervantes broke with this literary condemnation, bringing gypsies into full focus in the first of his *Exemplary Novels*. The success of this experiment would be attested to by Victor Hugo in *Notre Dame de Paris,* whose female protagonist is the gypsy girl Esmer-alda, and in our century by Federico García Lorca in his *Primer romancero gitano,* where the second *romance* is precisely called "Preciosa y el aire" ["Preciosa and the Air"], Preciosa being the name of Cervantes's protagonist in "La gitanilla." To this day the gypsy remains a social outcast, but he has been saved from literary oblivion by the magic art of Cervantes.

But there is more to it than that. "The Gypsy Maid" begins with these words: "It would seem that gypsies, men and women alike, came into the world for the sole purpose of thieving." By 1613, the date of publication of the *Exemplary Novels,* Spanish literary history knew a canonical literary form dedicated to thieves and thieving—the *novela picaresca* [picaresque novel], the romance of roguery, adumbrated by *Lazarillo de Tormes,* that anonymous novel published in 1554, and brought to full fruition by Mateo Alemán in his two-part *Guzmán de Alfarache* of 1599 and 1604. So "The Gypsy Maid" begins with the clear insinuation that the reader is about to enter a picaresque world sui generis. But the world we enter is one of ro-mantic love and travel. If we look at Spanish literary history again, we will see that the literary genre dedicated to narrating travels and studying ro-mantic love was the Byzantine novel, which I prefer to call the novel of adventures, which would constitute, precisely, the subject of the posthumous novel of Cervantes, his *Persiles y Sigismunda.* So "The Gypsy Maid" offers the reader kaleidoscopic literary possibilities, incarnated in a group of social pariahs, redeemed by love. I think that Cervantes was quite right in thinking that "The Gypsy Maid" would be the successful snare to keep the reader glued to the pages of the *Exemplary Novels.*

Now let us turn to the last piece in the collection, "El coloquio de los perros" ["The Dialogue of the Dogs"]. This "novel" has two immediate and distinctly unique qualities, which I want to emphasize now, although I will return later to the narrative as a whole. First, let us consider that this text is exactly what its title implies: the dialogue between two dogs, Cipión and Berganza, outside the hospital in Valladolid. The subject of their dialogue is, mainly, the autobiographical reminiscences of Berganza, interspersed with philosophical comments by Cipión. Talking animals, of course, will take us to the opposite extreme of literary realism and, for that matter, completely outside the realm of reality. We are in a world of fantasy and satire that had been previously explored, many centuries earlier, by the Greek satirist Lucian. But it is highly unlikely that Cervantes could have known Lucian, because the very few works of Lucian that circulated in Spanish had been printed outside Spain, in Lyon and in Strasburg. Cervantes could have known, however, *The Golden Ass* of Apuleius, translated into Spanish by Diego López de Cortegana in 1513, with various reprintings. The golden ass, however, is a former human being now devoid of the faculty of speech, and he does not come into contact with any other animal of similar characteristics. The possible model for talking animals in the medieval, Aesopic fables was too elementary in its conception and functions to be of effective use to the Cervantine imagination. In other words, when reading "The Dialogue of the Dogs" we are confronted with the imagination of its author completely untrammeled and in absolute freedom, abandoning the norms of realism and from the outlines of reality. These have been the boundaries of the other eleven *Exemplary Novels,* but upon reaching the last one, the one that will act as a golden brooch to close the collection so auspiciously opened by "The Gypsy Maid," Cervantes will abandon reality as a literary nourishment, and with the most graceful of intellectual pirouettes will openly embrace fantasy. Plato never dreamed of putting one of his philosophic dialogues to the use that this one is being put to by these two Cynic philosophers, and when I say Cynic I am referring to all possible meanings of the word.

The second unique characteristic of "The Dialogue of the Dogs" is that it literally has no beginning, an extraordinary occurrence in the annals of literary history. The way that Cervantes has manipulated things for this remarkable occurrence to take place has to do with the characteristics and plot of the eleventh of the *Exemplary Novels:* "El casamiento engañoso" ["The Deceitful Marriage"]. The protagonist of this novel is a soldier, Alférez Campuzano, who illustrates in his life and artistic development the folkloric tale of the deceiver deceived. On the streets of Valladolid, Campuzano meets an old friend of his, Licenciado Peralta, who asks him about his dejected and sickly appearance. The gist of the story told by Campuzano concerns his plan to deceive a woman, who in turn tricks and dupes him, leaving him with a most embarrassing social disease. To cure himself of this, Campuzano repairs to the local hospital. The treatment he undergoes there puts him in a feverish state, and in the ensuing delirium he thinks or imagines that he hears two guard dogs, under his window, exchanging in human voices their life stories. When he comes out of his delirium Campuzano jots down the conversation he thinks he has heard, and at the moment of the narrative he brings forth his jottings and places them in front of his friend, Licenciado Peralta. Peralta sits down comfortably, takes the sheaf of papers, and tells his friend that he will read the notes, out of curiosity if for no other reason. And he begins his reading. So, *sensu stricto,* "The Dialogue of the Dogs" is nothing but the act of reading on the part of the Licenciado Peralta. This process of reading has already begun in "The Deceitful Marriage," which ends with the following words: "The Alférez leaned back, the Licenciado opened the notebook, and at the very top he read the following title." Thus "The Dialogue of the Dogs" begins with no formal beginning.

But this is not the only structural innovation that Cervantes makes in "The Dialogue of the Dogs." He engages in structural telescoping carried to dizzying extremes. Let me try to explain myself. As I said before, the subject matter of the dialogue is mainly the autobiographical reminiscences of Berganza. At one point in his narrative Berganza recalls how he got to the Andalusian village of Montilla, famous at that time for its witches. There he ran into a witch named Cañizares, who recognizes him, in his canine form, as the long-lost son of another witch named La Montiela. At this point we are told that Berganza's real name is Montiel, and we get an outline of the life of La Montiela. Now the story of La Montiela is a function of the story being told of his life by Berganza, which functions as only part of "The Dialogue of the Dogs," which, as we have seen, is the product of the reading of Licenciado Peralta, a secondary character in "The Deceitful Marriage," which is in turn the product of the retelling of his own recent past by Alférez Campuzano to Licenciado Peralta. So we have this dizzying structural telescoping: a story (that of La Montiela) within a story (that of Cañizares) within a story (the life of Berganza) within a story (the dialogue of the dogs) within a story (the reading of Licenciado Peralta) within a story (the artful deceit played on the sickly Alférez Campuzano). At this point we can say that we are light-years away from the elementary structure of the folk motif of the deceiver deceived, or of the Aesopic fable, which is where it all began.

Now I wish to turn to some of the other uses to which Cervantes put literary tradition in his *Exemplary Novels.* I will try to be very specific, and to that end I will concern myself with only one literary tradition and the imaginative uses Cervantes made of it. The literary tradition I have in mind is that of la novela picaresca, the rogue's story, which I have mentioned earlier. As I said before, this tradition was set into motion in the Spanish peninsula by the anonymous author of *Lazarillo de Tormes* in the year 1554. Three editions came out in that year, in Alcalá, Burgos, and Antwerp. This little masterpiece was immediately continued by various authors, but in the climate of new moral and religious strictures during the reign of Philip II (1556–98), it lost its popularity, was thoroughly censured and refurbished, and reappeared as *El Lazarillo castigado* [*Lazarillo Punished*], attributed to the pen of the royal officer Juan López de Velasco. Nowadays there is a raging polemic as to whether *Lazarillo* is a picaresque novel or not. I will not take sides, at least not here. I will only point out that Cervantes recognized it as such (more about this later), which allows me to consider it as such for my purposes. Whatever its dominant genre, *Lazarillo* effectively outlined the standard form of the picaresque novel, which was brought to its perfection in the *Guzmán de Alfarache* of Mateo Alemán.

The narrative form of the picaresque novel became conventionalized and canonized in a hieratic form from the first moment. Its subject matter was intended to seem autobiographical. The picaro, the rogue, told his life from birth to a time that usually did not coincide with the actual moment of writing. For example, *Lazarillo* ends at a time considerably prior to the time of writing. As Lázaro is made to say: "At that time I was at the height of my good fortune"; these are the last words of his autobiography. *Guzmán de Alfarache*, with its illusion of autobiography, ends with the repentance of the picaro, that is to say, his metaphorical death; the repentant Guzmán will write his life to set an example for others.

In dealing with his first moments in life the picaro dwells especially on his ancestry. Lázaro tells us that his father was a thieving miller, captured, tried, condemned, and sentenced, while his mother quickly became the concubine of a Negro slave. It is at this point that Lázaro sets out into the world. Guzmán de Alfarache, for his part, was the son of a Jewish, Genoese merchant, with the very serious consequences that such a background had in Golden Age Spain, given the national, suicidal obsession with "limpieza de sangre [blood purity]." As if these factors were not sufficiently alienating, the Genoese, Jewish merchant becomes a convert to Islam, marries a rich Moorish woman, steals all her money, escapes to Spain, and reconverts to Christianity. At this point he meets the woman who is to become Guzmán's mother. She is the concubine of a very rich and very old nobleman. Although her ancestry, as far as it can be traced, consists of whores, she deceives her old paramour with Guzmán's father, and Guzmán is, naturally, born out of wedlock.

The elements that the picaro wants to stress about his ancestry are those that will accentuate the sense of "infamy [a nativitate]." But, as can also be seen, the infamy of Lázaro is only social, whereas the infamy of Guzmán is social, racial, and religious. This gradual stress on the all-pervading infamy of the protagonist will become a characteristic of the genre as it unfolds in time, as has been richly demonstrated by the fine study of the late Marcel Bataillon.

The autobiography of someone who is an infamous scoundrel from birth cannot but have a very jaundiced outlook on society. The point of view of the picaro, as Francisco Rico has suggested, is exclusive and completely negative. This is of paramount importance to the texture of the picaresque novel as a genre, for the point of view of the picaro is the only functional one in his autobiography. This last characteristic is, of course, proper to all autobiographies as a literary genre. Furthermore, the autobiography of the picaro will be highly selective, another characteristic of the genre. In the case of Lázaro, for example, the speaker selects from his life only those elements that in his own opinion, will serve to explain his success in life. For Lázaro success in life consists of the fact that he no longer has to work for a living, because his wife is the concubine of a priest from Toledo.

That Cervantes knew well the models of the picaresque genre is a foregone conclusion. Although he paid no compliments to Mateo Alemán and his *Guzmán de Alfarache* (not even in his all-embracing literary catalogue of Spanish men of letters, which he entitled *Viaje del Parnaso*), this was due to the fact that *Guzmán* had preceded his *Don Quixote* and was its main competitor in the novelistic field. But Cervantes did mention and praise *Lazarillo de Tormes,* in a passage to which I shall return.

In the works of Cervantes we can collect a rich gallery of roguish types. Leaving aside the *Exemplary Novels,* two of his literary characters are very particular prototypes of the picaro as interpreted by his creative mind. The first one is Pedro de Urdemalas, the protagonist of a play of the same title, who winds up his life of roguish antics as the head of a tribe of gypsies, which should draw our minds subtly back to "La gitanilla." The other wonderful picaro created by Cervantes is Ginés de Pasamonte, a character in both parts of *Don Quixote,* a special and distinguishing characteristic since he is one of the very few characters, other than the two protagonists, to appear in both parts. In *Don Quixote* of 1605 Ginés de Pasamonte is a galley-slave, and his antics in that part will lead to a tremendous textual confusion that should not concern us today. Because of his many crimes Ginés has been sentenced to the galleys, but while in jail he has been writing his autobiography, which, as he says, will enter into direct competition with *Lazarillo de Tormes.* He is then asked if his autobiography is finished. He laughs this off, asking how he could have finished it when he is still alive.

This last observation is worth considering from a few different viewpoints. In the first place, Ginés alludes to his autobiography, but we never see it, it is unfinished. In point of fact, Cervantes never wrote any kind of autobiography, fictional or nonfictional, a point I will have to return to later on. In the second place, Ginés appears in the novel in midlife, as a full-fledged picaro, a tried and sentenced criminal; we do not follow his education in crime but rather see its consequences. And in the last place, the novel focuses on Ginés de Pasamonte at a time in his life when he is totally un-repentant—he is almost proud of being a galley-slave—a fact which places him at the opposite extreme from Guzmán de Alfarache, who had by then become the picaro par excellence. In the second part of *Don Quixote* Ginés de Pasamonte continues to be completely unrepentant. In 1615 Ginés makes his reappearance as Maese Pedro el titerero [Master Peter the Puppeteer], and in this guise he hoodwinks his audience, most particularly Don Quixote and Sancho Panza, his main victims in the first part.

I said that Cervantes had an obvious dislike for autobiography as a literary genre, since he never wrote one. The closest he came was in the first part of *Don Quixote,* in the story of the captive captain, and even then his story, told in the first person by the captain himself, centers on the episode of his captivity in Algiers and his escape. Before passing on to the analysis of the picaros in the *Exemplary Novels,* I want to approach briefly this Cervantine dislike for autobiography. As I said before, and this is by way of insisting on a basic truth, autobiography presents us with but one viewpoint, that of the author of the autobiography. In the course of the narrative other viewpoints might be presented, but they are alway subordinated to the teller's point of view, because of narrative exigencies if for no other reasons. That is to say, autobiography constitutes an extreme form of literary dogmatism, because it presents one point of view to the exclusion of all others.

José Ortega y Gasset, the famous twentieth-century Spanish philosopher, once said that truth is but a point of view. And if that point of view remains motionless, truth will inevitably be distorted, with parts of it out of focus; it will suffer. A conjunction of points of view, on the other hand, will enhance truth, will help to clear up its outline. In an intuitive and artistic way Cervantes knew this long before Ortega y Gasset; multiple points of view constitute the fundamental tenet of his narrative art. This is why he spurned autobiography, which is the presentation of truth and reality from a single point of view, without the possibility of a challenge. On the contrary, he favored dialogue, explicit or implicit dialogue, because dialogue, as Plato had so admirably demonstrated, is the presentation of two or more different points of view. If Cervantes had but known it, he would have enthusiastically subscribed to Plato's statement in the *Republic*: "Dialogue is the coping stone of the sciences."

This is why *Don Quixote* as a novel really gets under way only after the creation of Sancho Panza, who becomes immediately a verbal sparring partner for his master. From now on, nature, reality, and truth will be seen from at least two different points of view. This, of course, is enhanced by the hallucinatory nature of Don Quixote's mind, which distorts reality while in the process of apprehending it, whereas Sancho's prosaic nature refuses any distortion whatsoever. This is why *Don Quixote* has become the greatest novel-dialogue ever written. The novel is conceived and executed as an exchange of viewpoints, as an immense dialogue, which can take place even at a great distance, as when Sancho, in the second part, goes to govern the famous island of Barataria. While discharging this illustrious duty Sancho is aided and abetted by the ever-present advice and letters of his master, which is a way of maintaining alive an implicit dialogue. There is no point in illustrating the almost eternal, explicit dialogue that occurs between master and servant at other points in the book, so full of merry verbal pranks and most serious intellectual queries.

This is another way of saying that Cervantes's mind had an intellectual thirst for dualities, dualities at minimum, because he considered the presentation of a single viewpoint a pauperization of reality. This was the great discovery of *Don Quixote,* and Cervantes would remain faithful to it throughout his creative career. This is why he could never bring himself to write a picaresque novel, which in its autobiographic, canonical form represented precisely that pauperization of reality that inhibited his creative imagination. The intellectual necessity for multiple viewpoints very likely explains Cervantes's love for the theater, an early love that he still avowed very late in life, when he published a selection of plays in 1615, the year before he died. In the prologue he wrote for this selection, "Ocho comedias y ocho entremeses nunca representados" ["Eight Comedies and Eight Interludes Never Shown"], he confirms much of what has just been said.

There is no point in going any further into Cervantes's dual intellectual necessities or his demand for multiple viewpoints. It can be seen even in the titles of so many of his texts. I will choose but a few, taken exclusively from his *Exemplary Novels*—"The Two Damsels," for instance, or "Rinconete y Cortadillo," or "The Dialogue of the Dogs," The last one, to be sure, appears in explicit dialogue form. All this should explain why Cervantes had an actual abhorrence to writing a truly picaresque novel.

This is not to say that Cervantes restrained himself from experimenting with the picaresque genre. I have already mentioned some of the wonderful picaresque types he created. The creation of these types was bound to lead him to experiment with the genre, to see if it could yield the possibility of multiple viewpoints. One thing to remember, at this juncture, is the fact that from the start of his literary career Cervantes demonstrated a wonderfully fertile, experimental turn of mind. One must only look back to *La Galatea,* his first published novel, a pastoral, which at the opening of its idyllic, bucolic world presents a brutal murder of one shepherd by another shepherd.

The frustrated autobiography of Ginés de Pasamonte could be considered one such experiment with the picaresque genre. But in the *Exemplary Novels* we have two such full-scale experiments, which it is time to consider. I am referring to "Rinconete y Cortadillo" and to "The Dialogue of the Dogs." I have mentioned the fact that "Rinconete y Cortadillo" is known to us in two different versions, one printed in 1613 and one before 1605, both contained in the manuscript of Francisco Porras de la Cámara. I repeat this because it demonstrates the early intellectual need that Cervantes felt to experiment with the picaresque genre. And also because it demonstrates the artful care that Cervantes took with his literary experiments.

"Rinconete y Cortadillo" tells the story of two teenagers who meet by happenstance at an inn in La Mancha and decide to make their way together to Sevilla. There they perform some minor thefts in San Salvador Square. But they are detected by Ganchuelo, a member of the fraternity of thieves and criminals presided over by Monipodio; Ganchuelo decides to take them to the house of Monipodio to be examined, pay their dues, and join the fraternity. This is precisely what happens. The last two-thirds of the novel are dedicated to the description of the kind of human beings who attend a soirée in the patio of Monipodio's house. That is to say, we are dragged into the heart of the criminal life of Sevilla, which is an extension of the kind of life into which Guzmán de Alfarache was born. But the presentation of this world could not be more diametrically opposed to the technique adopted by Mateo Alemán. The consideration of these differences will serve to emphasize the dimensions and scope of Cervantes's experiment with the picaresque genre.

From the very first words of Cervantes's tale we can detect a veritable gulf between his concept of the picaresque and that of his predecessors: "One of these hot days of summer two lads chanced to find themselves in the Molinillo Inn." This is to say, the fate of these two boys is going to be molded by chance ("acaso," in the original). But the action, the intervention, of chance, fortune, or whatever you want to call it is unthinkable in the picaresque genre. The life of the picaro is governed exclusively by predetermination, indeed by predestination, as is made only too clear by the morose care with which the speaker describes his criminal ancestry. The picaro is a criminal because he cannot be any other way; he faces a destiny of crime because he was predestined to it by his ancestry. To a certain extent this literary predestination can be seen as a result of the original conception of the picaresque novel as an antichivalric novel. Amadís de Gaula, the greatest chivalric hero produced in Spain, was predestined to be such, for he was the son of the heroic king Perión de Gaula and of the most beautiful princess Elisena. Similarly, Lazarillo de Tormes was predestined to be a petty criminal, because his father was a thieving miller and his mother something just this side of being a prostitute. Chance cannot play any part whatsoever in any picaresque novel; if it did, then by chance the picaro might turn out to be good—in other words, he might cease to be a picaro. Hence the novel would lose its raison d'être. The conversion of the picaro, Guzmán, for example, has nothing to do with chance; it is, instead, allied with the contemporary theological polemic *de auxiliis*. But from its first line "Rinconete y Cortadillo" opens its doors widely to the action of chance, because Cervantes, as I have demonstrated repeatedly, had an almost religious respect for human free will in its literary representation. The life of Don Quixote richly demonstrates this: on account of physiological reasons he becomes mad, and after he is mad he chooses to call himself Don Quixote—but much later, on his deathbed, he chooses freely to abdicate, to give up, his freely chosen identity of Don Quixote.

The role of chance in the first line of "Rinconete y Cortadillo" serves a purpose analogous to free will in the world of Don Quixote. But it also serves its own very definite and subtle literary purpose. At the end of the novel Rinconete "made up his mind to advise his comrade that they should not linger in that vicious and evil life." In other words, Cervantes's picaros are free to abandon their evil way of life at any time they feel like it; the entrance into, and the exit from, the picaresque life of Sevilla is an exercise of the will for Rinconete and Cortadillo. Neither Lázaro nor Guzmán were given, or could have been given, that option, for the reasons already mentioned.

The criminal life into which Lázaro and Guzmán were born is described only from their viewpoint, since each is writing his own autobiography, as is the case in the canonical picaresque novel. But, obviously, such is not the case with "Rinconete y Cortadillo," which spurns the simplistic approach to literary reality by having a double protagonist and, consequently, a double perspective on literary reality. For example, upon their entrance into Sevilla each youth enters the life of crime in his separate way, and the narrative thread will at first follow one and then the other. During the long episode on the patio of Monipodio's house, the literary viewpoint will alternate between youthful protagonists. And at the end of the novel the literary point of view will rest squarely with Rinconete. The last paragraph begins: "Although nothing but a boy, Rinconete had a good head on his shoulders, and was decent by nature." Toward the end of the same paragraph the author intervenes to tell us that "we must leave for some other occasion the account of his life and adventures," with the implied promise of a future unicity of literary viewpoint. Let us note in passing that this personal intervention of the author in the novel, this sort of narrative distance and control, is impossible by definition in the picaresque novel, where the distance is permanently fixed by the autobiographer's point of view.

Another significant divergence from the canonical picaresque lies in the fact that the novela picaresca is eminently an urban novel, because to practice his tricks the picaro needs the city mobs. By contrast, "Rinconete y Cortadillo" begins with a completely rural setting: "One of those hot days of summer two lads chanced to find themselves in the Molinillo Inn, which stands on the outskirts of the famed plains of Alcudia on the way from Castiel to Andalusia." Only after this significant start does the novel move leisurely to its urban setting of Sevilla.

For the sake of brevity I will point out one last divergence, this time between Cervantes's tale and *Guzmán de Alfarache*. Upon leaving his house, Guzmán's first adventure is his encounter with a mule driver who victimizes him and steals from him. Guzmán asks for the help of justice, but gets no redress, which demonstrates his complete impotence before the world. He has to learn and practise deceit in order to defend himself in the world. The first adventure of Cervantes's youthful protagonists also involves a mule driver at the Molinillo Inn, but here it is the boys who trick the mule driver, steal his money, and when attacked by the mule driver defend themselves successfully against him. The importance of the different dénouement to identical adventures is considerable. The young boys do not need to learn deceit in order to defend themselves successfully against the world; they fall back upon their combined strength and succeed; they are self-sufficient. At the bottom of this significant difference lies the fact that on account of Guzmán's early impotence and defeat, the tone of his tale is pessimistic, melancholy, and bleak. But the early show of self-sufficiency and victory makes the tone of the lives of Cervantes's characters happy, gay, graceful.

Now to "The Dialogue of the Dogs," which I consider to be Cervantes's other experiment with the form of the canonical picaresque tale in the *Exemplary Novels*—and by far the most ingenious and artful. The audacity of this experiment is extraordinary. To point out just some of the most obvious differences with the canonical picaresque, one need only recall that the protagonists are not human beings but rather two dogs, a most original and unique development of an Aesopic fable. The lonely protagonist of the novela picaresca is replaced by two, and its autobiographical form by a dialogue, with its consequent alternation of viewpoints.

But Cervantes has left enough characteristics of the picaresque genre in "The Dialogue of the Dogs" to make it easily identifiable as his most audacious and daring experiment with that genre. I will go one step farther and state that "The Dialogue of the Dogs" is Cervantes's travesty, ironization, and reworking of Mateo Alemán's *Guzmán de Alfarache*. Some other points of comparison will emerge later, but for the moment I want to stress only one. A major criticism addressed to the *Guzmán de Alfarache* is that each adventure is followed by lengthy passages of moralizing and philosophizing, passages invariably longer than the adventure itself. To be sure, this characteristic makes the reading of *Guzmán de Alfarache* quite an arduous experience. Of course, adventure and moral are all related from the same first-person viewpoint, with its categorical denial of any possible variation in the narrative tone. But in "The Dialogue of the Dogs" Berganza tells his own life from the moment of birth, with a passing reference to his ancestry ("this would lead me to believe . . . that my parents must have been mastiffs"), but his main role is to attend to the narrative of his life. He does not usually stop to philosophize or moralize about himself or his adventures. Such philosophical commentaries are usually supplied by Cipión. Such alternating viewpoints and functions give variety and spice to the sum total of the narrative, solving in the most dexterous and innovative way the enormous artistic problem that Alemán had created for himself in adopting the single point of view of an autobiographer's narrative.

As I have just mentioned, as in any picaresque novel Berganza begins the story of his life with a reference to his ancestry. He tells us, also, that he was born in Sevilla, like Guzmán; like Guzmán he was born into a life of crime. Berganza was born in the slaughterhouse of Sevilla, which he describes in the following terms: "All who work there, from the lowest to the highest, are persons of elastic conscience, cruel, fearing neither man nor devil; most of them are married without benefit of the clergy; they are birds of prey, and they and their doxies live on what they steal."

In a way analogous to Guzmán de Alfarache, the first adventure of Berganza consists of being tricked and duped, not by a mule driver, but by a beautiful girl, in a way somewhat reminiscent of *La Celestina*. The deceit into which he has fallen brings about the wrath of his first master, and gets him into deep trouble with the master, a butcher from Sevilla. Berganza runs away to save his skin and goes into the service of some shepherds, safely removed from the city. This suggests two characteristics of "The Dialogue of the Dogs," each worthy of comment. First, with each new master he serves, Berganza changes his name. At various times he is known as Gavilán, Barcino, Montiel, or Berganza, the name under which he is known in Valladolid. I have discussed at length this characteristic in relation to *Don Quixote,* and my conclusions will remain the same. Cervantes gives his protagonist various names, or, better still, the protagonist gives himself various names, to identify some deep-set, vital change. From the semianonymity of the beginning (what was his real name after all? Quijada? Quesada? Quejana?), the protagonist proceeds to call himself Don Quijote de la Mancha, and at various times in his life he will be known as The Knight of the Sad Countenance, The Knight of the Lions, Shepherd Quijotiz, and finally, on his deathbed, he will identify himself forever as Alons Quijano the Good. This *polinomasia,* this changing of personal names, has its roots in the Judeo-Christian tradition, and we know that Israel is the name given in the Old Testament to Jacob after he wrestled the angel of the Lord. In the New Testament, Saul of Tarsus was a bitter Christian-hater, but after the vision on the road to Damascus and his conversion, he came to call himself Paul. The use to which Cervantes puts this form of polionomasia is analogous, in the sense that the change of personal name differentiates the various stages of a man's life, or of a dog's life, for that matter. This, of course, goes against the grain of the picaresque, because the life of the picaro is one continuous reality, that of the life of crime.

The second characteristic that I want to point out is that in telling his autobiography we see Berganza serving various masters. Beside the two already mentioned, Berganza serves, to mention just a few, a rich merchant in Sevilla, a constable, a soldier, and a dramatist. This characteristic of the picaro serving a chain of masters became canonical in the picaresque genre as early as *Lazarillo de Tormes,* where we see the protagonist first serving a blind beggar, then the stingy priest of Maqueda, then the hungry and miserable nobleman of Toledo, then a friar of dubious reputation. In fact, each of the seven chapters of *Lazarillo de Tormes* presents the protagonist serving a different master. This characteristic became so ingrained in the picaresque genre that it was to serve as the title of a late Spanish picaresque novel: *Alonso, mozo de muchos amos* [*Alonso, Servant of Many Masters*], by Jerónimo de Alcalá, who published the first part in 1626 with such great success that he quickly had to publish a second one later the same year. To this extent, Cervantes is quite willing to go along with classical features of the canonical picaresque. This one feature he found most useful to air his views on literature, narrative technique, contemporary society, and even the burning issue of the day, the expulsion of converted Moors, which was going on at the very time of the publication of the *Exemplary Novels*.

There is no question, having read "The Dialogue of the Dogs" with the picaresque structure in mind, that Cervantes utilizes the novela picaresca with the same overwhelming irony as he utilizes in *Don Quixote* the romances of chivalry. There were standard situations and human types in both genres that he could use, imitate, parody, ironize. He did all of these things to the canonical picaresque in his minor masterpiece of "The Dialogue of the Dogs." Maybe the most valuable lesson that this tale can present to us lies in the demonstration that Cervantes could put to some remarkable uses the autobiographical form of the picaresque. The truth of the matter is that in "The Dialogue of the Dogs" he invented a new literary genre of such extraordinary novelty that it has had no followers: the autobiography in dialogue form.

RUTH EL SAFFAR

Tracking the Trickster
in the Works of Cervantes

Certain realms of human experience expose us to powers of the spirit which reveal, or suggest, the existence of pure forms, uncontaminated by the presence of neutralizing alloys. Philosophers, poets, and psychologists throughout the ages have intuited the presence of such unalloyed forces, which they have variously called essences, noumena, gods, and archetypes. Whether psychic forces are entities with their own discrete reality or are abstractions created by the analytic mind in order better to describe the phenomena of the real world need not be decided here. For the purposes of literary study, it is enough to grant that certain terms have achieved sufficient common currency to be useful in discussing specific texts. The objective reality of the referents of such terms is a matter that must be taken up elsewhere. The term that will be called into service for the present study is "trickster," a term much more frequently used by anthropologists and psychologists than by students of literature, though it has crept into critical texts from time to time.

The figure of trickster has become widely known since Paul Radin published his study of the trickster cycles in North American Indian stories. Carl Jung, whose essay "On the Psychology of the Trickster Figure" is appended in the Radin book, has also given the term depth and resonance. For Jung, the trickster is an archetypal figure whose chief characteristics are his unconsciousness, his unrelatedness, and his stupidity. The trickster represents

---

From *Symposium* 37, no. 2 (1983). © 1983 by the Helen Dwight Reid Educational Foundation.

what Jung has also called the shadow—a figure which can cause all sorts of damage when unrecognized, but which can, if confronted in the full light of consciousness, point the way to a higher integration, to what he calls the savior. In his shadow form, the trickster personifies all those traits of personality that consciousness has suppressed. Since the trickster exists in compensatory relation to the conscious personality, he is most likely to make his presence felt in the face of a highly constricted conscious attitude. Sly, protean, amoral and anarchical, the trickster will erupt from time to time to expose the limitations of a consciousness too circumscribed to be appropriate to the whole of experience.

In the Middle Ages, when society was ordered according to strict monarchical and ecclesiastical hierarchies, the trickster was abundantly evident in such public events as the Feast of Fools, Carnival, and the Feast of The Ass, events which became so popular and so violent that the Church eventually went to great lengths to stamp them out. Mikhail Bakhtin portrays Europe in the Middle Ages as a place in which laughter and carnival regularly exploded the myths of hierarchy that otherwise ordered the world. The hilarity that trickster produced provided a much needed counterbalance to the solemnity that prevailed in a rigified world order. The intense period of clerical reform that characterized the sixteenth century in Europe worked to subdue, among other things, trickster's more disruptive appearances in Carnival. But trickster himself is not so easily dispensed with. In fact, if we are to believe Jung when he says that trickster is an archetype and that he works through the unconscious to compensate for an imbalance in consciousness, we can well expect that when the front door is closed he will come around through the back.

Sociological and anthropological studies of the sixteenth and seventeenth centuries reveal a tremendous activity related to magic, superstition, and witchery running right through the period of persecutions, culminating, as is well known, in the witch-hunting and heretic-burning fevers of seventeenth-century Europe. Caro Baroja gives some idea of the kinds of collective activity in which the trickster was engaged.

We can also find, not surprisingly, traces of magic and superstition in the literature of the Spanish Golden Age. Cervantes's works are a veritable catalogue, as a close look at "El retablo de las maravillas" ["The Marvelous Pageant"] and "La cueva de Salamanca" ["The Cave of Salamanca"], *Don Quixote* and the *Persiles* would reveal. *La Celestina,* and the works of Quevedo and Calderón are also rich in data regarding the shapes and guises trickster took in the collective experience of the sixteenth and seventeenth centuries in Spain.

But the issue here is not to observe the traces of the trickster as a datum of sociological, historical or anthropological interest. One thing is the trickster's changing role as rebel and disruptor in the highly conflicted historical period of the Renaissance; another is the way he manifests through the consciousness of some of its most evolved individuals. Edith Kern points out that the male and female tricksters "seem to share Hermes' desire to oppose society and its gods whenever these favor the strong and disregard the weak. Yet their triumphs as well as their defeats—like those of all tricksters—belong to the realm of fantasy and imagination and are far from being mimetic." Trickster may best be understood in his many facets by a look at the way he manifests himself in works of art.

Trickster opposes established society, and operates wherever desire is hidden. And yet we need to keep firmly in mind that the opposites are always conjoined in this world. Desire is an integral, if suppressed aspect of established society. What happens in the dark recesses of the collective order has consequences which will manifest in the full light of its public face. Trickster's disruptions, so understood, are not all bad. Leo Salingar notes that although the trickster (in Greek Old Comedy) seems often motivated by self-interest, his public import is evident. He serves "to revive the peace and prosperity of the city, to purge it of false policies, wrong-headed philosophy or bad poetry." The Old Comedy dramatizes the opposition between the up-start trickster and the members of the old regime, who decry the trickster's shamelessness and insolence.

There is in the trickster, then, something that allies him with the most frightful antisocial forces, and which yet associates him with healing. Such is the role of the shaman, a figure who embodies the trickster, and who, working with mask and illusion, serves in tribal societies as healer. Such is also the role of many female tricksters, some of whom Frederick D'Armas has described [in *The Invisible Mistress*]. The task undertaken by the trickster in every case is to create an alternate reality in which the rules of everyday life no longer apply. Trickster's alternate reality renders helpless those individuals who are deeply identified with social hierarchies and values.

There is clearly something magical, something healing about entering the nonrational world where desire has its home. Lévi-Strauss, commenting on tribal societies which make extensive use of masks, notes that the primary significance of wearing a mask is not to hide the wearer's everyday personality but to change and transcend it, by bringing him into contact with images of the supranormal powers in nature, in the animal world, and in the dead.

Trickster, for better or for worse, is the guide to the unconscious. He does indeed activate another realm, one we could call fantasy, dream, desire, fear, hell, or even heaven. Whatever the context, he lifts the mask of reality from our waking world by donning a mask of his own. No one in Cervantes's vast gallery of characters better shows the effects of trickster than Don Quixote himself. It is trickster operating within him that drives him off his own beaten path and that causes him to put on the mask of knight-errant. And it is through that mask that his everyday personality is changed and transcended.

The Don Quixote of part 2 experiences a deeply troubling sense of being in masquerade as knight-errant. In the costumed party that is *Don Quixote* part 2, Don Quixote is exposed to successive images of magic, disguise, play-acting, the animal world, and the dead. Altisidora, for example, literally takes him through hell, after he has been stripped of his armor, trampled by pigs and bulls, and ridiculed by dancing ladies and carousing townspeople in Barcelona. It is clear by part 2 that Alonso Quijano's decision to wear the mask of knight-errant is now understood by Cervantes as the means by which the personality of his hero will change. *Don Quixote* part 2 is for its main character an experience in the world of tricks and delusions whose effect is to destroy, not for the world, but for himself, the "máquina mal fundada de los caballerescos libros [ill-founded machinery of chivalric romances]" [*Don Quixote,* part 1, prologue. This and all subsequent quotations from *Don Quixote* are taken from the edition by Juan Bautista Avalle-Arce (Madrid: Alhambra, 1979).], which have taken such a firm hold over his consciousness.

Although Don Quixote is very much a figure activated by trickster in both parts of the novel, his relation to that unconscious disruptive element differs interestingly from the one part to the other. But we need not focus exclusively on the personality of the hero himself to understand the way things have changed from 1605 to 1615. Cervantes has made it easy for us by providing two glimpses, one in each part of his novel, of the trickster figure himself. That figure, the *only* minor character to appear in both parts of *Don Quixote,* is none other than Ginés de Pasamonte.

In part 1, Ginés shows his trickster characteristics in his penchant for thievery, his slipperiness, his skill with language, and his role as would-be author of the story of his life. In order to understand him properly with relation to the hero, we must recognize that Ginés represents in pure form many traits also characteristic of Don Quixote: both are escapees, devotees of language, potential authors, and characters who are in essence alienated from the social order and in rebellion against it. The difference is that Ginés comes to us unencumbered by other complicating traits of character. All we see of him is his slippery antisocial nature. We could say of Ginés, then, that he embodies the trickster that works indirectly through Don Quixote.

Cervantes has given us a basis of inquiry into the trickster through

Ginés. To understand the role of the trickster in the entire work, we do well to take a close look at those places in it where Don Quixote meets Ginés face to face. Don Quixote first finds Ginés in chapter 22 of part 1, among the galley-slaves he has determined to set free. Ginés displays the wit and ingenuity appropriate to the trickster in his brief conversation with Don Quixote, but reveals his utter disregard of his liberator a moment later by stoning him and later stealing Sancho's donkey. The trickster whom Don Quixote releases burns quickly, like a brush fire out of control, when once free of his chains. Far from showing gratitude and submission, Don Quixote's inner trickster turns on him, making the main character's already uncertain existence away from home even more precarious. Don Quixote's encounter in part 1 with the trickster results in pushing him further from society, into the wilds, where he will fall quite literally into the labyrinth of fiction, from which only fiction (in the form of Dorotea's Micomicona) can extract him. Through Ginés we understand that Don Quixote is trickster's fool. Don Quixote has set the trickster free without understanding him. As an unconscious, autonomous figure, the trickster has literally robbed him of his goods and led him toward his destruction. The same unrelated, antisocial forces are at work, needless to say, on the other characters in part 1—Grisóstomo and Cardenio, for example—and provoke similarly disastrous results.

But let us look more closely at Ginés himself. Like the picaresque predecessors to whom Ginés explicitly alludes, Ginés in part 1 is caught in a dialectic of rebellion and dispossession that exposes an unconscious attachment to the dominant social values, including an unconscious *acceptance* of the alienated position to which society has relegated him.

Ginés, who appears as a pure trickster figure, contains within him the very hated authority of the social order against which he is constantly rebelling. As mentioned earlier, each element in the conflict of opposing forces contains, unrecognized, its opposite within it. The conflict cannot be resolved because each participant in it is governed not by an external other, but by the unconscious other within. The endless nature of the conflict is pointed out by Nancy Regalado [*Essays in Criticism* 16 (1976)], who notes that the trickster's desire is insatiable "because what he wants does not and cannot belong to him." The trickster, therefore, is confined to a tale that is episodic, repetitive, inconclusive in structure, in which he succeeds in acquiring forbidden objects only to have them taken away. What he is really enacting, as we shall see, is a battle between consciousness and the unconscious, a battle that can only end when one seeks to take possession not of the goods of the other, but of oneself.

The short step between the trickster and the hero can only be taken when the subject realizes that what he desires does not in fact already belong to him. In order to make that step, however, the subject must undergo a total revaluation of his attitude toward himself and society, a revaluation which in Cervantes's case occupied the whole of his writing life. In 1605 Cervantes was not ready to give legitimacy to the desires of anyone—from Don Quixote right on down to Ginés. Like Ginés, in fact—Cesáreo Bandera has seen this well—Cervantes reveals through *Don Quixote* part 1 his own unconscious overvaluation of society's values, and along with it, his unconscious *attraction* to the desires of his "mad" hero. The dialectic between desire and the social order that ranges across the whole of *Don Quixote* part 1 and burrows into every episode and sub-episode of it, tells the tale of its author's own imbalance. Like Lázaro's tale, like Ginés's autobiography, the story of Don Quixote's exploits cannot truly come to an end in 1605. As with the trickster's tale that Nancy Regalado describes, *Don Quixote* part 1 itself "tends to break apart into separate episodes [which do not] lead functionally to the end of the narration, but only to its own conclusion."

The alternations between rebellion and captivity reveal the compulsive, unconscious nature of the dialectic in which Ginés and Don Quixote are engaged. The sharp commentary Cervantes makes of the picaresque through Ginés—that it is unending because it is too attached to the life of its teller—is surprisingly applicable, therefore, to *Don Quixote* part 1 itself. This is not to say that *Don Quixote* part 1 is a picaresque tale. It is, however—as can be seen in its lack of conclusion, and in its episodic, unintegrated nature—a work in which the trickster's disruptive presence is evident. *Don Quixote* part 1 is a work, in other words, in which the archetypal struggle between desire and the social order remains untranscended; in which the world is still conceived of as a place consisting of "good guys" and "bad guys"; in which the essential identity between the self and the other has yet to be fully realized by the author.

Ginés, though still very much the trickster, has gained respectability by part 2 of *Don Quixote*. He appears there, in the guise of Master Peter, as puppeteer and magician. Jung has said of the trickster as forerunner of the savior that he is "God, man, and animal all at once. He is both sub-human and super-human, a bestial and divine being. . . ." Ginés in part 2, as in part 1, seems to sum up the nature of desire as it operates in the novel. He shows the animal side of his nature through the monkey that serves as his seer. As puppeteer he plays a god-like role, and as Master Peter he represents the man through whom the bestial and the divine are expressed.

The effect of Ginés's—Master Peter's—presence on Don Quixote is further to confound that character already severely disoriented by such events as Dulcinea's transformation and his experience in Montesinos's Cave. Don Quixote exposes his doubts to Master Peter, and is dumbfounded to discover that Master Peter, through his divinatory monkey, knows all his secrets. The reaction is not unlike that by Don Quixote when he learned in chapter 3 of part 2 that a book containing events that happened to him when he was alone had been published. Master Peter with his talking monkey takes a place in Don Quixote's mind beside that of the sage who is his author.

Ginés deepens his implied relation to the author in the next episode, when he exchanges his role as magician for that of puppeteer. He demonstrates his ability to manipulate Don Quixote through the unconscious, to reduce him, in fact, to the status of puppet. On his puppet stage, Ginés presents the world of knights and ladies that dominates Don Quixote's consciousness. He focuses in his story, however, on the problem of the captive lady and the lackadaisical knight that are the main characters of Don Quixote's own inner drama, as the dream in the Cave of Montesinos revealed. It is no wonder that Don Quixote finally jumps out of his seat in the audience and onto the puppet stage, hoping somehow to alter the course of the action taking place there. But it is also no wonder that he fails. He is a puppet himself, pulled by the one who rules him, the "Lord of Misrule," trickster himself.

The Ginés of part 2 shows that for him desire is no longer at loggerheads with the social order except in a very secondary way. As Master Peter, Ginés earns money; he is welcomed wherever he goes; he gives people something they want rather than taking what they have away from them. Ginés, in other words, is now desire's master, not its plaything. Through magic and artistry he represents to others the mechanics of the world of desire. Through the puppets he reveals the automatism of the actions that take place when one is caught in that mechanism.

Don Quixote, of course, is the most extreme example of a character caught in a trickster's net. If part 1 offered hosts of secondary characters who re-enacted in different keys Don Quixote's own rebelliousness, part 2 is filled with minor characters who fall into the familiar pattern of the "burlador burlado," the trickster tricked. It happens whenever an automatic re-action intrudes in a situation that the character knows otherwise is contrived. Like Freud's slips of the tongue, the automatic response reveals a gap in consciousness through which the unconscious escapes. I have detailed instances of this elsewhere. It needs only be said here that never once is Ginés's guise penetrated by another character. He walks into and out of the inn as Master Peter, his own desires as Ginés de Pasamonte kept entirely out of sight. As Master Peter he has made the whole world this theater, of which the puppet stage is a perfect simulacrum. Don Quixote, as long as he refuses to see the trickster who rules his life, will be as effective in achieving his desires as he is when he slashes away at plaster puppets on a tiny stage.

In part 2 we can see a marked change in the nature of the trickster. He allows us, as George Haley has shown, to see the way author, character, and reader function in the work itself, and he also shows us something interesting about the relation of the unconscious to consciousness, or of desire to the social order, as that dialectic is represented in part 2. Cervantes reveals through the confrontation of Don Quixote and the trickster in part 2 that the trickster—who represents desire and the unconscious—knows more about Don Quixote than Don Quixote knows about him. In part 1 the two were mutually opaque, combative forces. In part 2, Ginés is to Don Quixote as bullfighter to bull. He stands aside and lets his antagonist flail away at empty obstacles, much as the untrained combatant did when confronted with the master fencer in chapter 19 of part 2. The trickster, now an image of the author, is fully in charge of Don Quixote's world in part 2, leading him inexorably to the point where he will turn his sword against himself, and, dying, be reborn as Alonso Quijano the Good.

A beautiful example of what is expected of Don Quixote, and what he cannot really do until chapter 73 of part 2, is offered through Basilio in chapter 21 of part 2. Like Master Peter, Basilio has learned to transform desire into art, and has shown, in the process, that, through art, the trickster, otherwise dangerous, turns ally, if not savior. Basilio finds himself caught in the typical triangular love situation. His beloved, Quiteria, has been promised to a richer rival. Unlike Cardenio, who faced the same problem in part 1, however, Basilio takes charge by deciding to *act the part* of the distraught lover. Throwing himself on his sword at the wedding ceremony, he asks, and is granted as his "dying wish" that Quiteria be given to him in marriage. When the vows are stated, he jumps up and declares himself the winner, not by miracle, as the onlookers believe, but by trickery. He quite literally turned the sword on himself. But what he killed in his mock suicide was not his being, but the *image* of that frustrated desirer projected on him by an audience accustomed to the illusions of the social order.

When Ginés in part 1 said that the book of his exploits could not end because his life had not, he was saying more than he knew. The trickster in Don Quixote, Cervantes seems to have known in 1615, had to die in order for the book about Alonso Quijano to come to an end.

The trick that makes Ginés successful is his ability to separate illusion and reality. When the two are *not* kept clearly apart, the devil in all his legions comes into the house. The case is clearly made with, for example,

Cardenio, who was unable to decide whether Luscinda's "yes" in promise of marriage to Fernando was said in truth or falsehood. In the "Curioso impertinente" ["Tale of Foolish Curiosity"] illusion and reality overlap in such confusion that eventually the one is taken for the other and all who are engaged in their dangerous juxtaposition are destroyed.

Illusion, as Cesáreo Bandera has pointed out in the introductory chapter to his *Mimesis conflictiva,* is the realm of the gods. Unleashed in the world of society, those gods—those unconscious forces—are capable of incredible violence. Cervantes has shown the process well in his one-act play "El ratablo de las maravillas." Chanfallas and Chirinos present themselves in the play as theater managers capable not only of manipulating village after village for their own gain, but of throwing its citizens into chaos by working on nothing other than the villagers' own suppressed fears. Telling the town magistrates that their theater is visible only to those who are neither bastards nor *conversos,* Chanfallas and Chirinos bring onto their imaginary stage rats, lions, and torrents of magical rain, all through the power of suggestion. The most responsible members of the village, controlled by their fears, act exactly as if they were puppets on Master Peter's stage.

The lesson seems to be clear enough. If the demons on the underside of society remain hidden, they can be manipulated by anyone who understands them. They can be set loose, like the pigs and bulls that trampled Don Quixote in part 2, to tear down all the values that society holds dear. The magician and the artist are simply the ones who have become aware of their own unconscious, and who therefore *recognize* the mechanics of desire.

We have looked so far at the trickster, both as an unconscious force working through a basically unconscious fool figure—as in the case with Don Quixote—and as a character who has identified with the unconscious and who appears as deceiver or manipulator, as with Ginés de Pasamonte and with Chanfallas and Chirinos. Both roles are destructive, bringing into the social realm forces that society has, with good reason, built itself up to avoid. The question then emerges, since the trickster is such an essential figure in art: Can the trickster work through a character for positive ends, or through an artist with beneficial results? In the prologue to his *Exemplary Novels,* published in 1613, Cervantes claimed for his work a socially valuable purpose. He said, "Heles dado nombre de *ejemplares,* y si bien lo miras, no hay ninguna de quien no se pueda sacar algún ejemplo provechoso; y si no fuera por no alargar este sujeto, quizá te mostrara el sabroso y honesto fruto que se podría sacar, así de todas juntas como de cada una de por sí [I have given them the name *exemplary,* and if you read well, there is not one of them that does not offer some beneficial example; and if it weren't for my

not wishing to belabor the issue, perhaps I would show you the delicious
and honest fruit which you could find in them, all of them together or each
one by itself]."

The purpose, however, is not didacticism in an obvious sense. From all
that has been said so far it seems clear that didacticism of the sort someone
like Avellaneda, the author of the spurious second part of *Don Quixote,*
might condone is far from Cervantes's mind. The instruction that Cervantes's
late works offer is clearly distinguished from either the socioeconomic or the
spiritual. In the same prologue to the *Novelas ejemplares,* Cervantes adds:
"Sí, que no siempre se está en los templos, no siempre se ocupan los ora-
torios, no siempre se asiste a los negocios. Horas hay de recreación, donde
el afligido espíritu descanse [Yes, one is not always in temples, nor occupying
oratories, not always engaged in business. There is a time for recreation,
when the afflicted spirit may rest]."

The sense of Cervantes's often discussed commentary in the prologue
to *Novelas ejemplares* is that a work of art must be true to itself as a work
of art. Its role, as Ginés demonstrates in his presentation of himself as Master
Peter, is to *represent* desire, and not allow desire, unchecked, to express
through it. As thief, Ginés ritually failed because his disguise and skill were
always being used in the service of his own conflicted unconscious aspirations. Desire is the expression of lack, and if one acts out of desire alone,
sooner or later—the untranscended dialectic of part 1 shows this—one is
caught in the very lack one thinks one is filling. That is why the rogue is
always taking something that is not rightfully his. Unconsciously, the rogue
identifies with the social order that rejects him. Defining himself in their
terms, he sees himself as an outsider whose desires are basically illegitimate.

As Master Peter, Ginés was successful because he was no longer pro-
jecting his own desire into the world, but exposing, instead, the mechanics
by which desire works in the world. He could only do that by distinguishing
clearly the boundaries between reality—his hunger, his needs as Ginés de
Pasamonte—and illusion: the world of desire. It is here that Cervantes as
moralist can be understood. Cervantes's effort throughout his career was to
put space between himself as author and the world of desire that his works
revealed. In *Don Quixote* part 1 the transparency of the effort—the multiple
layers of authors, their ambiguity and lack of internal consistency—betrays
his failure. The hostility toward the social order so evident in the Prologue
to part 1 does find its way into the work itself, showing up in the unredeemed
nature of both hero and world, in the absurdity of desire, and the equal
absurdity of the social order which would deny it.

The highest representation of a character who has learned to disidentify with desire and its obstacles appears in the form of the clairvoyant Soldino in book 3 of the *Persiles*. The wise old man Soldino, for whom present, past, and future are as one, and who has passed through the phases of soldier and man of letters to that of hermit, completes the series of trickster figures who appear in Cervantes's works. Soldino says of the cave and hermitage in which he lives: "Aquí, huyendo de la guerra, hallé la paz; la hambre que en ese mundo de alla arriba . . . tenía, halló aquí la hartura . . . aquí soy yo señor de mí mismo . . . [Here, fleeing from war, I found peace; the hunger I felt in that world above . . . here found satiety . . . here I am master of myself . . .]." Unlike the pícaro, he realizes, in other words, that in truth there are no prohibitions, no forbidden objects. The delights of life are *rightfully* his. The hero and heroine who meet him on their journey to Rome represent the process by which one *discovers* the emptiness of the dialectic of desire and its obstacles.

How did Cervantes reach the point where such a work as the *Persiles* was posssible, where the dialectics of desire could be circumvented? The best place to look for an answer is in that double *novela* with which he closes his collection of exemplary stories, the "Casamiento engañoso" ["The Deceitful Marriage"] and the "Coloquio de los perros" ["The Dialogue of the Dogs"]. It is there that we find the clearest image of the process by which the artist is reborn out of the rogue. In that portrait, we shall come to see how closely allied for Cervantes are literature and morality, or rather, how important to both is *integrity,* in the essential sense of that word.

Both the "Casamiento engañoso" and the "Coloquio de los perros" represent the trickster in primitive aspect, and each shows how, out of the shambles of illusory desire, a new figure, in the role of author, can emerge. The double novela at the end of the *Novelas ejemplares* is so important in the subtle alchemy of Cervantes's work that it is worth taking a little space here to discuss the emergence and transformation of the trickster figure within it.

We should note from the beginning—something Blanco Aguinaga has shown to be essential in distinguishing Cervantes's work from that of the true picaresque—that Campuzano's story of this deceitful marriage is told to a *listener,* his friend the Licenciate Peralta. The presence of the listener takes immediate impact away from the narrative itself. Unlike Lázaro in *Lazarillo de Tormes,* whose "story" is far from disinterested, being itself an item of exchange in a world in which authority and the social order are the dominant force in Lázaro's life, Campuzano's tale of misfortune is not designed for the sake of self-justification. Between the time of the telling and the time of the events being told there exists an abyss in the life of Campuzano. Campuzano, as author, is totally divorced from the desires and motives of the Campuzano who figures as his character. The Hospital of the Resurrection from which he has just emerged when he meets Peralta represents the locus of transformation, the place wherein Campuzano-character died, to be replaced by Campuzano-author.

At the very moment of transition, when Campuzano-character is undergoing a cure in the hospital, he is enlightened by a dream (which he swears is real) in which two dogs talk. The dogs' conversation runs over two nights and so absorbs Campuzano's attention that he takes down every bit of it the next day, offering it to his skeptical friend Peralta as gospel truth. The story is the "Coloquio de los perros," which we read along with Peralta, while Campuzano, weary from his story and comfortable after his meal, takes a nap. Although Peralta cannot accept the idea that dogs talk, he takes Campuzano's manuscript as fantasy and declares it an excellent piece of art. His response launches Campuzano definitely into a new phase, one in which rogue will be abandoned, and author will take his place.

The dream of the talking dogs, both in its content and in its form, is obviously part of the transformation process. Campuzano's capacity to believe in the dream's truth, against the prejudices of his conscious mind, indicates that the socialized attitudes which had led him to his deceitful marriage had been broken down sufficiently to allow a dream to express and be taken on its own terms.

Not only the dream *per se,* but its substance is revealing. The dog Berganza, like Campuzano, has an interlocutor, his companion Cipión. Like Campuzano, Berganza has run through a life of desire until the frustrations of its constant unfulfillment led him finally to renounce service to "los señores de la tierra [the lords of the earth]" in favor of "el Señor del Cielo [the Lord of Heaven]." Both stories, then, that of Campuzano and that of Berganza, are pseudo-picaresque tales, representations of the life of illusion and of desire that are tellable because they have been transcended.

Cipión's role as restrainer and corrector of Berganza's otherwise chaotic story line reveals the positive relationship that can exist between desire and the social order. The listener forces into order the chaos of everyday experience, controlling, but also making possible, the expression of that experience. The limiting presence of Cipión, in other words, is also an enabling presence.

Berganza's story shows that the process of transforming desire from something unconscious that leads to failure and deception to something conscious that leads to success is an on-going one. Berganza's job throughout his narration of the evils of the social world is to describe it dispassionately, without malice or slander. If he falls into a pattern of resentment, it is implied, he will lose his position of control and revert to the pattern from which he has escaped. Campuzano, too, has a tenuous hold on his newfound freedom, and depends very much on the appreciative response of his interlocutor to maintain his position as one reborn out of the world of unconscious desire—of one who has made the transition from soldier to author.

Aside from the fact that the "Casamiento-Coloquio" documents as closely as one could hope Cervantes's own transformation from soldier to author, the stories also reveal clearly the fundamental difference between desire and its representation in literature. To the extent that desire—in the form of resentment, anger, or any other sentiment betraying a sense of lack on the author's part—intrudes on the work of art, it confuses literature and life and becomes dangerous. Theoretically, Cervantes realized this long before he was able to practice it perfectly in his own work. He showed his concern to separate the work of art from the unconscious desires of its author explicitly in *Don Quixote* in his overt attack on the pastoral and chivalric romances, and implicitly long before that, in his efforts to cure the pastoral of some of its worst shortcomings in his *La Galatea*.

Literature must preserve, Cervantes can be interpreted as saying, the very tension between desire and the social order that human beings experience in their everyday lives in their struggles to create harmony between religious aspirations and economic need, between love and marriage, between festival and work. But what literature can offer that the social and religious spheres cannot is the opportunity to contemplate, without direct participation, the functioning of desire in a social context. Literature, for Cervantes, must contain desire within the context of the forces that work against it, showing desire as part of a process of exchange.

If the desire is indulged, however, if it is presented largely cut off from its interaction with the forces that work to inhibit it, the work of art can be said to participate in the imbalance of the social order. Such is clearly the case with the pastoral or the chivalric, where no forces are strong enough to kill the hero, and no fathers or kings are present to interrupt the lover's ardor. True literary discourse is impaired when the author and reader follow the path of desire unchecked. In the picaresque, the imbalance between desire and the social order is reversed, with the same damaging effects to the integrity of the literary text. In neither case can the reader or author peer safely into the imaginative world. For to do so when that world is out of balance is to fall into an imbalance of one's own.

I am influenced, in what I am presenting here, by Felix Martínez-

Bonati's view of the relation of language to literature [*Fictive Discourse and the Structures of Narrative*]. Martínez-Bonati establishes a clear distinction between *reality,* wherein we engage in a communicative situation made up of speaker, listener, and world, and *fiction,* in which *both* author and reader stand apart from another complete communicative situation which, because it is imaginary, they are free to observe. Fiction, as he explains, invites contemplation, and is misunderstood in its essence if it is taken as an instrument of communcation.

I have taken Bonati's tripartite linguistic configuration and superimposed on it Girard's model for the discourse of desire. Very similar to Bonati's speaker/listener/world triangle, Girard's three-sided structure for desire introduces into the apparently bi-polar world of lover and loved one (desirer and object of desire) an essential third term, the rival. It is the third term that in fact makes exchange between lover and loved one possible, just as the listener makes possible the speaker's awareness of and communication about the objects in the real world.

In the discourse of desire, the rival takes the listener's place and functions as both inspirer and prohibitor. The "speaker" from Martínez-Bonati's model would correspond with the lover or desirer; the "world" with the loved one or object of desire. Girard's contribution to our understanding not only of literary works but of ourselves in relation to our myths, our rituals, and our conflicts, has been to insist on the decisive importance of the rival's place in the discourse of desire. What real-life situations blind us to, Girard has shown, is the interchangeability of our roles as lover and rival, and of the complexity of the exchange taking place between the two. Martínez-Bonati also analyzes with great subtlety the impact of the listener's presence on the speaker's discourse, proposing in fact that all sentences are best analyzed when examined for the relative weight given the speaker's self-expression, his desire to refer to an object in the real world, and his appeal to the listener, all three of which are present in some combination in any discourse.

Martínez-Bonati points out that only when the discourse is unreal, that is, when it is presented, usually through literature, as discourse taking place between others, discourse in which we are not participants, are we free to see the process of exchange. Because the literary text is a self-enclosed entity, we can allow ourselves to enter it *via* the imagination, knowing that it has all the earmarks of a real situation except that it is suspended from time and space and is therefore safe.

Going back now to my assertion that Cervantes criticized all the prevailing fictional forms—implicitly—failing to distinguish fiction and reality, we are now on stronger ground to understand that criticism and to see it at work in his own fiction. What the pastoral lacks, in its escape to the countryside, is the presence within it of the prohibitor—the listener who would force the speaker/desirer to come to terms with the world/object of his desire. Cervantes tried to solve the problem of the pastoral's imbalance on the dream side by importing to the shepherd's idyllic retreat on the banks of the Tagus refugee lovers from the strife-torn cities and towns where their love life had blossomed. Cervantes's *La Galatea* (1585) bulks so large with interpolated tales that its ostensible hero and heroine, Elicio and Galatea, all but disappear. Their love, in fact, makes very little progress in the midst of all the secondary characters' activity. Elicio's would-be rival makes a very poor obstacle for Elicio's aspirations, acknowledging at the outset that he has no chance of winning Galatea's affections. Without Erastro's inhibitory presence, Elicio's own desire is scarcely stirred. The whole central story seems finally to be leading nowhere when Cervantes calls upon Galatea's father. The latter assigns an unknown Portuguese shepherd to the role of fiancé for his daughter, thereby precipitating Elicio into something resembling a lover's resolve. Elicio's energies finally marshaled, Cervantes abruptly ends his experiment with the pastoral, noting years later in print what he must have felt from the beginning, that his maiden voyage into fiction "proposed much, but concluded nothing."

Fiction should be a place where one is safe to experience desire. In order to feel safe, however, the fiction must be complete unto itself, which means that it must contain in balance all three of the elements of discourse—whether based on language or desire—that have been discussed already. If the elements are in balance, one of the signs will be a clearly defined opening and closure for the work of art. Folktales and fairy tales, which offer strong doses of the imaginary, often with a lot of violence and cruelty that our rational minds find hard to accept—are safe, even salutory, because they clearly mark the doors that lead in and out of that world. Formulaic beginnings and endings—"Once upon a time"; "They all lived happily ever after"—demarcate firmly the realms of the imagination and the real. When, as in the chivalric, the pastoral, and the picaresque, the story finds no way of ending, we find ourselves in the dangerous in-between world where fantasy and reality are confused. When they are confused, we are automatically caught in the trickster's net.

At the beginning of this article, I affirmed that the trickster can become the savior, that his disruptions can lead to peace and a higher social order. We are now in a position to see how that theoretical observation is reified in the works of Cervantes.

Cervantes's last hero, Persiles, is born into the usual world of unfulfilled and unfulfillable desire. Like his predecessor, Don Quixote, he takes on an assumed name and role, and leaves home in pursuit of what his social world has denied him. But there is a difference between the two: Persiles, unlike Don Quixote, *uses* his disguise as the pilgrim Periandro. The trickster works in him all right, and as Periandro, Persiles is not above lying and deceiving. But Persiles uses trickery consciously, and never forgets that his disguise is not an end but a means. He is, in other words, a little like Master Peter, who carries Ginés de Pasamonte hidden beneath his disguise.

Persiles is also different from Don Quixote in that he knows what he wants. He wants to marry Sigismunda, and is not swayed to the contrary by the declaration of his older brother that she should be his. Like Campuzano when confronted with the phenomenon of talking dogs, Persiles takes his dream seriously, and gives its truth priority over that competing social truth which declares that older brothers have rights and powers denied to younger brothers. Don Quixote did not know what he really wanted. His journey was as much an escape as a search. As escape, it revealed an avoidance of his desires, a sense that they were illegitimate. Nancy Regaldo distinguishes between a trick and a hero's deed, pointing out that "the hero desires an object which it is legitimate for him to win. No matter how hard the task, the object is his for the taking."

The hero's only real travail is to kill within himself the illusory structure of mediated desire, that is, to break up the hold on consciousness that the structure of the social world has imposed on him. The many metaphors of death and rebirth in the *Persiles* testify to the importance of that process. When the process is complete, the object of desire and its prohibition can be seen as equally illusory, projections from an unconscious that perceives *being* as lack. When being is understood as fullness and completion, as Soldino experiences it, life in time becomes open, like Don Quixote's life, to full apprehension. As the many tricksters who run through Cervantes's work show, the material world, with all of its aggressiveness, is subject to manipulation and, if need be, to overturning. Trickster, master manipulator, is the figure by whom tragedy is transformed into comedy, struggle and lack, into plenitude.

Cervantes loves to leave a glimpse of himself as author within the works of his imagination. The last portrait he leaves us must have been composed very close to the end of his life. It appears at the beginning of the last book of the *Persiles,* when he was rushing to complete the work knowing death was near. In this final self-portrait, Cervantes appears to the pilgrims in Rome in the guise of a pilgrimming author. He tells them:

> Este traje de peregrino que visto, el cual trae consigo la obligación

de que pida limosna el que lo trae, me obliga a que os la pida, y tan aventajada y tan nueva, que, sin darme joya alguna ni prendas que lo valgan, me habéis de hacer rico. Yo señores, soy un hombre curioso: sobre la mitad de mi alma predomina Marte, y sobre la otra mitad, Mercurio y Apolo; algunos años me he dado al ejercicio de la guerra, y algunos otros, y los más maduros, en el de las letras; en los de la guerra he alcanzado algún buen nombre, y por los de las letras he sido algún tanto estimado; algunos libros he impreso, de los ignorantes no condenados por malos ni de los discretos han dejado de ser tenidos por buenos.

[This pilgrim's garb I am wearing, which requires the wearer to beg for alms, obligates me to ask them of you, and will be so excellent and so new, that, without giving me any jewel or valuable garments, you will make me rich. I, gentlemen, am a curious man: half my soul is governed by Mars, and the other half by Mercury and Apollo; I have spent some years dedicated to the exercise of war, and other years, the later ones, to the exercise of letters; in the war years I achieved some renown, and in those of letters I have been somewhat esteemed; I have published some books, not condemned as bad by the ignorant nor held to be other than good by the discreet.]

He goes on to explain that his new book project, prompted as always by need, and fed by his genius "que tiene un no sé qué de fantástico e inventivo [which has a fantastic and inventive I-don't-know-what]," will be written entirely by others, and that what he asks on his pilgrimage is a collection of aphorisms. All the pilgrims write, from their limited understandings, what they take for truth. They then ask him what saying of the many he has collected most represents his own ideas. He responds: "No desees, y serás el más rico hombre del mundo [Do not desire and you will be the richest man on earth]."

Trickster, in his final appearance as author, is pure representation of the desires of others, his own desires having been entirely absorbed into his awareness of completion. Trickster at the end of Cervantes's life is the supplier of genius, through whom "el trabajo es ajeno, el provecho mío [work is foreign, the benefit mine]." Like Soldino, the ex-soldier, ex-literary man is fulfilled by his transformation from manipulator to pure representer. His salutory effect can also be seen in the role of the pure actor and healer played by Pedro de Urdemalas in Cervantes's excellent play of the same title. *Pedro de Urdemalas* deserves a study of its own not possible here. Suffice it to say that Pedro carries out, in the realm of the actor, the role of trickster in his highest form that Soldino and the pilgrim author do with the *Persiles*. Through him, we can catch a glimpse once again, of the positive effect Cervantes's trickster was able to effect out of his own disillusion, desire, and disorder.

Northrop Frye says in *The Secular Scripture,* "we are not awake when we have abolished the dream world: we are only awake when we have absorbed it again." When we track the trickster in Cervantes, we follow his traces right into the forbidden world of dream, through all its nightmare and violence, to the place where, if we have persevered, we find ourselves awake within it.

ALBAN FORCIONE

The Descent into the Grave:
Cervantes's Apocalypse

The house of clay (which is the grave) is the school of true wisdom,
the place where God is wont to teach his doctrine to his own. . . .
Descend then, oh man, with your spirit to this house, and there you
will see who you are!

—LUÍS DE GRANADA

The depiction of the witch Cañizares at the center of the "Colloquy of the
Dogs" is one of the most powerful scenes in Cervantes's entire literary production. We have reached the monster at the center of the labyrinth, and, as
we move through the aborted anagnorisis and witness the two dogs groping
futilely for a correct exegesis of the prophecy that holds the promise of
release, the narrative grinds toward a halt, leaving us with the impression of
a dreamer mesmerized by a relentlessly oppressive nightmare. The briskly
paced flow of episodes and the enlivening movement of the retrospective
commentary, which have swept us along rapidly if somewhat aimlessly, are
suddenly suspended, and the analytical texture of the work thickens toward
the density of a metaphysical treatise. The tightening involutions of the tale,
its continuing thrusts inward from dream into dream and from confession
into confession, appear to be approaching a climactic dead center of con-
vergence, and the narrative itself seems to exert that menacing, constrictive
force that we observe everywhere in the imaginary space of the novella and
that becomes stifling in the tiny cell and in the spiritual abysses (the "sima
de su miseria") from which the hag vainly attempts to extricate herself. At

From *Cervantes and the Mystery of Lawlessness: A Study of* El casamiento engañoso
y El coloquio de los perros. © 1984 by Princeton University Press.

169

this moment of maximum narrative enclosure we find ourselves, together with the dreamer and his persona, in the depths of the grave, compelled to share with them the horror and the elation of their discoveries. As Cañizares proceeds monotonously through her interminable confession, we experience a recollection of numerous elements, which, scattered chaotically throughout the preceding narrative, here coalesce and obtrude with the intensity and concentrated symbolic power of dream visions. As she considers such philosophical and theological mysteries as the origin of suffering and the troubling complicity of the powers of evil in God's providential design and as she probes the psychology of the sinner in her unsparing self-analysis, laying bare the spiritual disease of the sick soul in the "triste noche del pecado [sad night of sin]," we plunge into the most profound strata of meaning infolded in the tale. Cañizares's confession is Cervantes's most spectacular epiphany of evil, and it forms the poetic heart of his final novella, the source of the imaginative energy that pulsates in all the details of its multiple episodes. Here we confront directly the central vision that animates the entire work, and we hear most clearly the dark tonic chord of its principal theme, which is echoed in numerous motifs playing across its surface. . . .

In her stature, centrality, and imaginative dominance of the tale in which she appears, and as the embodiment of a profoundly disturbing vision of evil, Cañizares has no parallel in Cervantes's other works. It is as if Cervantes the writer for once could not resist the mysterious appeal of the realm of sinfulness and destruction about which he had expressed his uneasiness when referring to probably its most spectacular literary exploration in the age— Fernando de Rojas's *Celestina*: "a book, in my opinion, divine, if only it would conceal the human more than it does." To be sure, if we were to look for literary characters resembling Cañizares in her hideously insensitive conscience, in her capacity to pervert sacred knowledge, in her dedication to the pleasures of the flesh, and in her diabolical connections and activities, we would have to turn to the *Celestina*, Quevedo's *Buscón,* and perhaps *Lazarillo de Tormes* to find her congeners. However, it must be emphasized that even in his most somber work Cervantes situates his own exploration of evil within the metaphysical framework provided by orthodox Christianity and celebrated in consolatory and confessional writings from the Book of Job and Augustine's *Confessions* to innumerable contemporary devotional and ascetic treatises, as well as in such popular literary works reflecting their influence as *Guzmán de Alfarache* and *La conversión de la Magdalena* [*The Conversion of the Magdalen*]. All confirm the paradoxical notion that the miseries which afflict the human being in his life on earth—whether the result of man's sinfulness or the natural infirmities and catastrophes to which

he is heir—are somehow necessary ingredients in the highest good to which
he can aspire and are part of an ultimately benevolent providential design.
As Pedro de Rivadeneira put it in his consolatory *Treatise on Tribulation*
(1589), man's miseries, when properly understood in the light of the grand
mystery of lawlessness, are in reality "the gentlest of fruits," "the richest
treasures of inestimable valuables," the "sweetest honeycomb in the mouth
of the dead lion," and the medicine that "perfects and refines the spirit." In
a conceit much more abstract but equally characteristic of the metaphysical
style of contemporary religious oratory, Cervantes turned to geometry for
his most concise expression of the religious paradox. Toward the end of his
prose epic of tribulations, *Los trabajos de Persiles y Sigismunda* [*The Trials
of Persiles and Sigismunda*], his sententious narrator introduces the climactic
resolution by invoking the venerable mystery: "good and evil are separated
so slightly from one another, that they are like two concurrent lines, which,
although they spring from separated and different beginnings, yet end in a
single point." All the unfathomable mysteries surrounding the complicity of
God and the forces of darkness which are latent in the orthodox Christian
vision of evil are powerfully evoked in Cervantes's monster. She reminds us
that "all the misfortunes that befall men, kingdoms, cities, and villages, and
sudden deaths, shipwrecks, and falls—in short, all the evils that are termed
disasters, ['males de daño']—come from the hand of the Almighty and His
permissive will," insists that her murder of innocent children and all of our
"disasters and evils that are termed of culpability ['males de culpa']," while
we must ultimately bear responsibility for them, are nonetheless permitted
by God ("all of this God permits because of our sinfulness; for without His
permission, I have seen by experience, the devil cannot hurt an ant"), and
suggests that there is a great mystery lurking behind her pronouncement,
which Berganza will be privileged "to understand when he becomes a man."
It is as if it were given to the monsters of the Book of Job to speak from the
whirlwind in justification of the destruction that they must wreak in fulfilling
God's darkest designs. As in the much less elaborate incident in the *Persiles,*
in which a wolf emerges from the darkness to reveal to the wrathful Antonio
the mysterious workings of Divine Grace even while reminding him of the
loathsomeness of his sins, the appropriateness of the grotesque scene must
be sought in the decorum of the nightmare with its concentrated symbolic
language and its readiness to collapse the categories and distinctions by
which we maintain our precarious hold on reality in waking life. In these
cases we glimpse the nightmare of the Christian soul tormented by the unen-
durable contiguity of good and evil, by all the truth that is concealed beneath
the paradox of fruitful evil.

Throughout Cervantes's age writers and thinkers were obsessed with the mystery of lawlessness. They continually exhorted men to consider the "logicality" and justness of evil and suffering according to God's most lofty purposes, and they ridiculed the foolishness of those who would hope to render that justice intelligible in terms of man's capacities for understanding. Thus Luis de León recalls Paul's statement that Christ was perfected and crowned with glory through sufferings (Heb. 2:9–10) and suggests that every man must make Christ's discovery that "scarcely has the light been born when evil begins to persecute it," if he is to know the glory of the blessed. . . .

Cervantes's contemporaries were intent on opening their eyes to what Erasmus, in his meditations on the Psalms, called the "other face of God," the "clouded face which human infirmity can not endure," a countenance etched with the most troubling mysteries of the divine will and universal justice. The fiction of the age—with its picaros, penitents, converts, sinners, saints, and tormented visionaries—bore eloquent witness to the depth and pervasiveness of this cultural preoccupation. In the enormous survey of disorder and depravity, *Guzmán de Alfarache,* in which Mateo Alemán claims that he wishes to depict the development of a perfected human being, the protagonist moves through a world of evil toward a miraculous conversion, and at the climactic moment of his inner illumination and deliverance, he introduces the profound theme with an analogy which, like Cervantes's monster, suggests that there is something unnatural at the heart of the mystery of fruitful evil and suffering. The narrator recounts an anecdote of a man who orders a picture of a horse, discovers that the artist has painted it upside down, and, on complaining, is advised by the "discreet painter" simply to invert the painting. The repentant picaro's interpretation of the analogy offers the vision of God as a supremely demanding, "baroque" artist, who provokes his public by paradoxical expression and encodes the most profound secrets of his text within startling conceits: "God's works will often appear to us like this horse which lies wallowing in the mire." However, if we invert "the painting made by the sovereign Artificer," we discover a perfect work:

> As we have said just now, ordeals seem harsh to us; we fail to grasp their true significance, for we understand little of them. But when he who sends them reveals the mercy that he has stored in them and we see them right side up, then we will take them for pleasures.

According to the workings of logic, the paradox, like most other paradoxes, is ridiculous, and it remained for Quevedo to exploit its ridiculousness in creating one of the most abject of the hoards of contemporary literary sin-

ners—Pablos, the "Buscón." Of all the actions and utterances that contribute
to the sense of moral revulsion which the reader feels on beholding this
"stinking Lazarus," who is incapable of emerging from his grave, one of the
most striking is his blasphemous perversion of the traditional consolatory
paradox. On reading the humorously eloquent letter from his uncle, the
hangman, describing the execution, mutilation, and cannibalism of his father
and the sentencing of his mother for witchcraft, the lowly picaro, following
the practices of Guzmán de Alfarache and Berganza and the recommenda-
tions of countless preachers, meditates on his sufferings and finds consolation
in contemplating the significance of the catastrophe: "I cannot deny that I
was deeply moved by the new disgrace, but I took comfort in the consolation
which it provided: parents' vices can achieve so much that they console their
children for their misfortunes, however great they may be." The curious
piece of nonsense makes sense only as a sardonic deformation of commonplaces of consolation which surround the depiction of sin in contemporary
fiction, as a deliberate play with the convention and the readers' informed
expectations concerning it, and as one of Pablos's numerous profanations of
the sacred, in this case, the venerable notion of fruitful evil and the form of
literature that gives it expression.

The cultural obsession with the paradoxes of divine justice was inti-
mately connected with the current hysteria concerning witchcraft, which
infested the spiritual life of the whole of Europe and in Spain reached its
maximum intensity precisely during the period in which the "Coloquio de
los perros" was conceived. Cañizares's account of her nocturnal flights to
the mountain sabbats in the Pyrenees, the orgies of feasting and sexuality,
the distorted sermons of the goat-god, the murder and cannibalism of children, and the various *maleficia* that give her pleasure and do honor to Satan,
matches in all details the official versions of the witches' sabbat, which
haunted the popular fantasy and was attested to by innumerable confessions
which inquisitors extracted, frequently through torture, from accused
witches in the sixteenth and seventeenth centuries. The origins of this sce-
nario, as well as its powerful hold on the European mind for two centuries,
have yet to be fully explained by historians, but it is clear that it provided
the imagination of the period with a powerful mythology of evil and enabled
an embattled religious authority, in an age of schism, complex spiritual tur-
moil, and increasing secularization, to draw together its ranks and pursue a
satisfying crusade against its most ancient and easily identifiable adversary.
If the enemy was engendered in large part by the anxieties of those in need
of victory, his imputed powers were no less spectacular and his predictable
defeat no less reassuring.

The nocturnal armies of Satan were unleashed all over Europe, and the successes which they enjoyed under his banner were readily explained by theologians according to the traditional Christian doctrine of providential evil. As I have pointed out above, Cañizares's confession is marked by a peculiar doctrinal self-consciousness, which she displays in analyzing herself as a sinner and offering a metaphysical *apologia* for the suffering she and her cohorts inflict on human beings. The doctrine that she invokes thoroughly penetrated contemporary thinking concerning witchcraft, and one of the most interesting testimonies to its importance can be found in the refreshing arguments of Pedro de Valencia against the enthusiasm, cruelty, and superstition of the Inquisition's witch hunters. While acknowledging that there have always been witches, that demons exist with powers to perform "marvelous acts," and that God allows their success in order to punish man's evil and subject his faith to trial, Valencia calls for the exercise of prudence in dealing with the cases of accused individuals, and urges skepticism concerning the popular myth of witches' sabbats. He openly expresses his doubts about the possibility of the alleged transformations of men into beasts, their invisible penetration of walls, their flights through the air, and their sexual encounters with a supernatural being known as the goat-devil. He insists that inquisitors seek explanations of the origins of the marvelous phenomena, which so many swear to have experienced, in natural causes—charlatanism, debauchery, opportunistic exploitation of fear and ignorance, hallucination rooted in physiological processes, and forced confessions—and he reminds them that there have been analogous cases of superstition and mass hysteria in pre-Christian history. However, the most eloquent part of Valencia's argument is addressed to the theological foundation of the belief in witchcraft, a matter that he considers so important that he feels obliged to include absolutely everything relevant to a "true judgment" and to ask his readers to suffer his prolixity on the subject. While he grants the existence of the devil, the rationalistic Valencia finds deeply perverse the fundamental belief in "God's permission," a belief which, as we have seen, Cañizares underscores and which the orthodox portrayals of witches' activities, such as the influential encyclopedia of demonology of the Jesuit Martín del Río (1599–1600), repeatedly invoked to account for the spread of witchcraft and the spectacular successes of Satan. With a possible trace of irony Valencia notes that del Río and others "presuppose the harshest permissions which have ever been heard about the divine goodness" and proceeds to argue that "in regard to God's permission mountains of difficulties present themselves." The conception that God would tolerate such triumphs by the devil and visit such afflictions on helpless women and children would appear to be at odds with the belief in His omnipotence and goodness, and Valencia recoils from a bewildering paradox with indignation:

> I fail to understand how those people who affirm this view of God's permissive will and defend it by referring to it as a great piety while denouncing as a victim of an impious fancy anyone who refuses to believe it can themselves maintain with proper piety and reverence the doctrine of divine goodness and abominate with proper hatred and contempt the devil. I at least do not wish to believe the words of those who have offered to him the submission that they confess. . . . Did ever God grant to the devil so that he might use it against Indians, devourers of human flesh, or Egyptians, worshippers of garlic and onions, such an infamous power as that which is given to him by these tales of evil old crones for his use against Catholic Christians? And can it be said that one honors God by believing this?

Without having to endorse the uncompromising skepticism of the "political thinkers, the Epicureans, and the Lucianists, who believe in no more than nature and the physical things which they experience in the course of life," one can legitimately refuse to lend credence to "all the old wives' tales," "all the pagan fables," "all the metamorphoses in Ovid," and of course, all the extravagant marvels detailed in the infamous confessions.

Valencia's penetrating critique of the superstitions of his contemporaries is animated by the powerful skeptical spirit of a man who is repelled by the irrationality and inhumanity about him, who is not prepared to account for such suffering by praising the mysteries of a darkened divine countenance, and who perhaps senses the sinister potential for ideological tyranny lurking in the traditional consolatory doctrines of Christianity such as sanctified affliction and fruitful evil. In Cervantes's "Colloquy of the Dogs" we observe a similar skeptical spirit informing the dogs' discussion of the fantastic metamorphoses of the witches' world and the enigmatic oracle, which Cipión describes as "fairy stories or old wives' tales, like those about the headless horse and the magic wand, with which people while away the long winter nights beside the hearth." But Cervantes does not focus his skepticism on the theological mysteries that emerge in Cañizares's confession and Berganza's anguished meditation over the lifeless husk of the hag, from which the spirit has evidently departed on its travels to the orgiastic sabbat. Whether or not Cervantes actually believed in witches—and the dogs' sarcastic rejection of the oracle, its promise of metamorphosis, and any kinship with the crone would indicate that he was certainly skeptical about the miraculous events commonly said to transpire at the demonic sabbats—it is nevertheless clear that he was well aware of the imaginative power of the myth of witchcraft, that he effectively introduced its vision of annihilating energy and its vocabulary of horrible inversion at the moment of climactic disintegration in his narrative, and that he exploited its theological implications to pursue to its most profound depths his major theme of the nature of evil. When Berganza meditates on the loathsome cadaver of the witch in the darkness of the night, the series of troubling questions that he poses—"Who made this wicked old woman so wise and so evil? From where does she know which are evils of calamity and which are evils of culpability? How does she come to know so much about God and speak of Him so often, while her works are those of the devil? Why does she sin so much out of pure malice, not being able to offer the excuse of ignorance?"—far from exposing the contradictions in a perverse theology, intimates rather the mystery of a paradox which conceals a dread but liberating secret.

II

At this point, rather than directly pursuing the theological implications of Cañizares's presence and confession, I turn to the imagery and motifs that are concentrated about the witch, for the scene provides the imaginative center of the work, the source of life that radiates to all points of its circumference. Once we have possessed it, we can see much more clearly the relationships among its apparently disorderly parts and between its parts and the unified whole that they compose. If Cervantes's plot construction reveals a mastery of what I have called a grammar of narrative disorder, which is intelligible to all readers, but which depends to some extent for its most powerful effects on their recognition of the specific principles of plot structure manifest in certain narrative forms that were popular in his age, his principal imagery is drawn from the archetypal imagery of the literature of disorder, but a full, correct response to it depends on the readers' awareness of a distinctive body of associations and themes that surround it in the contemporary Christian literature of sinfulness and divine retribution. [Among] the central images [are] the tomb, confinement, night, sleep, physical infirmity, animality, mutilation, torture, cannibalism, and disorientation. . . .

I would stress at the outset that the imagery and the themes with which it is charged are in themselves commonplaces, as they derive for the most part from the Bible and are always close to the surface of any anatomy of sin, whether in didactic or imaginative writing, within the Christian tradition. It is precisely because they are commonplaces, orchestrated with particular frequency and intensity in Cervantes's own religious culture, with a tremendous impact on the literary production of the age—an age that we remember for the beast-man and the fortunate thieves of Calderón, the sleep of Segismundo and Tirso's "Desconfiado," the repentant and nonrepentant picaresque heroes, the theological trickster, Don Juan, the contrite Magdalena, the martyr, and the saint—that they resonate with such power throughout his tale and organize its total design. For these very reasons I would also emphasize that when I call attention to the presence of such traditional imagery and to its associative values in the religious writing of Cervantes's age, I am not at all arguing for the causal connections which have interested traditional source studies. There is only one true source of the "Coloquio de los perros," and that is Cervantes's own vision of evil and its forms, powers, consequences, origins, and necessity in the redemptive process, as well as whatever personal and existential factors were responsible for shaping that vision. I am concerned only with meaning, expressive power, and imaginative impact and resonance in the vocabulary that gives literary shape to Cervantes's vision, and, although his vocabulary remains our vocabulary, its range of associations is much less precisely defined in our culture, its imaginative power much more diffuse, and its metaphysical resonance much more muted. If we are to respond intensely to the rich imagistic texture of Cervantes's literary world or if our response to it is to be directed at what is central to his text rather than at peripheral details which are more immediately striking and more readily intelligible according to the priorities of our "modern" imagination and critical interests, our own philosophical orientation and moral values, or our own conceptions of Cervantes and Cervantes's Spain, then we must recognize how its overwhelming vocabulary of disorder draws power and meaning from the Christian culture of the age, and we can do this effectively only by glancing at works representative of that culture.

At the center of the Cañizares episode we watch as the witch moves from a "room that was dark, narrow, and low-ceilinged, illuminated only by the feeble glow of a clay lamp," into a "tiny room even narrower than the other," where she anoints herself, "stretches out on the floor like a dead woman," and falls into a trance. Berganza can detect no breathing in her motionless form, and, as he stares at the "skeleton of bones," he is seized with an uncontrollable fit of terror. Before entering the room, Cañizares describes the diseased condition of her soul, a state in which she can recognize with a keen intelligence her sinfulness and yet summon no energies from a totally flaccid will that would free her from her bondage in sensuality. She describes herself as a typical sinner, her soul wallowing and "sunken in the profound abyss of its own misery," incapable of lifting a hand upward toward the hand that God is extending in her direction. The images of moving into the grave and sinking into the abyss, with their strong associations of constricted space and bottomlessness, certainly add powerful visual support to the effects of the narrative movement of the work, which at this climactic point plunges deeper and deeper into central recesses that appear to hold the promise of clarification and release from suspense only to become sources of greater confinement and mystery. As I have pointed out above, both the confessions within the confession and the dreams within the dream lead us to a central void.

However, the images of the grave and the abyss, as well as the cadaverous body whose foul-smelling mouth has repelled Berganza, are primarily meaningful as traditional symbols of the condition of sin as a state of death in life. This fundamental Christian view, expressed so forcefully in Paul's epistles, is omnipresent in the devotional and ascetic writings of the sixteenth century. For example, at the beginning of his widely read manual for the true Christian warrior, the *Enchiridion,* Erasmus surveys the powerful enemies he must confront and repeatedly describes sinfulness as a "death of the soul." He invokes the fifth psalm—"their throat is an open sepulcher"—exploits the similarity in the Greek words for body and grave to suggest a link based on etymological reasoning, and alludes to the four-day death and stink of the entombed Lazarus, a Christian archetype of spiritual regeneration which was to enjoy a spectacular resurrection in the devotional and literary writings of the following one hundred years. . . .

If the description of the naked Cañizares in the dark, narrow chamber is the most important elaboration of the central imagery of the tomb and death and reveals quite explicitly the themes embodied in it, the scene is at the same time the climax in the development of another closely related body of imagery—that of sleep, night, and awakening. This is undoubtedly the most complex image pattern in the work, and the particular effects of derangement which Cervantes achieves in its articulation require special consideration. Again it is necessary to emphasize the archetypal character of these elements within Christian tradition.

I would point to two fundamental symbolic associations of sleep, both of which Cervantes exploits at the climactic moments of the "Colloquy of the Dogs." On the one hand sleep is imaginatively equated with death and sinfulness. The notion appears repeatedly in the New Testament, where the awakening to the light of day is invoked to express most vividly the process of the redemption and rebirth of the new man through Christ's grace: "Awake, O sleeper, and arise from the dead, / and Christ shall give you light" (Eph. 5:14); "Besides this you know what hour it is, how it is full time now for you to wake from sleep. For salvation is nearer to us now than when we first believed; the night is far gone, the day is at hand. Let us then cast off the works of darkness and put on the armor of light" (Rom. 13:11–14); "For since we believe that Jesus died and rose again, even so, through Jesus, God will bring with them those who have fallen asleep" (1 Thes. 4:14). Now, precisely because sleep is the prelude to awakening to new life, it is also viewed traditionally as a restorative force which renders the soul open to the infusion of divine grace and capable of undergoing the mysterious healing metamorphosis of redemption and conversion. It is a darkness that nourishes the "eyes of the soul" with a light that clarifies the deepest mysteries of existence, even as it blinds the "eyes of the body," riveted as they are on the things of this world. And it is, of course, the time when God can reward the sleeper with the higher vision, even if his dream, like that of Cervantes's Ensign, is a torment of purgation. As Elihu tells Job, "For God speaks in one way, / and in two, though man does not perceive it. / In a dream, in a vision of the night, / when deep sleep falls upon men, / while they slumber on their beds, /then he opens the ears of men, / and terrifies them with warnings" (Job 33:14–16). Thus Augustine interprets Adam's sleep as the sleep of illumination, and in the *Confessions*, a work that had a significant impact on the religious culture of Cervantes's age and the major literary modes by which it gave expression to the Christian mysteries of sin and redemption—the picaresque novel and religious drama—he describes his own difficulties in arising from the sleep of death and sinfulness. The passage resembles Cañizares's analysis of her own *acedia*, the spiritual sickness that poisons her soul, and, as it is important to see that Cervantes's witch, for all the sensationalism and grotesque effects that she brings to the work, is a vehicle for the introduction of profound and venerable theological concerns, it is worth looking at Augustine's words.

> Thus by the burdens of this world I was sweetly weighed down, *just as man often is in sleep.* Thoughts wherein I meditated upon you were like the efforts of *those who want to arouse themselves but, still overcome by deep drowsiness, sink back again.* . . . I had no answer to give to you when you said to me, "Rise, you who sleep, and arise from the dead, and Christ will enlighten you." . . . In vain was I delighted with your law according to the inward man, when *another law in my members fought against the law of my mind, and led me captive in the law of sin which was in my members. For the law of sin is force of habit, whereby the mind is dragged along and held fast, even against its will but*

still deservedly so, since it was by its will that it had slipped into the habit. *Unhappy man that I was!* Who would deliver me from the body of this death, unless your grace through Jesus Christ our Lord?

As she prepares for her sleep, Cañizares confesses to Berganza how habit has made sin second nature to her, how the pleasures of the flesh have so dulled her soul that it has lost its faith and forgotten its Christian identity and God's laws, and how she strangely can understand what has happened to her but nevertheless do nothing to remedy her plight, since her will, hopelessly enslaved by her appetite, refuses to respond to her understanding. She too is tormented by the traditional *tristitia vitae,* the unhappiness of the sinner who despairs in his ineffectual efforts to extricate himself from the "manacles on his will" and to rise from the "profound abyss of misery" into which he has sunk and who fails completely to understand the mysteries of God's mercy and the hope that it provides. "Let death come and take me from this weary life . . . thus my thoughts are bound always to be evil, and yet I know that God is good and merciful and that He knows what is in store for me; so that is enough, and let us drop this conversation, for it truly saddens me."

It makes little difference for our purposes whether or not Cervantes read St. Augustine's *Confessions;* for these essential Christian ideas and symbolic images and motifs were undoubtedly mediated to him through sermons, devotional works, and popular fiction, notably the picaresque novel and the best seller of the age, *Guzmán de Alfararche.* From the very origins of the genre, the death and resurrection, the sleep and awakening of Lazarus can frequently be glimpsed in the backgrounds of the picaresque narratives. The myth was a favorite of religious writers of the time, as it had been since the earliest eras of Christianity, for the symbolic representation of the mystery of sinfulness and redemption and the powers of grace and God's mercy. There were few contemporary discussions of sinfulness that failed to introduce the tomb, the sleep, the sickness, the stink, the voice of Christ, the cure, and the awakening. "Lazarus, however, was already rotting in the tomb. . . . It was not difficult for the Lord to raise up one who had been dead for four days. It is a more difficult matter to raise up someone who has lived in sin all his life and has become rotten as well. . . . Every day He calls, 'Maiden arise!' 'Young man, arise!' 'Lazarus, come forth!' But there are many who are more than dead, who do not hear Him when he calls them back to life." Fray Luis de Granada writes that the call of grace has the power to awaken the most hardened sinner, to transform him into a new Lazarus, and to summon him forth from the "tomb of his wickedness." The concluding scene of Juan de Luna's somber picaresque novel, *La segunda parte de la vida de Lazarillo de Tormes,* depicts the protagonist in a state of utter misery but presumably on his way toward conversion, huddled in a church and covered by a mantle which the priest has taken from a sepulcher. In the sprawling panorama of disorder and vice of Alemán's novel, the confessor refers to the necessity of opening the "eyes of the understanding" and awakening from the sleep of sinfulness ("if with all of this I would not awaken from the sleep of my sins"), and at the moment of his conversion, in the darkness and stillness of the night aboard the galley, he ponders his sinfulness and God's grace, exhorts himself to "wake up from his sleep," sheds tears of contrition, falls asleep, and awakens to a new identity and a new life: "I fell asleep, and, when I awakened I found myself another man, no longer I and no longer the person with that old heart of before."

If St. Augustine's struggles with the sleep of sinfulness lead him to an awakening to the new life and if his spiritual descendants in the picaresque novel are occasionally rewarded with the same experience, it must be noted that there are also unregenerate sleepers who discover no way out of the nightmare. Writers fascinated with their spiritual malaise did not shrink from evoking the promise of Augustine's and Lazarus's destinies in order to underscore their failures. Following her confession, Cañizares sinks into her sleep, a sleep of orgiastic communion with the devil in which we witness a hideous climax to all the scenes of carnal indulgence and bestiality, banqueting and sexuality, running through the "Colloquy" ("there he gives us dull, saltless food, and there certain things take place which . . . are filthy and indecent"). For her there is no release from the manacles of sin, and her awakening in rage and violence is a demonic parody of the awakening to new life which traditionally rewards the redeemed Christian and which in the tale rewards the Ensign following his night of expiation and, by implication, his double, the reader, who imaginatively shares his slumbers. Similarly her "ointments" ["unturas"], which enable her to sink into that sleep and make rapturous contact with her devil-goat, represent a grotesque inversion of the divine grace which inspires the visionary sleeper and enables the redeemed Christian to "turn the wheel of good works."

In the description of Cañizares's sleep Cervantes is, then, releasing in his text the powerful negative energies of a travesty of the sacred. He is employing a basic technique for the full orchestration of horror which had emerged as a convention in Spain's literature of disorder of the previous century and which his contemporary, Francisco de Quevedo, was developing for unprecedented effects in narrative. . . . The basis of this method of travesty is the association of the act or speech of a character which arouses disgust and moral outrage with something that is sacred or valued. The valued model may, of course, be anything which the writer's audience esteems—sacred myths, legends, rituals and texts, historical and religious figures, venerated actions and gestures, moral doctrines, lofty institutions, or literary conventions. Through the process of association the action described becomes an incongruous incarnation of what is sacred, and its impact is all the more disturbing as it defiles its model and activates about itself in the text the destructive energy always generated by the violation of taboos. The procedure is undoubtedly as old as literature itself, and the medieval Christian literature of sinfulness certainly developed a rich tradition of disorderly imaginary worlds which exploit the vocabulary and the power of profanation.

Chronology

1547   Miguel de Cervantes Saavedra born to Rodrigo de Cervantes and Leonora de Cortinas. Family poor and possibly of New Christian origin.

1568   Composes *Elegia* for Queen Isabel de Valois.

1569   Apparently condemned to ten years exile; serves the future Cardinal, Giulio Acquaviva; enlists.

1571   Wounded in the battle of Lepanto. Wound to right hand leaves him partially disabled for life.

1575   Embarks on the ship *Sol* with his brother Rodrigues. Captured by Turks and enslaved to Dali Miami. Carried off to Algiers.

1576   Rodrigues released.

1577   Cervantes composes *Epistola a Mateo Vazquez* (*Letter to Mateo Vazquez*).

1580   Ransomed by Trinitarian monks; returns to Spain.

1581   Begins work on *La Galatea*.

1583   Completes *La Galatea*.

1584   Daughter, Isabella de Saavedra, born to Anna Frana de Rojas; marries Catalina de Salazar Vozmedian y Palacios.

1585   Writes *El Trato de Argel* (*The Legend of Argel*). Publishes *La Galatea*.

1587   Enters public service as a commissary for provisions.

1588   Writes *Dos Odas sobre L'Armada* (*Two Odes on the Spanish Armada*).

1590   Financial difficulties as salary falls into arrears.

1591   Accountants determine that Cervantes owes 27,406 maravedis to the government.

1597   Cervantes arrested and imprisoned; released on the first of December.

1602   Arrested for a second time and transferred to a prison at Valladolid, the capital of Spain; in prison Cervantes begins writing *Don Quixote*.

1605   Publication of *Don Quixote,* part 1.

1606   Writes *La Tia Fingida* (*The Deceitful Aunt*).

1607   Following Isabella, Cervantes and his family move to Madrid. Begins work on *Novelas ejemplares* (*Exemplary Novels*).

1613   Publication of *Novelas ejemplares*.

1614   Licentiate Alonso Fernandez de Avellaneda publishes apocryphal conclusion to *Don Quixote*.

1615   Enraged, Cervantes completes *Don Quixote,* part 2. Writes *Ocho comedias y ocho entremeses* (*Eight Comedies and Eight Interludes*).

1616   Cervantes dies April 23.

1617   Posthumous publication of *Persiles y Sigismunda* (*Persiles and Sigismunda*).

Contributors

HAROLD BLOOM, Sterling Professor of the Humanities at Yale University, is the author of *The Anxiety of Influence, Poetry and Repression,* and many other volumes of literary criticism. His forthcoming study, *Freud: Transference and Authority,* attempts a full-scale reading of all of Freud's major writings. A MacArthur Prize Fellow, he is general editor of five series of literary criticism published by Chelsea House.

LEO SPITZER was an American linguist and philosopher. His books include *Linguistics and Literary History, Essays in Historical Semantics,* and *Essays on English and American Literature.*

ERICH AUERBACH was Librarian of the Prussian State Library, Professor at Marburg, and a member of the Institute for Advanced Study at Princeton University. His best-known works are *Dante als Dichter der irdischen Welt* and *Mimesis: The Representation of Reality in Western Literature.*

JOSÉ ORTEGA Y GASSET was a Spanish philosopher and the founder of influential periodicals, including *España* and *El Sol.* His works include *Meditaciones de Quijote, España invertebrada,* and *La Rebelion de las Masas.*

JORGE LUIS BORGES was an Argentine poet and short story writer, and one of the most eminent Latin American writers. His best-known works are *Ficciones* and *Inquisiciones.*

MICHEL FOUCAULT was a French historian, sociologist, critic, and philosopher. His best-known works are *Les Mots et les choses* (*The Order of Things*), *L'Archeologie du savoir* (*The Archaeology of Knowledge*), *L'Histoire de la folie* (*Madness and Civilization*), and *L'Histoire de la sexualité* (*The History of Sexuality*).

MANUEL DURÁN is Professor of Spanish at Yale University. He has written widely on the Spanish Golden Age and is editor of *Lorca: A Collection of Critical Essays.*

ROBERTO GONZÁLEZ-ECHEVARRÍA is Chairman of the Department of Spanish and Portuguese at Yale University. His books include *Alejo Carpentier, The Pilgrim at Home.*

MARY GAYLORD RANDEL teaches in the Department of Romance Studies at Cornell University.

JUAN BAUTISTA AVALLE-ARCE is Professor of Spanish at the University of California, Santa Barbara. His works include *El Persiles de Cervantes, Conocimiento y vida en Cervantes, La Galatea de Cervantes,* and *Deslindes cervantinos.* He is editor of *Suma Cervantina.*

RUTH EL SAFFAR is Professor of Spanish at the University of Illinois. Her works include *Distance and Control in Cervantes* and *Beyond Fiction: The Recovery of the Feminine in the Works of Cervantes.*

ALBAN FORCIONE is Professor of Spanish and Comparative Literature at Stanford University. His works include *Cervantes, Aristotle and the Persiles, Cervantes' Christian Romance,* and *Cervantes and the Humanist Vision.*

Bibliography

Allen, John J. *Don Quixote: Hero or Fool? A Study in Narrative Technique.* Gainesville: University Presses of Florida, 1969.

———. *Don Quixote: Hero or Fool? A Study in Narrative Technique,* part 2. Gainesville: University Presses of Florida, 1979.

Aylward, E. T. *Cervantes, Pioneer and Plagiarist.* London: Tanesis Books, 1982.

Bates, Margaret J. *"Discreción" in the Works of Cervantes: A Semantic Study.* Washington, D.C.: Catholic University of America Press, 1945.

Bell, Aubrey. *Cervantes.* Norman: University of Oklahoma Press, 1947.

Bell, Michael. "The Structure of *Don Quixote.*" *Essays in Criticism* 18 (1968): 241–57.

Bjornson, Richard, ed. *Approaches to Teaching Cervantes'* Don Quixote. New York: Modern Language Association of America, 1984.

Blanco Aguinaga, Carlos. "Cervantes y la picaresca: notas sobre dos tipos de realismo." *Nueva Revista de Filología Hispánica* 11 (1957): 313–16, 328–42.

Bradbury, Gail. "Lope, Cervantes, a Marriage Trick and a Baby." *Hispanofila* 28, no. 1 (September 1984): 11–19.

Byron, William. *Cervantes, A Biography.* Garden City, N.Y.: Doubleday, 1978.

Calcraft, R. P. "Structure, Symbol and Meaning in Cervantes' *La Fuerz de la Sangre.*" *Bulletin of Hispanic Studies* 58, no. 3 (July 1981): 197–204.

Cascardi, Anthony J. *The Bounds of Reason: Cervantes, Dostoevsky, Flaubert.* New York: Columbia University Press, 1986.

Castro, Américo. *An Idea of History: Selected Essays of Américo Castro.* Translated and edited by Stephen Gilman and Edmund L. King, with an introduction by Roy Harvey Pearce. Columbus: Ohio State University Press, 1977.

———. *El pensamiento de Cervantes.* Madrid: Hernando, 1925.

Church, Margaret. *Don Quixote: The Knight of La Mancha.* New York: New York University Press, 1971.

Close, Anthony J. "Don Quixote as a Burlesque Hero: A Reconstructed Eighteenth Century View." *Forum for Modern Language Studies* 10 (1974): 365–78.

———. *The Romantic Approach to* Don Quixote: *A Critical History of the Romantic Tradition in Quixote Criticism.* Cambridge: Cambridge University Press, 1978.

———. "Sancho Panza: Wise Fool." *Modern Language Review* 68, no. 2 (1973): 344–57.

Cox, Ralph Merrit. *The Rev. John Bowle: The Genesis of Cervantean Criticism.* Chapel Hill: University of North Carolina Press, 1971.

Drake, Dana B. Don Quijote *in World Literature: A Selective Annotated Bibliography.* New York: Garland, 1980.

Durán, Manuel. *Cervantes.* New York: Twayne, 1974.

Efron, Arthur. *Don Quixote and the Dulcineated World.* Austin: University of Texas Press, 1971.

El Saffar, Ruth S. *Beyond Fiction: The Recovery of the Feminine in the Novels of Cervantes.* Berkeley: University of California Press, 1984.

———. *Distance and Control in* Don Quixote: *A Study in Narrative Technique.* North Carolina Studies in the Romance Languages and Literatures, no. 147. Chapel Hill: University of North Carolina Department of Romance Languages, 1975.

———. "The Function of the Fictional Narrator in *Don Quixote.*" *MLN* 83 (1968): 165–77.

———. "*La Galatea*: The Integrity of the Unintegrated Text." In *Cervantes: Su Obra y Su Mundo: Actas del I Congreso Internacional sobre Cervantes,* edited by Manuel Críado de Val. Madrid: ED1–6, 1981.

———. "Montesinos' Cave and the *Casamiento engañoso* in the Development of Cervantes' Prose Fiction." *Kentucky Romance Quarterly* 20, no. 4 (1973): 451–67.

Entwistle, William J. *Cervantes.* Oxford: Clarendon, 1940.

Flores, Angel, and M. J. Bernardete, eds. *Cervantes across the Centuries: A Quadricentennial Volume.* New York: Dryden Press, 1947.

Flores, Ralph. "Deconstructing Authors: *Don Quixote.*" *New Orleans Review* 10, nos. 2–3 (Summer–Fall 1983): 100–109.

Forcione, Alban K. *Cervantes, Aristotle, and the* Persiles. Princeton: Princeton University Press, 1970.

———. *Cervantes' Christian Romance: A Study of* Persiles y Sigismunda. Princeton: Princeton University Press, 1972.

———. *Cervantes and the Humanist Vision: A Study of Four Exemplary Novels.* Princeton: Princeton University Press, 1982.

———. *Cervantes and the Mystery of Lawlessness: A Study of* El casimiento engañoso y El coloquio de los perros. Princeton: Princeton University Press, 1984.

Fox, Dian. "The Critical Attitude in *Rinconete y Cortadillo.*" *Cervantes: Bulletin of the Cervantes Society of America* 3, no. 2 (Fall 1983): 135–47.

Frank, Waldo. *Virgin Spain.* New York: Boni & Liveright, 1926.

Frazier, Harriet C. *A Babble of Ancestral Voices: Shakespeare, Cervantes and Theobald.* The Hague: Mouton, 1974.

Friedman, Edward H. "Dramatic Structure in Cervantes and Lope: The Two 'Pedro de Urdemalas' Plays." *Hispania* 60 (1977): 486–97.

Fuentes, Carlos. Don Quixote: *Or, The Critique of Reading.* Austin: Institute of Latin American Studies, University of Texas at Austin, 1976.

Gilman, Stephen. "The Death of *Lazarillo de Tormes.*" *PMLA* 81 (1966): 149–64.

Glannon, Walter. "The Psychology of Knowledge in *El licenciando Vidriera.*" *Revista Hispanica Moderna: Columbia University Hispanic Studies* 40, nos. 3–4 (1978–79): 86–96.

Grismer, Raymond L. *Cervantes: A Bibliography.* New York: Kraus, 1946.

Guillén, Claudio. *Literature as System.* Princeton: Princeton University Press, 1971.

Haley, George. "The Narrator in *Don Quijote:* Maese Pedro's Puppet Show." *MLN* 80, no. 2 (1965): 145–65.

Hart, Thomas R. "Versions of the Pastoral in Three *Novelas ejemplares.*" *Bulletin of Hispanic Studies* 58, no. 4 (October 1981): 283–91.

Herrero, Javier. "Renaissance Poverty and Lazarillo's Family: The Birth of the Picaresque Genre." *PMLA* 94 (1979): 876–86.

Ihrie, Maureen. *Skepticism in Cervantes.* London: Tanesis Books, 1982.

Immerwahr, Raymond. "Structural Symmetry in the Episodic Narratives of *Don Quixote,* part 1." *Comparative Literature* 10 (1958): 121–35.

Jiminez Fajardo, Salvador. "The Sierra Morena as Labyrinth in *Don Quixote* 1." *MLN* 99, no. 2 (1984): 214–34.

Johnson, Caesar. *The Great Quixote Hoax, or Why Was Cervantes Burned at the Stake?* New York: Exposition Press, 1972.

Johnson, Carroll. *Madness and Lust: A Psychoanalytic Approach to* Don Quixote. Berkeley: University of California Press, 1983.

Karl, Frederick R. "Don Quixote as Archetypal Artist and *Don Quixote* as Archetypal Novel." In *The Adversary Literature.* New York: Farrar, Straus & Giroux, 1974.

Kossoff, A. David, and José Amero y Vásquez, eds. *Homenaje a William L. Fichter. Estudios sobre el teatro antiguo hispánico y otros ensayos.* Madrid: Castalia, 1971.

Krutch, Joseph Wood. *Five Masters: Boccaccio, Cervantes, Richardson, Stendhal, Proust: A Study in the Mutations of the Novel.* London: J. Cape, 1931.

Larsen, Kevin S. "Observations on the Animals and Animal Imagery in Cervantes' Theater." *Modern Language Studies* 14, no. 4 (Fall 1984): 64–75.

Lázaro Carreter, Fernando. *Lazarillo de Tormes en la novela picaresca.* Barcelona: Ariel, 1972.

Ledesma, Francisco Navarro. *Cervantes: The Man and the Genius.* Translated and revised by Don Gabriela Bliss. New York: Charter House, 1973.

Levin, Harry. "The Example of Cervantes." In *Contexts of Criticism.* Cambridge: Harvard University Press, 1957.

Lewis, Dominic Bevan Wyndham. *The Shadow of Cervantes.* London: Hollis & Carter, 1962.

Linsalata, Carmine Rocca. *Smollet's Hoax:* Don Quixote *in English.* Palo Alto: Stanford University Press, 1956.

Madariaga, Salvador de. Don Quixote: *An Introductory Essay in Psychology.* Rev. ed. London: Oxford University Press, 1961.

Mades, Leonard. *The Armor and the Brocade: A Study of Don Quixote and the Courtier.* New York: Las Americas, 1968.

Mancing, Howard. *The Chivalric World of* Don Quixote: *Style, Structure and Narrative Technique.* Columbia: University of Missouri Press, 1982.

Marianella, Conchita Herdman. *"Duenas" and "Doncellas": A Study of the "Dona Rodriguez" Episode in* Don Quijote. North Carolina Studies in the Romantic Languages and Literatures, no. 209. Chapel Hill: University of North Carolina Department of Romance Languages, 1979.

McGaha, Michael D., ed. *Cervantes and the Renaissance: Papers of the Pomona College Cervantes Symposium, November 16–18, 1978.* Easton, Pa.: Juan de la Cuesto Monographs, 1980.

McKendrick, Melveena. *Cervantes.* Boston: Little, Brown, 1980.

Murillo, Louis Andrew. *The Golden Dial: Temporal Configuration in* Don Quijote. Oxford: Dolphin Books, 1975.

Nabokov, Vladimir. *Lectures on* Don Quixote. Edited by Fredson Bowers, with an introduction by Guy Davenport. New York: Harcourt Brace Jovanovich, 1983.

Nelson, Lowry, Jr., ed. *Cervantes: A Collection of Critical Essays.* Englewood Cliffs, N.J.: Prentice-Hall, 1969.

Ortega y Gasset, José. *Meditations on Quixote.* Translated by Evelyn Rugg and Diego Marin, with introduction and notes by Julian Marias. New York: Norton, 1961.

Parker, Alexander A. *Literature and the Delinquent: The Picaresque Novel in Spain and Europe.* Edinburgh: University Press, 1967.

Plaja, Arturo Serrano. *"Magic" Realism in Cervantes:* Don Quixote *as Seen through* Tom Sawyer *and* The Idiot. Translated by Robert S. Rudder. Berkeley: University of California Press, 1970.

Predmore, Richard Lionel. *Cervantes.* New York: Dodd, Mead, 1973.

———. *The World of Don Quixote.* Cambridge: Harvard University Press, 1967.

Randel, Mary Gaylord. "Ending and Meaning in Cervantes' *Persiles y Sigismunda.*" *Romantic Review* 14, no. 2 (March 1983): 152–69.

Rapaport, Herman. "*Atopos:* The Theater of Desire." *New Orleans Review* 11, nos. 3–4 (Fall–Winter 1984): 43–46.

Read, Malcolm K. "Language Adrift: A Re-Appraisal of the Theme of Linguistic Perspectivism in *Don Quijote.*" *Forum for Modern Language Studies* 17 (1981): 271–85.

Rico, Francisco. *La novela picaresca y el punto de vista.* Barcelona: Seix Barral, 1970.

Riley, Edward C. "Cervantes: A Question of Genre." In *Medieval and Renaissance Studies on Spain and Portugal in Honor of P. E. Russell,* edited by F. W. Hodcroft. Oxford: Society for the Study of Medieval Languages and Literature, 1981.

———. *Cervantes's Theory of the Novel.* Oxford: Clarendon, 1962.

———. "'El Alba bella que las perlas cria': Dawn-Description in the Novels of Cervantes." *Bulletin of Hispanic Studies* 33 (1956): 125–37.

Robert, Marthe. *The Old and the New: From* Don Quixote *to Kafka.* Translated by Carol Cosman, foreword by Robert Alter. Berkeley: University of California Press, 1977.

Selig, Karl-Ludwig. "Cervantes' *Rinconete y Cortadillo* and the Two 'Libros de memoria.'" *Revista Hispanica Moderna: Columbia University Hispanic Studies* 40, nos. 3–4 (1978–79): 126–27.

Siciliano, Ernest A. *The Jesuits in the* Quijote *and Other Essays.* Barcelona: Ediciones Hispam, 1974.

———. "Satire in the Inversion of Rules in the *Quijote.*" *Romance Notes* 22, no. 1 (Fall 1981): 64–68.

Sobejano, Gonzalo. "El coloquio de los perros en la picaresca y otros apuntes." *Hispanic Review* 43 (1975): 25–41.

——. "Un perfil de la picaresca: el pícaro hablador." In *Studia Hispanica in Honorem R. Lapesa*, vol. 3. Madrid: Gredos, 1975.

——. "De Alemán a Cervantes: monólogo y diálogo." In *Homenaje al Profesor Muñoz Cortés*. Murcia: Nogués, 1977.

Stern, Charlotte. "Dulcinea, Aldonza, and the Theory of Speech Acts." *Hispania* 67, no. 1 (March 1984): 61–73.

Torbert, Eugene Charles. *Cervantes' Place-names: A Lexicon*. Metuchen, N.J.: Scarecrow Press, 1978.

Ullman, Pierre L. "Romanticism and Irony in *Don Quixote*: A Continuing Controversy." *Papers on Language and Literature* 17, no. 3 (Summer 1981): 320–33.

Unamuno y Jugo, Miguel de. *Our Lord Don Quixote: The Life of Don Quixote and Sancho, with Related Essays*. Translated by Anthony Kerrigan, introduction by Walter Starkie. Princeton: Princeton University Press, 1967.

Van Doren, Mark. *Don Quixote's Profession*. New York: Columbia University Press, 1958.

Wardropper, Bruce W. "*Don Quixote*: Story or History?" *Modern Philology* 63, no. 1 (August 1965): 1–11.

——. "The Strange Case of Lázaro González Pérez." *MLN* 92 (1977): 202–12.

——. "El trastorno de la moral en *Lazarillo*." *Nueva Revista de Filología Hispánica* 15 (1961): 441–47.

Weiger, John G. "Cervantes' Curious Curate." *Kentucky Romance Quarterly* 30, no. 1 (1983): 87–106.

——. "The Curious Pertinence of Eugenio's Tale in *Don Quijote*." *MLN* 96, no. 2 (1981): 261–85.

——. "*Don Quixote*: The Comedy in Spite of Itself." *Bulletin of Hispanic Studies* 60, no. 4 (October 1983): 283–92.

——. *The Substance of Cervantes*. New York: Cambridge University Press, 1985.

Williamson, Edwin. "Romance and Realism in the Interpolated Stories of the *Quixote*." *Cervantes* 2 (1982): 43–67.

——. *The Half-Way House of Fiction: Don Quixote and Arthurian Romance*. New York: Oxford University Press, 1984.

Willis, Raymond Smith. *The Phantom Chapters of the Quijote*. New York: Hispanic Institute, 1953.

Wilson, Diana de Armos. "Cervantes' Last Romance: Deflating the Myth of Female Sacrifice." *Cervantes* 3 (1983): 163–220.

Acknowledgments

"Linguistic Perspectivism in the *Don Quijote*" by Leo Spitzer from *Linguistics and Literary History: Essays in Stylistics* by Leo Spitzer, © 1948, © 1976 renewed by Princeton University Press. Reprinted by permission of Princeton University Press.

"The Enchanted Dulcinea" by Erich Auerbach from *Mimesis: The Representation of Reality in Western Literature* by Erich Auerbach, translated by Willard R. Trask, © 1953, © 1981 renewed by Princeton University Press. Reprinted by permission of Princeton University Press.

"Master Pedro's Puppet Show" by José Ortega y Gasset from *Meditations on Quixote* by José Ortega y Gasset, translated from the Spanish by Evelyn Rugg and Diego Marin, © 1961 by W. W. Norton & Company, Inc. Reprinted by permission of W. W. Norton & Company, Inc.

"Pierre Menard, Author of *Don Quixote*" by Jorge Luis Borges from *Ficciones* by Jorge Luis Borges, © 1962 by Grove Press. Reprinted by permission of Grove Press and George Weidenfeld & Nicholson Publishers. This essay was translated by Anthony Bonner.

"Representing: *Don Quixote*" (originally entitled "Representing") by Michel Foucault from *The Order of Things: An Archaeology of the Human Sciences* by Michel Foucault, translated by Alan Sheridan-Smith, © 1970 by Random House, Inc. Reprinted by permission of Pantheon Books, a division of Random House, Inc. The original French version of this essay appeared in *Les Mots et les choses*, © 1966 by Editions Gallimard.

"Cervantes's Swan Song: *Persiles and Sigismunda*" by Manuel Durán from *Cervantes* by Manuel Durán, © 1974 by Twayne Publishers. Reprinted by permission of Twayne Publishers, a division of G. K. Hall & Co., Boston.

"The Life and Adventures of Cipión: Cervantes and the Picaresque" by Roberto González-Echevarría from *Diacritics* 10, no. 3 (September 1980), © 1980 by The Johns Hopkins University Press. Reprinted by permission of The Johns Hopkins University Press.

"The Language of Limits and the Limits of Language: The Crisis of Poetry in *La*

Galatea" by Mary Gaylord Randel from *MLN* 97, no. 2 (March 1982), © 1982 by The Johns Hopkins University Press. Reprinted by permission of The Johns Hopkins University Press.

"*Novelas ejemplares*: Reality, Realism, Literary Tradition" by Juan Bautista Avalle-Arce from *Mimesis: From Mirror to Method, Augustine to Descartes,* edited by John D. Lyons and Stephen G. Nichols, Jr., © 1982 by the Trustees of Dartmouth College. Reprinted by permission of Dartmouth College and the University Press of New England.

"Tracking the Trickster in the Works of Cervantes" by Ruth El Saffar from *Symposium* 37, no. 2 (1983): 106–22, © 1983 by the Helen Dwight Reid Educational Foundation. Reprinted by permission of the Helen Dwight Reid Educational Foundation, and published by Heldref Publications, 400 Albemarle St., N.W., Washington, D.C.

"The Descent into the Grave: Cervantes's Apocalypse" (originally entitled "Cervantes' Apocalypse: The Descent into the Grave") by Alban Forcione from *Cervantes and the Mystery of Lawlessness: A Study of* El casamiento engañoso y El coloquio de los perros, © 1984 by Princeton University Press. Reprinted by permission of Princeton University Press.

In providing bracketed translations for *Don Quixote,* Sandra Ferdman has relied on the work of J. M. Cohen and Samuel Putnam as well as her own translations.

Index